Rhetoric, Religion, and Tragic Violence

Speaking of Religion

Daniel S. Brown
Series Editor

Vol. 4

Christopher J. Oldenburg and
Adrienne E. Hacker Daniels

Rhetoric, Religion, and Tragic Violence

Sacred Succor and Rancor

Afterword by
Sergio Peña

New York · Berlin · Bruxelles · Chennai · Lausanne · Oxford

Library of Congress Cataloging-in-Publication Data

Names: Oldenburg, Christopher J., editor. | Hacker Daniels,
Adrienne E., editor. | Peña, Sergio (Communication scholar),
writer of afterword.
Title: Rhetoric, religion, and tragic violence :
sacred succor and rancor / edited by Christopher J. Oldenburg
and Adrienne E. Hacker Daniels ; afterword by Sergio Peña.
Description: New York : Peter Lang, 2025. |
Series: Speaking of religion ; volume 4 | Includes bibliographical references.
Identifiers: LCCN 2024031294 (print) | LCCN 2024031295 (ebook) |
ISBN 9781433190230 (hardback) | ISBN 9783034351836 (paperback) |
ISBN 9783034351812 (ebook) | ISBN 9783034351829 (epub)
Subjects: LCSH: Speeches, addresses, etc. | LCGFT: Speeches.
Classification: LCC PN6122 .R44 2025 (print) | LCC PN6122 (ebook) |
DDC 808.5/1–dc23/eng/20240708
LC record available at https://lccn.loc.gov/2024031294
LC ebook record available at https://lccn.loc.gov/2024031295
DOI 10.3726/b22168

Bibliographic information published by the Deutsche Nationalbibliothek.
The German National Library lists this publication in the German
National Bibliography; detailed bibliographic data is available
on the Internet at http://dnb.d-nb.de.

With thanks to Alice H. Engelbach Memorial Endowment for Peace Studies Fund,
Mr. Friedrich Engelbach, Christine Hitchcock, and the Illinois College Faculty Awards and
Grants Committee.

Cover design by Peter Lang Group AG

ISSN 2575-9124 (print)
ISSN 2575-9132 (online)
ISBN 9783034351836 (paperback)
ISBN 9781433190230 (hardback)
ISBN 9783034351812 (ebook)
ISBN 9783034351829 (epub)
DOI 10.3726/b22168

© 2025 Peter Lang Group AG, Lausanne
Published by Peter Lang Publishing Inc., New York, USA
info@peterlang.com - www.peterlang.com

All rights reserved.
All parts of this publication are protected by copyright.
Any utilization outside the strict limits of the copyright law, without the permission of the
publisher, is forbidden and liable to prosecution.
This applies in particular to reproductions, translations, microfilming, and storage and
processing in electronic retrieval systems.

This publication has been peer reviewed.

Acknowledgments

If one were to generate a word cloud from news stories on cable news, network news, newspapers, and news magazines, the word "rhetoric" would certainly be one of the most often heard and seen. Regrettably, the preponderance of the time, the term rhetoric is ascribed to discourse and speeches promulgating divisiveness and animus, deploying religion within cultural, political, and geopolitical spheres as rancor to engender fear and hate. This brand of rhetoric makes no attempt to find common ground, aligning itself more with Wayne Booth's notion of rhetrickery, than his more succor-oriented paradigm of Rhetorology.

The discourse examined herein is a transhistorical, scholarly mosaic imbricating religious discourse, public address, and rhetorical criticism as instruments for confronting an American culture of increasing tragic violence experienced in the *topoi* of race, gender, sexuality, genocide, terrorism, school shootings, and indifference to, and antipathy for, the immigrant Other. The goal of this compendium aims to complicate the rhetoric/violence binary by adducing and analyzing manifold paradigms of speech texts whereby the critical interplay of sacred succor and rancor endemic to religious discourse demonstrates the invitation to both harm and harmonize, to revile and to relieve, to crush and to comfort the tragic corollaries of violence felt all too frequently by the human condition.

As is predictable, our indebtedness far surpasses our poor power to voice our gratitude to all those who assisted with this book. We are grateful to the Faculty Awards and grant Committee at Illinois College for a generous award from the

Alice H. Engelbach Memorial Endowment for Peace Studies Fund, to assist us with research expenditures.

Chris dedicates this book to my late mentor, Michael Leff. Learning Leff's bravura approach to rhetorical criticism known as "close reading" was a religious experience that permits me to practice my faith (both rhetorically and theologically) in pursuit of the paradox of rhetorical truth. The spirit of Leff's interpretive project of what has been called "the theory of the case" and what Leff himself expressed ironically as "concrete abstraction" inhabits much of this book. Not only do we examine the dialectical discursive inter-animation between the action of succor and rancor in historical, religious speech texts and contexts through traditional public address scholarship, but thematically and methodologically the diverse wholeness of Leff's critical intersections between theory and practice, tradition and change, intrinsic and extrinsic analysis, and the universal and the particular are cleaved by a similar, pharmakon-like homeopathy offering diagnostic prescriptions for allaying that which is antithetical to rhetoric, religion, and violence.

Adrienne dedicates this book to Stephen Lucas, Professor Emeritus at the University of Wisconsin-Madison. Professor Lucas played a pivotal role in her graduate school education, in his capacity as Director of the Public Speaking course, and as a scholar-teacher. Professor Lucas is the consummate embodiment of the best that the professoriate offers our students: transformative teaching, superb scholarship, and meaningful mentorship. I take unfettered satisfaction in lauding the impact that Professor Lucas has had on noted achievements in my academic career.

Let it also be acknowledged as with all of the research collaborations that Oldenburg and Hacker Daniels have produced over the years, the scholarly labor in publishing this volume is mutual, and this book should thereby be delineated as equally coauthored in every sense of the word. We are so fortunate to be the beneficiaries of the collegiality and scholarship of our former student and alumnus of Illinois College, Sergio Peña. Sergio has worked with us while he was an undergraduate student, and currently as a graduate student. How consummately satisfying it is to have seen the ways that he has stretched himself intellectually, and we are so fortunate that he made the commitment to write the Afterword in addition to his prodigious research and formatting assistance.

We extend our gratitude to Luke Beatty, former Director of Schewe Library at Illinois College, and Elora Angston, former librarian at Schewe Library, who were eminently helpful in locating and accessing needed research material. Currently Schewe library colleagues, Emma Norris, Jaeda Calaway, and McKenna Jacquemet provided invaluable assistance in processing material and engaging in edifying conversations. Adam Enz, Technical Services librarian at Schewe Library was of great assistance in searching out repositories for important scholarly articles and interlibrary loan books and affording us his technological acumen in helping us realize our vision for the book cover. We also extend profound thanks to our many encouraging and caring colleagues at Illinois College and elsewhere. In no particular order: Adam Jones, Mizuki Wyant, Anna Wright, Shawna Merrill, and John Saunders.

A special debt of gratitude must go to Daniel S. Brown, the series editor. Daniel provided the requisite latitude for the scholarly approach which we undertook, always on the ready to provide counsel when needed. What stands out to us is the trust that Daniel had in our vision and our ability for the project to comport with the vision that he created for the series.

Chris is also indebted to his coauthor, Adrienne Hacker Daniels. As colleagues working in the same department at the same institution for many years, Adrienne and I have collaborated on my scholarly projects, co-curricular events, and served on the same committees. I have learned much from her. I treasure her captious mind, her indefatigable work ethic, her razor-sharp sense of humor, and her kind heart. I'm also exceedingly grateful to Adrienne for hiring me and inviting an insecure assistant professor to collaborate on what has been a most extraordinary and meaningful scholarly career.

Chris is also grateful for his Irish Catholic mother, Cathie Malone Oldenburg, whose abiding sense of tragedy helps see us all through the ephemeral succories of life.

Chris also extends his thanks to his daughters, Cora, Annaliese, and Marin who enliven in me the most prodigious sense of pride. One of the greatest joys of my life is being your Dad. May you continue to love the play of language and the language of prayer and know that you all are my foremost purpose.

Chris wishes to express his immense gratitude for his wife, Carolyn, whose selflessness, unwavering support, and faith, humbles me, energizes me, and inspires me to love and live like she does. She is our cynosure. She is succor incarnate and the source of all my happiness. Nothing would be more bitter or painful than to be of a different mind than her. Carolyn, please accept my eternal thanks for being my editor, my interlocutor, my partner, my noble lover, and the other half of my soul.

Adrienne's husband Marc was very supportive of this project, as were her two sons, Isaak and Simon, without whom my life would be impoverished. I am so proud of the ways they live their lives, guided by succor in their relationships with others, and I know that they are already on the path of making the world a better place, living in the tradition of, and committed to practicing *tikkun olam*—repairing the world.

Sergio expresses his fondest gratitude and appreciation for the two authors of this book, Chris Oldenburg and Adrienne Hacker Daniels. Their infinitely generous mentorship and intrepid intellectual prowess remain an indelible force in my journey as a queer rhetorical scholar, and I could not be more grateful. Additionally, many thanks to Dr. Sam C. Tenorio for his expansive expertise in trans-of-color critique and mentorship that has inspired and shaped my perspective as a rhetorical critic.

It is our hope that readers of this volume find it edifying and worthy of further contemplation and discussion with colleagues and students.

Contents

Foreword   xi
List of Rhetors   xv

Introduction   1
Chapter 1: Race, Gender, and Violence
    Part 1: Joseph Biden, "100th Anniversary of Tulsa Race Massacre", 2021   11
    Part 2: Sojourner Truth, "Address at the Woman's Rights Convention in Akron, Ohio", 1851   35
Chapter 2: LGBTQ and Violence
    Part 1: "Harvey Milk vs. John Briggs" Televised debate transcription, 1978   47
    Part 2: Tony Kushner, "Matthew's Passion", 1998   67
Chapter 3: Geopolitics, Violence, and Remembrance: "Interfaith Meeting with Pope Francis at September 11 Memorial and Museum", 2015   79
Chapter 4: Education and Violence: Barack Obama and Interfaith Speakers, "Interfaith Prayer Vigil Address at Newtown High School," 2012   105
Chapter 5: Religion and Violence
    Part 1: Julius Streicher, "The Night of Broken Glass", 1938   125
    Part 2: Josef Schuster, "80th Anniversary of Reichspogromnacht", 2018   143

Chapter 6: Borders/Immigration and Violence
    Part 1: Jefferson Sessions, "Zero Tolerance Policy Speech", June 2018   153
    Part 2: Pope Francis, "Homily of His Holiness Pope Francis at Ciudad Juárez Fair Grounds" Ciudad Juárez, Mexico. February 17, 2016   167

Afterword   175
Notes   181

Foreword

Speaking of Religion: A Book Series advances the important principle that religious words and ideas continue to hold authority and power in an increasingly secular public sphere. Claiming that religious beliefs, symbols, and themes lack efficacy in public efforts to move listeners' beliefs, attitudes, or actions a significant plurality of intellectuals argue that we live in a post-Christian society. This historic turn echoes Nietzsche's "God is Dead" statement. The statement implicates not only historic Christianity, but suggests the rise of post-theism, apatheism, and even the understanding of human life is at a risk in society.

The segregation of private religious talk from public policy debates whether political or social is the presumed norm in scholarly quarters. The *Speaking of Religion* series, on the contrary, offers evidence that religion wields an outsized influence in the public sphere. Indeed, scholars of religion, sociology, communication, and rhetoric understand that religion broadly defined has either resurged or persisted as a controlling narrative in the public sphere. The public speaking of prominent influencers substantiates this claim. The present volume is, at the minimum, an argument that public communicators believe this is true and act as if it is true when they message their audience members.

The current volume, edited by Illinois College's Adrienne Hacker Daniels and Christopher Oldenburg, supported as they are by emerging rhetorical scholar (and Illinois College alumnus), Sergio Peña, provides an exploration of the rhetoric of tragedy. Tragedy originates in spoken words as surely as peace emerges from words spoken. Both lived experience and historical events demonstrate that rhetoric in the midst of tragic circumstances evokes both peace and violence. At a minimum the power to create peace or to provoke violence is embedded in rhetoric.

Nonetheless, the questions remain: "How do words accomplish their purpose? How are ideas crafted linguistically to create peace and to elevate violence?"

These are fundamentally religious questions. The origin narratives that support the three Abrahamic faiths, for example, are instructive here. Adam and Eve spoke the cataclysmic "No" to the Creator in Genesis creation narrative. Their "No" symbolizes all practices that reject goodness, righteousness, and justice. In this instance, their words perpetrate violence on the created, "good" order. The religious heritage of the Jewish tradition provides a corrective to violence which is, interestingly enough, also spoken. That word? Shalom. Shalom knits together the reality of God, humanity, and creation; it signals a hoped-for state of harmony, unity, justice, and righteousness. It is used both to refer to healthy relationships between groups or individuals as well as to a sense of wellness or safety of an individual or group.

Hacker Daniels and Oldenburg, the volume's editors, originally planned to develop a book that examined the American civil rights movement. Other speech texts continued coming to their attention and initially seemed to be peripheral to their project. Ultimately, the volume editors chose—and wisely so I believe—to expand their effort and include texts well-beyond the civil rights movement.

Furthermore, by placing in juxtaposition the carefully chosen speech texts noted in their proposal, Hacker Daniels & Oldenburg open the door to new understandings of religion, rhetoric, and tragic violence. (Not all violence is tragic; not all tragedy is violent. The book's focus is unique in curating these texts, placing them side-by-side.)

The notion that religious rhetoric (speech) in times of tragic violence generates *pharmakon*, both a remedy and a poison, during times of tragic violence is exclusive to this work as far as I know. There *may* be works that focus on religious rhetoric as a balm (i.e., a remedy), and other works that focus on such rhetoric as a weapon (i.e., a poison). To my knowledge, however, the proposed volume is exclusive in placing such texts in conversation with each other. Thus, the work has a dual emphasis on succor and rancor.

The late scholar of rhetoric and public affairs Martin J. Medhurst challenged "individual discourse communities to form their own canons through the process of rhetorical archaeology—the recovery of texts and discourses central to the self-understanding and public expression of specific groups and movements."[1] Medhurst's challenge is the continuing basis for the *Speaking of Religion* book series. In the case of this ongoing project, the discourse community is that of religious communication scholars. Specifically, scholars of religious communication, functioning as a broad discourse community, have banned together by means of the book series to generate a sequence of thematic volumes that address the roles and functions of religion within social movements and public policy debates.

This book you hold in your hands is a labor of love and persistence on behalf of the editors; it is a tribute to Professor Medhurst's vision. May contemporary readers listen carefully to the voices of the past as we chart our voyage into the future.

Daniel S. Brown, Jr.
Noblesville, Indiana

List of Rhetors

Joseph R. Biden
    Tulsa, Oklahoma. June 1, 2021.

John Briggs
    San Francisco, California. September 6, 1978.

Pope Francis
    Ciudad Juárez, Mexico. February 17, 2016.

Pope Francis
    New York City, New York. September 25, 2015.

Tony Kushner
    From *The Nation*. November 9, 1998.

Harvey Milk
    San Francisco, California. September 6, 1978.

Barack Obama
    Newtown, Connecticut. December 16, 2012

Josef Schuster
   Berlin, Germany. November 9, 2018.

Jefferson Sessions
   Fort Wayne, Indiana. June 14, 2018.

Julius Streicher
   Nuremberg, Germany. November 10, 1938.

Sojourner Truth
   Akron, Ohio. May 29, 1851.

Introduction

Twentieth century literary critic Kenneth Burke avers that the art of rhetoric "*is produced for the purposes of comfort, as part of the consolatio philosphiae. It is undertaken as equipment for living*, as a ritualistic way of arming us to confront the perplexities and risks. It would *protect* us."[1] Burke, true to the idiom of his theoretical system, explicated in the most Promethean of diction, always reveals contradiction. The idea that an individual or a culture wounded by violence would be consoled by violence through the piety of "arming" and "confronting" threats speaks to a homeopathic dialectic implicit in Burke's cycle of terms. René Girard, whom from Burke appropriated much, notes the mimetic scapegoat function is predicated on the "paradox of archaic religion… that, in order to prevent violence, it resorted to substitute violence."[2] Succor implies an oppositional rancor from which to protect against.

A monistic understanding of Burke's palliative theory has conventionally been augmented by religion, long evoked in the forms of eulogies, panegyrics, funeral orations, and memorials, to offer solace for sorrowful events, violence, and death. Such forms are magnanimous and are often exemplary instances of religiously inspired, epideictic oratory. In *The Rhetoric of Religion*, Burke concedes that "the history of religions has also been the history of great discord."[3] Burke's words ring true when one observes the religious rhetoric, currently manifested in Christian

Nationalist discourse enveloping much of the nation, has degenerated into a violent theological dystopia. Andrew Whitehead and Samuel Perry note, a volatile interface between "nativism, white supremacy, patriarchy, and heteronormativity, along with divine action for authoritarian control and militarism," has gripped out nation. "It is as ethnic and political as it is religious."[4] Decades earlier, political theorist Carl Schmitt concluded that "all significant concepts of the modern theory of the state are secularized theological concepts not only because of their historical development—in which they were transferred from theology to the theory of the state, whereby for example the omnipotent God became the omnipotent lawgiver, but also because of their systematic structure."[5] Schmitt's observation, expressed as the will of a nation-God, is succinctly emblazoned on MAGA endorsed T-Shirts: "Jesus is My Savior, Trump is My President." Moreover, Benedict Anderson in his seminal work *Imagined Communities* explains that the roots of nationalism are embedded in antecedent cultural systems, those of the religious community.[6]

A cursory viewing of the January 6th insurrection footage displays a multitude of sacred symbols emblematizing Jesus's will to empower insurrectionists' victory. Political rhetoric and religion have made for sometimes strange and violent bedfellows, where political violence (violence predicated on political ideologies) is committed predominantly in the name of religion—with religion providing the claims and the supporting evidence. G.O.P. Congressman Adam Kinzinger serving on the January 6 Committee, has opined on what he believes to be an outrageous equivalency: "And you have people today that, literally, I think in their heart—they may not say it—but they equate Donald Trump with the person of Jesus Christ. And to them, if you even come out against this 'amazing man Donald Trump,' which obviously quite flawed, you are coming out against Jesus, against their Christian values."[7] And in a *Time* article, Franklin Graham repudiated Republican congresspersons who voted to impeach Trump after the January 6 insurrection, calling them a collective "Judas."[8]

Adam Kinzinger released a compilation of hate-filled profane and threatening voicemails that were sent to his congressional office. As reported by Yahoo News, the callers' wrath was leveled at Kinzinger for "not buying into former President Trump's baseless election fraud lies."[9] A graphic instance introducing the vile and disgusting calls, states, "Keep in mind all voicemails and phone calls are received by my interns, high school or college level, attempting to learn about the legislative process."[10] One particular voicemail sent by a woman, employing the most religiously rancorous rhetoric in the most subdued tone stands out: "Wrath of the Lord God Almighty come upon you, your health, your family, your home your livelihood and I'll pray if it be God's will that you suffer."[11] The other messages are threats strung together with a veritable Carlinesque influence, but far removed from Carlin's witty and brilliant disquisition on language. The woman's threat is particularly chilling, intoning the threat to sound almost like a prayer.

Hent de Vries, employing a chiastic copula, states a profound verity, "No violence without (some) religion; no religion without (some) violence."[12] Sacredness and violence are inseparable and *sine qua non* to most major religious traditions. As Girard proclaimed in his celebrated book *Violence and the Sacred*, violence is the "heart and secret soul of the sacred."[13] In the current American milieu, Girard's premise is hardly clandestine. Socially mediated and contemporary instances of de Vries's chiasmus abound. Recently, *Atlantic* writer Daniel Panneton inquired, "Why are sacramental beads suddenly showing up next to AR-15s online?"[14] Panneton's article, like the title suggests, explains "How Extremists Gun Culture is Trying to Co-opt the Rosary." Bishop Daniel Flores of Brownsville, Texas, the diocese that includes Uvalde, bemoans the way some Americans have "sacralized death instruments."[15] Panneton argues sacred artifacts like rosaries are becoming weaponized. "The battle beads culture of spiritual warfare permits radical traditional Catholics to literally demonize their political opponents and regard the use of armed force against them as sanctified."[16] No where do we see this troubling linkage between religion and violence more than the increasingly visible and vocal forms of Christian Nationalism espoused by publicly elected members of the United States Congress and the Senate.

In June 2022, at the Family Camp Meeting's "All Things Are Possible" conference in Colorado Springs, Representative Lauren Boebert addressed an audience on the significance of speaking up for conversative beliefs as a means of combating cancel culture. She quipped that Jesus didn't have enough AR-15 rifles to "keep his government from killing him."[17] A bit later in referencing cancel culture specifically, Boebert remarked, "Cain canceled Abel." "And guess what, it wasn't with a big, scary AR-15, it was with a rock, so I don't think it's a firearm issue. I think it's a heart, a sin issue."[18] Anachronism, hypocrisy, and blasphemy notwithstanding, what is perhaps most disquieting about Boebert's rhetoric is how the so-called cancel culture phenomenon has been appropriated by the Christian Right to define their victimhood as well as demarcate cancel culture as a major battlefront in the latest culture war campaign.[19] Secondly, in the wake of repeated mass shootings where AR-15s— high capacity weapons engineered to kill people as efficiently as possible—the Christian Right invokes rancor and violence so readily as a response to any deliberative arguments about gun reform and assault rifle bans. The fallacious perversion of biblical references imbued with the incongruous glorification of violence alone attests to the lethal mélange of religion, violence, and political rhetoric being promulgated by elected officials.

Republican Congresswoman Marjorie Taylor Greene publicized a trip that she made in June to the Holocaust Museum in Washington, D.C., affording her the opportunity to express contrition for the faulty analogy heard around the world. In an appearance on David Brody's podcast in May, bemoaning the mask mandate put in place on the floor of the House of Representatives, Greene said,

"You know, we can look back at a time in history where people were told to wear a gold star and they were definitely treated like second-class citizen, so much so, that they were put in trains and taken to gas chambers in Nazi Germany."[20] Days after the podcast, Greene doubled down on Covid protocols implemented in private retail outlets and grocery stores, where they allowed employees to be mask free if they were vaccinated, communicating that status by wearing a badge to that effect. Greene then opined, "Vaccinated employees get a vaccination logo just like the Nazi[']s forced Jewish people to wear a gold star." But even after she apologized in June (following the Holocaust Museum visit), she still claimed that the forced wearing of masks and getting vaccinations amounts to "a type of discrimination and I'm very much against that type of discrimination."[21] In response to her original comments in May, the American Jewish Congress (AJC) said, "You can never compare health-related restrictions with yellow starts, gas chambers and other Nazi atrocities. Such comparisons demean the Holocaust and contaminate American political speech."[22] And Joel Rubin, the AJC Executive Director, characterized Greene's comments as hate speech and a trivialization of the Holocaust.[23]

    This volume is a compendium comprising both historic and contemporary speeches on the thematic imbrication of Religion, Rhetoric, and Violence. We endeavor to complicate the rhetoric/violence binary by interpolating religion, another foundational and cultural construct inextricably entangled with both rhetoric and violence, into the dialectic. Sacred words often provide succor, rhetorical emollient, summoned to comfort individual victims, and entire communities ravaged by acts of violence. However, history also demonstrates that religious discourse, like rhetoric itself, functions as a pharmakon—both as remedy and a poison. The Latin etymology for the word *sacred*, or *sacer*, originally meant something that is both simultaneously blessed and cursed.[24]

    The themes for the book were chosen for the ways that they are sacralized and desanctified. Over the millennia, religion has been a powerful instrument: to extol and execrate, to ameliorate or worsen, to valorize or demonize. In his introduction to the volume *Trialogue and Terror*, Alan Berger quotes Peter Berger, who argues that "very probably religion in the modern world more often fosters war, both between and within nations."[25] Alan Berger consummately captures the succor/rancor dualism of religion: "Religion is, however, a two-edged sword. On the one hand, religion can serve as a 'sacred canopy' for adherents providing a 'plausibility structure' against the absurdity of evil while giving meaning to their existence and a transcendent purpose to their death. Yet on the other hand, religion can also provide justification for terror and mass murder."[26] Religion is instrumentalized, providing moral entitlement, as sincere or disingenuous within a plethora of spheres, including the political, legal, and aesthetic. Religious discourse evoked to incite or justify violence functions as a kind of rancor that distorts reality, exacerbates harm, and eschews accountability of the perpetrators.

Moreover, religious rhetoric, employed to mitigate the pain of bloodshed, structural injustice, and spurring social reform, is emoted with righteous indignation, a synthesis of sacred succor and rancor operating as a productive tension. The past can inform and influence the future, but does not necessarily dictate the future, whereby the events to transpire in the future would be ineluctable. The texts that we have chosen communicate the fact that we can learn from the past, good, bad, or indifferent. In setting our sights on the chosen artifacts, we explore the ways that these texts ameliorate that which, worsen a situation (given the realities of the current circumstances), jeopardizing any good that could be reaped from the past—in short—the reader can decide—as we have attempted—to determine the degree to which these speeches are inculcative.

A vital edifice of the federal government in Washington, D.C., the National Archives Building, speaks to the necessity for preserving the past and learning from it. Two of the four sculptures gracing the building are located on the Pennsylvania side of the building. Engraved on the base of the "Future" sculpture is an uncontracted version of the passage in William Shakespeare's *The Tempest*, "what's past is prologue." As described in the National Archives: Pieces of History, "Future is a youthful woman gazing in contemplation of things to come. She holds an open book symbolizing what has yet to be written."[27] The "Past" sculpture includes the exhortative inscription "study the past," which is a truncated paraphrase of Confucius: "Study the past if you would divine the future." In the "Past" sculpture, "an old man [is] gazing down the corridors of time. He holds a closed book representing history."[28] The framing of each with a historical context served us most auspiciously in making links with more contemporary analogues. The texts examined not only to speak in their own times with their own temporally related contexts as part of history, but with more contemporary resonances, enabling the reader to understand and appreciate the fact that a speech is not only studied as an artifact in vacuo as part of the past—enjoying autonomy—but it is also a part of a more longitudinal history, traversing the ground of the future. We hope that these speeches and analyses provide fruitful avenues for reflection on the heuristic values of these texts spanning three centuries, and the ways that they speak to events in the present, and to those in the past.

A volume like this one can belie the myriad of challenges which annex themselves to such an enterprise. Some of the challenges are ostensibly more pedestrian than others. One significant task is obtaining copyright permissions from the appropriate individuals/entities, to ensure that the texts are published without fear of legal reprisal. Over the course of writing the book, we were thrilled upon receiving these legal "blessings." For the government documents, we did not have to garner permission for documents classified as those within the public domain.

However, Sojourner Truth's speech text(s) did pose considerable challenges. Multiple versions of Truth's speech text exist, and this volume includes two of the most documented and prominent versions of the speech, and curating these speeches was uniquely challenging, since no technology allowed for the memorialization of the speech as it was delivered, and in fact, the multiple versions complicate the rhetorical critic's work.

As the reader will no doubt conclude, we intend for the analyses to stand on their own, but we hope the reader discerns the not irrelevant linkages between and among the texts. We have offered up some of the more obvious, and from our perspectives, some of the more salient, but those concatenations can assuredly be expanded upon, bearing fruit that we had not produced. Although our analyses enjoy depth, and we hope, afford the reader edifying conclusions, we are certainly not suggesting that they are, to quote Shakespeare's *Macbeth*, "the be-all and the end-all." We think that they are instructive, critical roadmaps for your own work as you come to terms with a wide range of rhetorical texts.

Myth is the precursor of religion and the rhetorical vehicle by which humanity's socio-political civilization is told. Rhetoric, religion, and violence have been there since antiquity. The Bible serves as the religious vehicle revealing the origins of both rhetoric (in the beginning was the word) and violence first through the fratricide of Cain. The introduction of Mark Wallace's and Theophus Smith's edited volume *Curing Violence* opens with the question, "why does religion sometimes appear to be a 'cure' for social violence, and yet also and at the same time its cause?"[29] While these religious scholars turn to the works of French thinker René Girard's examination of religion as mimetic desire, we probe via paradigms and rhetorical analyses from the discursive roles religion plays in its response to and impetus for violence. According to Palaver, the three Abrahamic faiths: Christianity, Judaism, and Islam and their "concern for victims has led to the best and worst in our world. On the one hand, it has led to a strong emphasis on human rights. On the other hand, it has led to violent defenses of victims in the human rights struggle," arguing that taking up the cudgels for the victims as "an aggressive weapon" is left untethered to the "forgiveness of persecutors."[30] Palaver warns of "vengeful religious lamenting" in the Abrahamic religions, contributing to a "contemporary culture of radical victimology," a concept espoused by Girard with the "cult of the victim."[31]

Traditionally, rhetoric's relationship with violence is conceived as compensatory. Plato's Myth of Protagoras, for example, provides an etiology of democracy whereas Hermes' gift of logos is presented as a *deus ex machina*. Rhetoric delivers humanity from the savagery and scarcity of nature and from the violence of the physical agôn, thereby ensuring civilization and survival. Stephen Browne intones Isocrates', Aristotle's, and Cicero's classical hymns to logos, which echo the resounding chorus that rhetoric is an art which displaces violence.[32] Browne, then offers an interesting coda to "the eloquence as antithetical to violence frame" by inquiring as to how violence may be employed artistically as a means of rhetorical invention.[33] Attendant to Browne's approach, Erin Rand, in a *Rhetoric & Public Affairs* review of books titled "Thinking Violence and Rhetoric," also calls into question the assumption of violence and rhetoric as oppositional, advising that violence as a potential rhetorical *topos* may serve as a productive resource for agency.[34] More recently, Jeremy Engels, serving as a guest editor for a *Quarterly Journal of Speech Forum* on "The Violence of Rhetoric," notes that other thinkers held rhetoric and violence to be inseparably entangled.[35]

Gorgias, for example, characterized speech as a pharmakon, both tonic and toxin, and both cure and curse. In the same Forum piece, Nathan Stormer asks which came first, violence or rhetoric? He proceeds to trouble the traditional and logical view of language as post-violence by questioning the credulity of the genesis stories that established assumptions about the rhetoric/violence binary. Like Gorgias, Stormer sees rhetoric and violence as ubiquitous, iterative, and intertwined forces. Since origin stories are indeterminate and do not tell us the whole story, therefore neither rhetoric nor violence can be a privileged term in the binary. Moreover, he, similar to Girard, contends that the conventions reciprocal to both rhetoric and violence are negation and mimesis.[36] In his book *Rhetoric and Power*, Nathan Crick, following the lead of Hannah Arendt, differentiates violence from both power and speech by its complex active role, arguing that violence comprises "the whole sphere of instrumental means used to directly alter one's environment without the need for speech."[37]

Jennifer Mercieca investigates the conception of a "rhetoric of honor" that persuades by appealing to local community members, is devoted to rituals that reconfirm shared values, and is meant to restore reputation and status above all else based on the religious connotations of "devoted" and "rituals." Mercieca's definition is intentional, and such discourse may include appeals to broader religious ideologies.[38] If one of the rhetorical functions of a rhetoric of honor aims to unify a community, then religious appeals, recalling the word religion means "to bind together," would perform a central function in a culture of honor, as it did for the Greek poet Homer.[39] Religious consubstantiality, as Kenneth Burke reminds us, functions through mergers and divisions; therefore, as Mercieca notes, a rhetoric of honor also aims to scapegoat and silence outsiders by casting them as enemies and threats antithetical to the culture of honor.[40] These threats must be managed with violence. In fact, Mercieca further explicates that, a primary role of a rhetoric of honor is to promote what she calls "epideictic violence," "discourse that uses the mandates of community obligation to punish outsiders and control insiders."[41] Rhetoric formulated and disseminated through this paradoxical form performs in a parallel manner as our conceptualization of sacred succor/rancor embodied in the rhetorical potent chemistry of rhetoric, religion, and violence.

Even when one is a "practicing member" or a faithful adherent of a particular religion, one does not necessarily accept or abide by every codified or uncodified tenet, and certainly, from the outside looking in, particular theological beliefs and/or associative norms might be perceived as contravening one's belief system and values disallowing their incorporation. If one conceives of this belief system applying Milton Rokeach's hierarchy of beliefs, the willingness to incorporate those beliefs of others might be determined as to where those beliefs fall: primitive, unanimous consensus, primitive, zero consensus, authoritative, derived, and inconsequential. Reasonably, the more inconsequential the beliefs, the greater the willingness to entertain those beliefs for folding into one's belief system without undue conflict.[42]

Respect for religion and the religions of others, as observed by Christopher Lewis, does not negate the differences, and in fact, they are not distinctions without differences.[43] From the process of recognizing these differences, a determination should be made about the values inherent in those religions. Lewis says, "there is a need to be able to distinguish between good and bad religion…For example, good religion is open to new insights, fosters human flourishing, gives a proper place to women, cares for the world in which we all live, works for justice and against violence, protects the poor, fights suffering."[44] Lewis concedes that achieving this sort of "global ethic" has not been wholly successful, and that in fact, "the different religions have often been the context (or the rationalization for) the horrors of discrimination, injustice, oppression, and nationalism, for they are enmeshed in the world. Yet they are not 'drowned' in the world, for the same religions are challenging those horrors and making their principles, which sound abstract, become concrete in particular places."[45] Undoubtedly, these "vices" and "virtues" are interpreted by an eye and ear of the beholder. As consumers, relentlessly bombarded by digital mediated symbols and exposed to more and more egregious defacements of religion, we may be tempted to surrender the church, temple, synagogue, and mosque as nothing more than irredeemable Augean stables. For scholars of religion and rhetoric, as confounded and stunned as we are by the aberration of religious symbolism that produces a toxic and deeply disturbing sense of selfishness, sacrilege, and devastation, we owe it to ourselves, our students, and our own "good faith" efforts at inner-religious dialogue, political unity, and the common good to critically engage this Gordian knot taut with the strands of rhetoric, religion, and violence. As Heraclitus aphoristically proclaimed, "Religion is a disease, but it is a noble disease."[46]

As we approached these speeches, in our preliminary stages of coming to terms with them, we kept very open minds regarding the critical approaches that would best serve the texts. In *Philosophy of Literary Form*, Kenneth Burke exhorts the critic in their criticism "to use all that there is to use,"[47] and we hope that we have accomplished that.

The intersection between religion, rhetoric, and violence will be explored through the following themes: Race, Gender and Violence, LGBTQ+ Identity and Violence, Geopolitics, Remembrance and Violence, Education and Gun Violence, Antisemitism and Violence, and Borders/Immigration and Violence.

In Chapter 1, the Sojourner Truth analysis employs a close textual analysis through prophetic and feminist lenses; the applies genre criticism the Biden speech applies genre criticism. The Truth analysis explores racism and the speeches of Sojourner Truth prompt important discussions of women's rights, issues circumscribing slavery, and the ways that these historical issues influence the approaches to these subjects in classrooms across the country. The Biden speech also addresses issues of racism and the controversial issue of reparations.

In Chapter 2, the Kushner analysis uses an ironic version of jeremiad prophetic rhetoric. Kushner employs what Martin Luther King Jr. called "the sword that heals," exposing the hypocoristic discourse of both the religious and political right. The Milk interview applies theories of interviewing and genre criticism to illuminate the contested policy of California Proposition 6, advanced by John Briggs, repudiated by Milk, and placed on the 1978 ballot in California. The chapter brings to the fore current policies related to LGBTQ+ pedagogies and curricula, manifest most notably in Florida's "Don't Say Gay" bill and efforts to ban books in public schools and libraries with LGBTQ+ themes across the country.

Chapter 3 explores the September 25, 2015, 9/11 commemorative event under the auspices of the 9/11 Memorial and Museum, using interfaith, interreligious, and multi-religious theories of prayer, applied predominantly to the three Abrahamic faiths, with the analysis of Pope Francis's prayerful panegyrics, applying spatial-visual rhetoric. The September 25, 2015 event provides an opportunity for a microcosm of the world's religions through their representatives, to come together in prayer at the site of the fallen World Trade Center Towers, the inhabitants of the Towers who died, and the first responders who died saving lives on September 11, 2001. The September 25, 2015 prayer service also commemorates the first responders and the workers who suffered ill health in the ensuing years, with many ultimately succumbing to the physical and emotional tolls resulting from their unparalleled heroism.

Chapter 4 also applies interfaith, interreligious, and multi-religious prayer theories in tandem with the Sandy Hook memorial service, December 16, 2012. The Sandy Hook prayer service was an opportunity to offer spiritual consolation. The controversies surrounding gun violence and the easy availability of weapons that can decimate a community have not abated since 2012, as we have experienced with the Parkland, Florida massacre at Marjorie Stoneman Douglas High School, and the most recently in 2022 in Uvalde, Texas at Robb Elementary School. Adding to the tragedies they are the incidents of hate speech, defamation and death threats leveled against parents of slain children, obstructing parents' herculean efforts to heal in the wake of such tragedies, hoping to find a scintilla of healing through the legal system, and with lawsuits against individuals like Alex Jones of Infowars.

In Chapter 5, the Josef Schuster speech uses metaphorical criticism, as does the Julius Streicher speech, the latter with an embedded discussion of rhetoric and First Amendment constraints on hate speech. Chapter 5 hearkens back to the tragic events surrounding Kristallnacht, with a contemporaneous speech by Julius Streicher on November 10, 1938, whose soubriquet was "Jew-Baiter Number One," and a commemorative speech by Dr. Josef Schuster, President of the Central Council of Jews in Germany on the eightieth anniversary of Kristallnacht in 2018. Antisemitism is tragically thriving in the hate-filled recesses of our society, which have not remained in the dark, but have been visible in the light of day. They are trafficking in stereotypes, death threats and realized violence, accomplished all too efficiently with the aid of social media. Holocaust denial, a hallmark of antisemitic rhetoric, has been appropriated in the most abhorrent and perverted ways, through the cooptation of the holocaust metaphor to claim persecution and victimization for themselves.

In Chapter 6, Jeff Sessions' speech uses the Aristotelian canons as applied to a policy, and Pope Francis's speech applies a hermeneutic reading using prophetic narrative augmented with affect theory. This chapter provides a sort of point-counterpoint, with Jeff Sessions' speech advocating the heart-wrenching and inhumane Zero Tolerance policy, some aspects of which eerily hearken back to the parent-child separations during World War II, and Pope Francis's compassion-filled speech.

As a liberal art traversing two and a half millennia, our critical applications of rhetoric are indebted to the theory and praxis of rhetoric longitudinally—drawing from major thinkers from the time of Aristotle through the twenty-first century. We labored assiduously to choose the methodological approaches which would provide the most edifying analyses. But labor does not have to be laborious. As stated in Hebrews 6:10, "For God is not unrighteous to forget your work and labor of love." This labor of love, far from sapping one's energy, sustains and strengthens the work. Some definitive answers will remain elusive and the reconciliation in your own minds of conflicting ideas will remain unreconciled, and that is fine. But what an exciting and fulfilling journey!

CHAPTER 1: PART 1

Race, Gender, and Violence

The tragic incidents encompassing the Tulsa Race Riot/Massacre which occurred on the last day in May and the first day of June 1921, function as the impetus for President Joe Biden's speech commemorating the 100th Anniversary of the Tulsa Race Massacre, delivered, June 1, 2021, at the Greenwood Cultural Center in Tulsa, Oklahoma. At its heart, Biden's speech is commemorative, yet secured in profound ways with the principal precepts of deliberative and forensic speech. Joseph Biden's speech is remarkable for the intertwining of the three Aristotelian genres of rhetoric.

"REMARKS BY PRESIDENT BIDEN COMMEMORATING THE 100TH ANNIVERSARY OF THE TULSA RACE MASSACRE"[1]

Joseph R. Biden

Tulsa, Oklahoma. June 1, 2021

Lauren, thank you for that gracious introduction. And in case you were wondering, I—in Delaware—we're a small state—we have the eighth-largest Black population in America, and we have one of the most talented members of Congress. And so if I didn't walk around and pay my tribute to Lisa Blunt Rochester my congress woman—(applause)—immediately, that was—How are you, Rev? Good to see you.

We've got a distinguished group of people here, and I want to thank Lauren for sharing the powerful story and for helping the country understand what's happening here.

And to all of the descendants here today, and to the community and civil rights leaders, and members of the Congressional Black Caucus that are here: Thank you for making sure we all remember and we never forget.

You know, there's a verse in First Corinthians that says, "For now, we see in a mirror dimly, but then, face to face, now I know in part, then I shall know fully."

It is—I just toured the Hall of Survivors here in Greenwood Cultural Center, and I want to thank the incredible staff for hosting us here. And—(applause)—I mean that sincerely. Thank you. And if I didn't say what my father would insist on, please excuse my back. (Laughter.) I apologize.

But the tour—in the tour, I met Mother Randle, who's only 56 [107] years old. (Laughter.) God love her. And Mother Fletcher, who's 67 [106] years old. (Laughter.) And her brother—her brother, Van Ellis, who's 100 years old. (Laughter.) And he looks like he's 60. Thank you for spending so much time with me. I really mean it. It was a great honor. A genuine honor.

You are the three known remaining survivors of a story seen in the mirror dimly. But no longer. Now your story will be known in full view.

The events we speak of today took place 100 years ago. And yet, I'm the first President in 100 years ever to come to Tulsa (applause)—I say that not as a compliment about me, but to think about it—a hundred years, and the first President to be here during that entire time, and in this place, in this ground, to acknowledge the truth of what took place here.

For much too long, the history of what took place here was told in silence, cloaked in darkness. But just because history is silent, it doesn't mean that it did not take place. And while darkness can hide much, it erases nothing. It erases nothing. Some injustices are so heinous, so horrific, so grievous they can't be buried, no matter how hard people try.

And so it is here. Only—only with truth can come healing and justice and repair. Only with truth, facing it. But that isn't enough.

First, we have to see, hear, and give respect to Mother Randle, Mother Fletcher, and Mr. Van Ellis. (Applause.) To all those lost so many years ago, to all the descendants of those who suffered, to this community—that's why we're here: to shine a light, to make sure, America knows the story in full.

May 1921: Formerly enslaved Black people and their descendants are here in Tulsa—a boom town of oil and opportunity in a new frontier.

On the north side, across the rail tracks that divided the city already segregated by law, they built something of their own, worthy—worthy of their talent and their ambition: Greenwood—a community, a way of life. Black doctors and lawyers, pastors, teachers; running hospitals, law practices, libraries, churches, schools.

Black veterans, like a man I had the privilege to giving a Command Coin to, who fought—volunteered and fought, and came home and still faced such prejudice.(Applause.)Veterans had been back a few years helping after winning the first World War, building a new life back home with pride and confidence, who were a mom-and—they were, at the time—mom-and-plack [sic]—mom-and-pop Black diners, grocery stores, barber shops, tailors—the things that make up a community.

At the Dreamland Theatre, a young Black couple, holding hands, falling in love. Friends gathered at music clubs and pool halls; at the Monroe family roller-skating rink. Visitors staying in hotels, like the Stradford.

All around, Black pride shared by the professional class and the working class who lived together, side by side, for blocks on end.

Mother Randle was just six years old—six years old—living with her grandmom. She said she was lucky to have a home and toys, and fortunate to live without fear. Mother Fletcher was seven years old, the second of seven children. The youngest, being Mr. Van Ellis, was just a few months old. The children of former sharecroppers, when they went to bed at night in Greenwood, Mother Fletcher says they fell asleep rich in terms of the wealth—not real wealth, but a different wealth—a wealth in culture and community and heritage. (Applause.)

But one night—one night changed everything. Everything changed. While Greenwood was a community to itself, it was not separated from the outside.

It wasn't everyone, but there was enough hate, resentment, and vengeance in the community. Enough people who believed that America does not belong to everyone and not everyone is created equal—Native Americans, Asian Americans, Hispanic Americans, Black Americans. A belief enforced by law, by badge, by hood and by noose.

And it speaks to that—lit the fuse. It lit it by the spark that it provided—a fuse of fury—was an innocent interaction that turned into an in—a terrible, terrible headline allegation of a Black male teenager attacking a white female teenager.

A white mob of 1,000 gathered around the courthouse where the Black teenager was being held, ready to do what still occurred: lynch that young man that night. But 75 Black men, including Black veterans, arrived to stand guard.

Words were exchanged. Then a scuffle. Then shots fired. Hell was unleashed. Literal hell was unleashed.

Through the night and into the morning, the mob terrorized Greenwood. Torches and guns. Shooting at will. A mob tied a Black man by the waist to the back of their truck with his head banging along the pavement as they drove off. A murdered Black family draped over the fence of their home outside. An elderly couple, knelt by their bed, praying to God with their heart and their soul, when they were shot in the back of their heads.

Private planes—private planes—dropping explosives—the first and only domestic aerial assault of its kind on an American city, here in Tulsa.

Eight of Greenwood's nearly two dozen churches burned, like Mt. Zion—across the street, at Vernon AME.

Mother Randle said it was like war. Mother Fletcher says, all these years later, she still sees Black bodies around.

The Greenwood newspaper publisher A.J. Smitherton [sic]—excuse me—Smitherman penned a poem of what he heard and felt that night. And here's the poem. He said, "Kill them, burn them, set the pace … teach them how to keep their place. Reign of murder, theft, and plunder was the order of the night." That's what he remembered in the poem that he wrote.

One hundred years ago at this hour, on this first day of June, smoke darkened the Tulsa sky, rising from 35 blocks of Greenwood that were left in ash and ember, razed and in rubble.

Less than 24 hours—in less than 24 hours, 1,100 Black homes and businesses were lost. Insurance companies—they had insurance, many of them—rejected claims of damage. Ten thousand people were left destitute and homeless, placed in internment camps.

As I was told today, they were told, "Don't you mention you were ever in a camp or we'll come and get you." That's what survivors told me.

Yet no one—no arrests of the mob were made. None. No proper accounting of the dead. The death toll records by local officials said there were 36 people. That's all. Thirty-six people.

But based on studies, records, and accounts, the likelihood—the likely number is much more, in the multiple of hundreds. Untold bodies dumped into mass graves. Families who, at the time, waited for hours and days to know the fate of their loved ones are now descendants who have gone 100 years without closure.

But, you know, as we speak, the process—the process of exhuming the unmarked graves has started. And at this moment, I'd like to pause for a moment of silence for the fathers, the mothers, the sisters, sons, and daughters, friends of God and Greenwood. They deserve dignity, and they deserve our respect. May their souls rest in peace.

[Pause for a moment of silence.]

My fellow Americans, this was not a riot. This was a massacre—(applause)—among the worst in our history, but not the only one. And for too long, forgotten by our history.

As soon as it happened, there was a clear effort to erase it from our memory—our collective memories—from the news and everyday conversations. For a long time, schools in Tulsa didn't even teach it, let alone schools elsewhere.

And most people didn't realize that, a century ago, a second Ku Klux Klan had been founded—the second Ku Klux Klan had been founded.

A friend of mine, Jon Meacham—I had written—when I said I was running to restore the soul of America, he wrote a book called "The Soul of America"—not because of what I said. And there's a picture about page 160 in his book, showing over 30,000 Ku Klux Klan members in full regalia, Reverend—pointed hats, the robes—marching down Pennsylvania Avenue in Washington, D.C. Jesse, you know all about this. WashinWashington, D.C.

If my memory is correct, there were 37 members of the House of Representatives who were open members of the Klan. There were five, if I'm not mistaken—it could have been seven; I think it was five—members of the United States Senate—open members of the Klan. Multiple governors who were open members of the Klan.

Most people didn't realize that, a century ago, the Klan was founded just six years before the horrific destruction here in Tulsa. And one of the reasons why it was founded was because of guys like me, who were Catholic. It wasn't about African Americans, then; it was about making sure that all those Polish and Irish and Italian and Eastern European Catholics who came to the United States after World War One would not pollute Christianity.

The flames from those burning crosses torched every region—region of the country. Millions of white Americans belonged to the Klan, and they weren't even embarrassed by it; they were proud of it.

And that hate became embedded systematically and systemically in our laws and our culture. We do ourselves no favors by pretending none of this ever happened or that it doesn't impact us today, because it does still impact us today.

We can't just choose to learn what we want to know and not what we should know. (Applause.) We should know the good, the bad, everything. That's what great nations do: They come to terms with their dark sides. And we're a great nation.

The only way to build a common ground is to truly repair and to rebuild. I come here to help fill the silence, because in silence, wounds deepen. (Applause.) And only—as painful as it is, only in remembrance do wounds heal. We just have to choose to remember.

We memorialize what happened here in Tulsa so it can be—so it can't be erased. We know here, in this hallowed place, we simply can't bury pain and trauma forever. And at some point, there will be a reckoning, an inflection point, like we're facing right now as a nation.

What many people hadn't seen before or ha—or simply refused to see cannot be ignored any longer. You see it in so many places.

And there's greater recognition that, for too long, we've allowed a narrowed, cramped view of the promise of this nation to fester—the view that America is a zero-sum game where there is only one winner. "If you succeed, I fail. If you get ahead, I fall behind. If you get a job, I lose mine." And maybe worst of all, "If I hold you down, I lift myself up," instead of "If you do well, we all do well." (Applause.) We see that in Greenwood.

This story isn't about the loss of life, but a loss of living, of wealth and prosterity [prosperity], and possibilities that still reverberates today.

Mother Fletcher talks about how she was only able to attend school until the fourth grade and eventually found work in the shipyards, as a domestic worker.

Mr. Van Ellis has shared how, even after enlisting and serving in World War Two, he still came home to struggle with a segregated America.

Imagine all those hotels and dinners [diners] and mom-and-pop shops that could been—have been passed down this past hundred years. Imagine what could have been done for Black families in Greenwood: financial security and generational wealth.

If you come from backgrounds like my—my family—a working-class, middle-class family—the only way we were ever able to generate any wealth was in equity in our homes. Imagine what they contributed then and what they could've contributed all these years. Imagine a thriving Greenwood in North Tulsa for the last hundred years, what that would've meant for all of Tulsa, including the white community.

While the people of Greenwood rebuilt again in the years after the massacre, it didn't last. Eventually neighborhoods were redlined on maps, locking Black Tulsa out of homeownerships. (Applause.) A highway was built right through the heart of the community. Lisa, I was talking about our west side—what 95 did to it after we were occupied by the military, after Dr. King was murdered. The community—cutting off Black families and businesses from jobs and opportunity. Chronic underinvestment from state and federal governments denied Greenwood even just a chance at rebuilding. (Applause.)

We must find the courage to change the things we know we can change. That's what Vice President Harris and I are focused on, along with our entire administration, including our Housing and Urban Development Secretary, Marcia Fudge, who is here today. (Applause.)

Because today, we're announcing two expanded efforts targeted toward Black wealth creation that will also help the entire community. The first is: My administration has launched an aggressive effort to combat racial discrimination in housing. That includes everything from redlining to the cruel fact that a home owned by a Black family is too often appraised at a lower value than a similar home owned by a white family. (Applause.)

And I might add—and I need help if you have an answer to this; I can't figure this one out, Congressman Horsford. But if you live in a Black community and there's another one on the other side of the highway—it's a white community; it's the—built by the same builder, and you have a better driving record than they guy with the same car in the white community, you're—can pay more for your auto insurance.

Shockingly, the percentage of Black American homeownership is lower today in America than when the Fair Housing Act was passed more than 50 years ago. Lower today. That's wrong. And we're committing to changing that.

Just imagine if instead of denying millions of Americans the ability to own their own home and build generational wealth, we made it possible for them to buy a home and build equity into that—into that home and provide for their families.

Second, small businesses are the engines of our economy and the glue of our communities. As President, my administration oversees hundreds of billions of dollars in federal contracts for everything from refurbishing decks of aircraft carriers, to installing railings in federal buildings, to professional services.

We have a thing called—I won't go into it all because there's not enough time now. But I'm determined to use every taxpayer's dollar that is assigned to me to spend, going to American companies and American workers to build Ameri—to build American products. And as part of that, I'm going to increase the share of the dollars the federal government spends to small, disadvantaged businesses, including Black and brown small businesses.

Right now, it calls for 10 percent; I'm going to move that to 15 percent of every dollar spent will be spent (inaudible). (Applause.) I have the authority to do that.

Just imagine if, instead of denying millions of entrepreneurs the ability to access capital and contracting, we made it possible to take their dreams to the marketplace to create jobs and invest in our communities.

That—the data shows young Black entrepreneurs are just as capable of succeeding, given the chance, as white entrepreneurs are. But they don't have lawyers. They don't have—they—they don't have accountants, but they have great ideas.

Does anyone doubt this whole nation would be better off from the investments those people make? And I promise you, that's why I set up the—a national Small Business Administration that's much broader. Because they're going to get those loans.

Instead of consigning millions of American children to under-resourced schools, let's give each and every child, three and four years old, access to school—not daycare, school. (Applause.)

In the last 10 years, studies have been done by all the great universities. It shows that, if increased by 56 percent, the possibility of a child—no matter what background they come from; no matter what—if they start school at three years old, they have a 56 percent chance of going all through all 12 years without any trouble and being able to do well, and a chance to learn and grow and thrive in a school and throughout their lives.

And let's unlock more than—an incredible creativity and innovation that will come from the nation's Historically Black Colleges and Universities. (Applause.) I have a $5 billion program giving them the resources to invest in research centers and laboratories and high-demand fields to compete for the good-paying jobs in industries like—of the future, like cybersecurity.

The reason why they don't—their—their students are equally able to learn as well, and get the good-paying job that start at 90- and 100,000 bucks. But they don't have—they don't have the back—they don't have the money to provide and build those laboratories. So, guess what? They're going to get the money to build those laboratories. (Applause.)

So, instead of just talking about infrastructure, let's get about the—about the business of actually rebuilding roads and highways, filling the sidewalks and cracks, installing streetlights and high-speed Internet, creating space—space to live and work and play safely.

Let's ensure access to healthcare, clean water, clean air, nearby grocery stores—stock the fresh vegetables and food that—(applause)—in fact, deal with—I mean, these are all things we can do.

Does anyone doubt this whole nation would be better off with these investments? The rich will be just as well off. The middle class will do better, and everybody will do better. It's about good-paying jobs, financial stability, and being able to build some generational wealth. It's about economic growth for our country and outcompeting the rest of the world, which is now outcompeting us.

But just as fundamental as any of these investments I've discussed—this may be the most fundamental: the right to vote. (Applause.) The right to vote. (Applause.)

A lot of the members of the Black Caucus knew John Lewis better than I did, but I knew him. On his deathbed, like many, I called John, to speak to him. But all John wanted to do was talk about how I was doing. He died, I think, about 25 hours later.

But you know what John said? He called the right to vote "precious," "almost sacred." He said, "The most powerful nonviolent tool we have in a democratic society."

This sacred right is under assault with an incredible intensity like I've never seen —even though I got started as a public defender and a civil rights lawyer—with an intensity and an aggressiveness that we have not seen in a long, long time.

It's simply un-American. It is not, however, sadly, unprecedented. The creed "We Shall Overcome" is a longtime mainstay of the Civil Rights Movement, as Jesse Jackson can tell you better than anybody.

The obstacle to proc-—to progress that have to be overcome are a constant challenge. We saw it in the '60s, but with the current assault, it's not just an echo of a distant history.

In 2020, we faced a tireless assault on the right to vote: restrictive laws, lawsuits, threats of intimidation, voter purges, and more. We resolved to overcome it all, and we did. More Americans voted in the last election than any—in the midst of a pandemic—than any election in American history. (Applause.)

You got voters registered. You got voters to the polls. The rule of law held. Democracy prevailed. We overcame.

But today, let me be unequivocal: I've been engaged in this work my whole career, and we're going to be ramping up our efforts to overcome again.

I will have more to say about this at a later date—the truly unprecedented assault on our democracy, an effort to replace nonpartisan election administrators and to intimidate those charged with tallying and reporting the election results.

But today, as for the act of voting itself, I urge voting rights groups in this country to begin to redouble their efforts now to register and educate voters. (Applause.)

And in June—June should be a month of action on Capitol Hill. I hear all the folks on TV saying, "Why doesn't Biden get this done?" Well, because Biden only has a majority of, effectively, four votes in the House and a tie in the Senate, with two members of the Senate who vote more with my Republican friends.

But we're not giving up. Earlier this year, the House of Representatives passed For the People Act to protect our democracy. The Senate will take it up later this month, and I'm going to fight like heck with every tool at my disposal for its passage.

The House is also working on the John Lewis Voting Rights Act, which is—which is critical—(applause)—to providing new legal tools to combat the new assault on the right to vote.

To signify the importance of our efforts, today I'm asking Vice President Harris to help these efforts and lead them, among her many other responsibilities. With her leadership and your support, we're going to overcome again, I promise you. But it's going to take a hell of a lot of work. (Applause.)

And finally, we have to—and finally, we must address what remains the stain on the soul of America. What happened in Greenwood was an act of hate and domestic terrorism with a through line that exists today still.

Just close your eyes and remember what you saw in Charlottesville four years ago on television. Neo-Nazis, white supremacists, the KKK coming out of those fields at night in Virginia with lighted torches—the veins bulging on their—as they were screaming. Remember? Just close your eyes and picture what it was.

Well, Mother Fletcher said when she saw the insurrection at the Capitol on January the 9th [6th], it broke her heart—a mob of violent white extremists—thugs. Said it reminded her, what happened here in Greenwood 100 years ago.

Look around at the various hate crimes against Asian Americans and Jewish Americans. Hate that never goes away. Hate only hides.

Jesse, I think I mentioned this to you. I thought, after you guys pushed through, with Dr. King, the Voting Rights Act and the Civil Rights Act—I thought we moved. But what I didn't realize—I thought we had made enormous progress, and I was so proud to be a little part of it.

But you know what, Rev? I didn't realize hate is never defeated; it only hides. It hides. And given a little bit of oxygen—just a little bit oxygen—by its leaders, it comes out of there from under the rock like it was happening again, as if it never went away.

And so, folks, we can't—we must not give hate a safe harbor.

As I said in my address to the joint session of Congress: According to the intelligence community, terrorism from white supremacy is the most lethal threat to the homeland today. Not ISIS, not al Qaeda—white supremacists. (Applause.) That's not me; that's the intelligence community under both Trump and under my administration.

Two weeks ago, I signed into law the COVID-19 Hate Crimes Act, which the House had passed and the Senate. My administration will soon lay out our broader strategy to counter domestic terrorism and the violence driven by the most heinous hate crimes and other forms of vigorty [sic]—of bigotry.

But I'm going to close where I started. To Mother Randle, Mother Fletcher, Mr. Van Ellis, to the descendants, and to all survivors: Thank you. Thank you for giving me the honor of being able to spend some time with you earlier today. Thank you for your courage. Thank you for your commitment. And thank your children, and your grandchildren, and your unc-—and your nieces and your nephews.

To see and learn from you is a gift—a genuine gift. Dr. John Hope Franklin, one of America's greatest historians—Tulsa's proud son, whose father was a Greenwood survivor—said, and I quote, "Whatever you do, it must be done in the spirit of goodwill and mutual respect and even love. How else can we overcome the past and be worthy of our forebearers and face the future with confidence and with hope?"

On this sacred and solemn day, may we find that distinctly Greenwood spirit that defines the American spirit—the spirit that gives me so much confidence and hope for the future; that helps us see, face to face; a spirit that helps us know fully who we are and who we can be as a people and as a nation.

I've never been more optimistic about the future than I am today. I mean that. And the reason is because of this new generation of young people. They're the best educated, they're the least prejudiced, the most open generation in American history.

And although I have no scientific basis of what I'm about to say, but those of you who are over 50—how often did you ever see—how often did you ever see advertisements on television with Black and white couples? Not a joke.

I challenge you—find today, when you turn on the stations—sit on one station for two hours. And I don't know how many commercials you'll see—eight to five—two to three out of five have mixed-race couples in them. That's not by accident. They're selling soap, man. (Laughter.) Not a joke.

Remember ol' Pat Caddell? He used to say, "You want to know what's happening in American culture? Watch advertising, because they want to sell what they have."

We have hope in folks like you, honey. I really mean it. We have hope. But we've got to give them support. We have got to give them the backbone to do what we know has to be done. Because I doubt whether any of you would be here if you didn't care deeply about this. You sure in the devil didn't come to hear me speak. (Laughter.)

But I really mean it. I really mean it. Let's not give up, man. Let's not give up.

As the old saying goes, "Hope springs eternal." I know we've talked a lot about famous people, but I'm—my colleagues in the Senate used to kid me because I was always quoting Irish poets. They think I did it because I'm Irish. They think I did it because we Irish—we have a little chip on our shoulder. A little bit, sometimes.

That's not why I did it; I did it because they're the best poets in the world. (Laughter.) You can smile, it's okay. It's true.

There was a famous poet who wrote a poem called "The Cure at Troy"—Seamus Heaney. And there is a stanza in it that I think is the definition of what I think should be our call today for young people.

It said, "History teaches us not to hope on this side of the grave, but then, once in a lifetime, the longed-for tidal wave of justice rises up, and hope and history rhyme."

Let's make it rhyme. Thank you.

* * *

RHETORICAL ANALYSIS

A recent 30 second ad for Citi, entitled "Citi—New Black Wall Streets," provides the following text:

> One hundred years ago, a beautiful empire built on black excellence was booming. Black Wall Street—it was a sight to be seen. Until one day it was all burned to the ground. But fire is no match for the fire within Black dreamers everywhere. And so, New Black Wall Streets rise. Citi supports the development of New Black Wall Streets across the U.S. For the love of Black Entrepreneurship. For the Love of Progress. Citi is committed to helping build black businesses through banking, Citi. Learn more at citi.com/RacialEquity.[2]

This ad hearkens back to the events that took place May 31–June 1, 1921, known as the Tulsa Race Riot and alternatively as the Tulsa Race Massacre. Although this ignominious event has been characterized as "arguably the worst discrete incident of racial violence in American history,"[3] and "a dark and tragic disgrace for Oklahoma and the entire United States,"[4] the event has not achieved the comparable commemorative stature as other tragic events dotting the timetable in U.S. history.

The Citi commercial promotes Black enterprise by refamiliarizing and familiarizing people with the tragedy surrounding the events of 1921. The cachet of this event is its coalescence of the tragic loss of life, of property, of community, and legacy.

The events comprising the Tulsa Race Riot/Massacre which transpired over the course of the last day in May and the first day of June 1921, serve as the impetus for President Joe Biden's speech commemorating the 100th Anniversary of the Tulsa Race Massacre, delivered, June 1, 2021, at the Greenwood Cultural Center in Tulsa, Oklahoma. Nelson and Joselus note Biden's focus on the ways that systemic racism "impeded black economic progress and contributed to the substantial, persistent wealth and income gap between black and white Americans,"[5] and the "racial inequality" is ascribed "to external forces such as prejudice, discrimination, and lack of opportunity."[6]

With an eye on the historical frame, on June 6, 1921, President Warren G. Harding, en route from Valley Forge, Pennsylvania to Washington D.C., made a stop at Lincoln University and delivered a speech commemorating the African American soldiers who perished serving the country in World War I.[7] In his speech, Harding bemoaned the violence that ensued in Tulsa, Oklahoma just days prior. Lincoln University, founded in 1854 as Ashmun Institute, was renamed in 1860, enjoying the cachet as the first institution of higher learning named for Abraham Lincoln. Harding's remarks were evidently delivered extemporaneously, the passages of which were documented in the June 7, 1921 edition of the *New York Times*. In contrasting the sacredness and the honorableness of Lincoln University's mission with the rancor, profaneness, and shame of the perpetrators of the Tulsa Race Massacre, Harding said:

> I commend the valuable work that this institution is doing in that direction. It is a clear contrast to the unhappy and stressing spectacle that we saw the other day out in one of the Western States. God grant that in the soberness, the fairness and the justice of this country, we shall never have another similar spectacle.[8]

Biden's speech provides an interesting oratorical bookend to Harding's abbreviated but meaningful encomium to the African American citizens of the time (referring most pointedly to the veterans and the graduates of Lincoln University), in tandem with the obloquy leveled against the perpetrators of the Tulsa Race

Massacre. Here, the dual purposes of honor and shame are combined. At its core, Biden's speech is commemorative, yet anchored in significant ways with the foundational tenets of deliberative and forensic rhetoric.

As challenging as it is to capture the attention of the public with events that are contemporaneous with their lives, how much more challenging it is to instantiate an event from the past—let alone one from a century ago, imbuing it with relevance for a public that for the most part, does not even have a scintilla of knowledge about that event.

As described in the Report by the Oklahoma Commission, "For seventy-three years before the Murrah Federal Building was bombed, April 19, 1995, the city of Tulsa erupted into a firestorm of hatred and violence that is perhaps unequaled in the peacetime history of the United States."[9] As recounted by Scott Ellsworth in *The Ground Breaking*, the Today Show with Bryant Gumbel broadcast live for an entire week from Oklahoma City in the aftermath of the Oklahoma City bombing. Characterized as "the most devastating incident of terrorism to ever occur on American soil,"[10] prior to the events of September 11, 2001, 168 persons were killed, hundreds injured, with damage to 300 buildings in the vicinity of the bomb site perpetrated by Timothy McVeigh and Terry Nichols.[11] As a co-conspirator, Terry Nichols received a life sentence, Timothy McVeigh a death sentence in 1997, but he refused all appeals, and was executed in June 2001.[12] In Gumbel's encounter on the Today Show set with Dan Ross, a state legislator in the House of Representatives and representing North Tulsa at the time,[13] Ross said to Gumbel, "as horrible as this tragedy is, there was another tragedy even worse, that happened in Tulsa. And no news organization has ever given it the attention that it deserves."[14] The Oklahoma City bombing was duly commemorated, notably with one year and twenty-five year milestone ceremonies.[15] But the sesquicentennial anniversary of the Tulsa Race Riot/Massacre, coinciding with the one-year anniversary of the Oklahoma City bombing in the spring of 1996, is no testament to the historical memory and import of Tulsa, 1921. A modest service was held at one of the churches that had been rebuilt after it was torched and burned, and a monument titled, "Black Wall Street of America" was dedicated at the Greenwood Cultural Center.[16] For the fiftieth anniversary in 1971, Reverend G. Calvin McCuthen Sr., then the pastor of Mt. Zion Baptist Church, opined, "it's almost as if it never occurred."[17]

For what should have been annual events commemorating the Tulsa Race Massacre, the sad and even shameful reality is that commemorations were not even sporadic occurrences, for as the former mayor of Tulsa said in 1996, "it just wasn't something that people discussed,"[18] and admitted that even she did not know anything about it until she was an adult.[19] According to the Commission, "entire generations of Oklahoma school children were taught little or nothing about what happened."[20]

As tantamount as the Tulsa Race Massacre is to the Oklahoma City bombing in its tragic proportions, Ellsworth argues that "like the bombing of the Murrah Federal Building some seventy-three years later, there is simply no denying the fact that the riot was a true Oklahoma tragedy, perhaps our greatest."[21]

Joseph Biden's speech at the Greenwood Cultural Center in Tulsa, Oklahoma, June 1, 2021, in commemoration of the 100th anniversary of the Tulsa Race massacre is noteworthy for the interweaving of the three Aristotelian genres of rhetoric. Aristotle delineates the three kinds or genres of rhetoric: deliberative, judicial (forensic), and epideictic. The deliberative speech within a legislative arena used to exhort or dissuade for expediency or inexpediency, the judicial or forensic speech used to accuse or defend within a judicial arena for justice or injustice. As a speech of praise or blame, epideictic rhetoric, does, according to Lanham, engender a "classificatory problem,"[22] in that the "distinguishing features" of the epideictic speech can also be found in deliberative and forensic speeches. Generally, the epideictic speech purports to praise or blame, bringing to light honor or shame.[23] Complicating this classificatory conundrum is the extensive list of subclassifications of epideictic rhetoric, which Johannesen et al. describe as, "speeches that intensify social cohesion," of which eulogies and commemorative speeches are but two of twelve that are delineated.[24] They define a commemorative speech as one which "marks the anniversary of an event. It demonstrates the significance of the event considering present groups, values, beliefs, and goals."[25] All of the above epideictic subtypes, although different, "share the larger social purpose of intensifying social cohesion by paying tribute to the values of the group," and "invites members to reaffirm their commitment to the values, customs, and traditions that are at the heart of group life."[26] The epideictic speech is traditionally construed as the least controversial, with its goal to "intensify social cohesion," distinguished by a more archetypal foundation, and emphasizing the common ground in minimally contentious ways,[27] but that does not preclude the speech from possessing embeds from the forensic and deliberative speeches.

Scholarship within the communication discipline, provides an edifying entry point in understanding the complexities of the epideictic genre. As explained by Jamieson and Campbell, a fruitful way of understanding the characteristics of the three genres coalescing in one speech is with the "rhetorical hybrid."[28] They underscore that "genres are not only dynamic responses to circumstances; each is a *dynamis*—a potential fusion of elements that may be energized or actualized as a strategic response to a situation."[29] In rhetorical hybrids, one genre is predominant, and as exemplified in eulogistic discourse, for example—a subclassification of epideictic rhetoric, the eulogistic genre should predominate.[30] In their example, Campbell and Jamieson describe Lyndon Johnson's eulogy of John F. Kennedy, in which Johnson needed to "eulogize, legitimize, and advocate," in order "to satisfy the human and institutional needs created by Kennedy's death."[31] The subordinate but important policy dimension for Johnson must be the realization of Kennedy's aspiration to pass civil rights legislation, among other important pieces of legislation.[32]

Celeste Michelle Condit's edifying essay, "The Functions of Epideictic: The Boston Massacre Orations as Exemplar," identifies three paired functions which characterize "the epideictic experience for speakers and audiences"[33] in the message production: (1) definition and understanding, (2) sharing and creation of community, and (3) entertainment and display Condit notes that the former term for each pair functions on behalf of the speaker and the latter on behalf of the audience.[34]

With definition/understanding, the epideictic speech purports "to explain a social world," explicating a concept through a prism of the "audience's key values and beliefs."[35] The speaker's ethos is strengthened with the ability to render the issues more pellucid, producing a feeling of succor in the audience.[36] This "definitional authority" can furnish "immediate or pastoral gratification" or in pursuit of future "argumentative purposes."[37] In shaping and sharing community, the epideictic speaker crafts the speech with a focus on explaining the speech's raison d'être to the community and expounding upon how the "shared heritage" can be realized.[38] In the third pair, the speaker achieves "eloquence," through "truth, beauty and power in human speech."[39]

In Condit's paradigm, three perspectives augment the understanding of epideictic rhetoric: the message-centered, speaker-centered, and audience-centered perspectives.[40] An important but limited perspective is the mainstay of epideictic discourse—praise and blame. In the speaker-centered perspective, the two sub routes are argumentative and performance theory. As understood through Perelman and Olbrechts-Tyteca, the epideictic speech functions as preparation for action, lending "values heft" to the arguments for deliberative and forensic arguments.[41] The epideictic speech has the potential to "set the table" as it were, for the other genres, the latter, seemingly of greater import than the mere ceremonial nature of the epideictic speech.[42] With the performance theory subtype, the speech functions more like an aesthetic artifact as "art for art's sake," as opposed to a rhetorical artifact.[43] For the audience perspective, the audience's focus is on the speaker, adjudicating the speaker's success in achieving the purpose of praising and/or blaming.[44] Within the audience perspective, Rosenfield's distinguishing characteristic of the "radiance of being" is albeit rare, but as a more spiritually steeped notion, can be a potent aspect of the epideictic speech,[45] notwithstanding the Perelman and Olbrechts-Tyteca critique of the epideictic genre, where the genre is simultaneously predominant and relegated to a lower rung and an attenuated status on the genre ladder. As a commemorative speech under the rubric of epideictic rhetoric, Condit concludes that the epideictic speech is "an awesome humane tool."[46]

Rather than seeing Biden's speech as neither fish nor fowl, the speech is a kairotic event, in which each genre is more fully developed than one would usually find in a rhetorical hybrid, without the loss of the dominant epideictic genre, and without the dissipation of the deliberative and judicial purposes and treatments. Biden's speech is an exceptional example of a commemorative speech that does not downgrade the argumentative tenets as instantiated in the deliberative and judicial genres, providing fulsome treatments of all three purposes within all three genres: expediency/inexpediency (deliberative), justice/injustice (judicial), and honor/shame (epideictic).[47] The speech is an effective treatment of each pair of purposes within each genre, with commensurate emphasis for each pair. Although particular sections of the speech seem to provide a more overt treatment of one genre over the other, ultimately, when examining the speech holistically, the speech is an exemplar of a successfully realized "fusion" with distinctive hybridized properties.[48]

After acknowledging some dignitaries to the audience, Biden quotes a passage from First Corinthians, alluding to the importance of direct confrontation, in order to ascertain truth. He makes the claim that the only way healing, justice, and repair can be realized is through the ascertainment and acceptance of painful truths as a part of a painful past. On the heels of the spiritually embedded salutations, Biden says, "Only—only with truth can come healing and justice and repair. Only with truth facing it. But that isn't enough," and he continues by saying that it is incumbent upon all of us that "America knows the story in full."[49] The truth begins with bringing the history to light, in addition to setting the historical record straight, and in doing so, fostering a process of healing, and promulgating justice through the acts of reparations.

Hearkening back to the Zeitgeist of Tulsa, 1921, before the events of May 31–June 1, 2021, Biden regales the audience with a more sanguine part of Tulsa's past, although it must be noted that life in Tulsa was far from idyllic for its African American citizens. Biden then brings the events from 1921 literally to life, again recognizing the three sole survivors of the Tulsa Race Massacre: Mother Randle, Mother Fletcher, and Mr. Van Ellis, who, as told by Biden, were put to bed with peace in a beloved, thriving community, only to have awaken to experience the most tragic type of peripeteia.[50]

In his seminal work, *Death in a Promised Land*, Scott Ellsworth calls Tulsa "a boom city in a boom state."[51] Between 1910 and 1920, Tulsa's population increased from 18,182 to 72,075 with the greater Tulsa population at the latter year, 100,000.[52] Contemporaneous with achieving statehood in 1907, Oklahoma had the cachet as the top oil producer in the United States.[53] By 1913, not only did Oklahoma achieve recognition for "producing one-quarter of all the oil produced in the nation," but it also prospered as "an important commercial center tied to the state's agricultural industry, which claimed in 1920 about one-half of Oklahoma's work force."[54] Bestowed on the city were the soubriquets "Tulsey Town" and "Magic City," with its exponential growth in the Southwest sector of the country.[55] Although the Black population in Tulsa was significant, racism abounded, engendering two separate cities within its geographical limits: White Tulsa and Black Tulsa. In Black Tulsa, the intersection of Greenwood and Archer Avenues, known as "Deep Greenwood" was the "key spot of delineation between the city's black and white worlds."[56] A thriving community, prior to the riot/massacre, this area also enjoyed a soubriquet—"Negro's Wall Street", and as part of its history, is proudly called "Black Wall Street."[57]

Notwithstanding its veneer of wealth and prosperity, "Tulsa was a deeply troubled town."[58] White residents referred to the section where the 10,000 Black residents lived as "Little Africa."[59] Tulsa saw a significant amount of "Klan activity," with approximately 3,200 Klansmen operating out of Tulsa in December 1921, with the ownership of its own building called BENO Hall, thought to be a partial epithet laced acronym of sorts for "BE NO N*** BE NO JEW, BE NO CATHOLIC."[60] In August 1923, a Jewish Tulsan, Nathan Hantaman, was kidnapped by the Klan on Greenwood Avenue,[61] and the Catholic Tulsans were also in the Klan's crosshairs, where the latter attempted to coerce businesses "to fire their Catholic employees."[62]

What precipitated the tragic events in Tulsa and how did they unfold? What is known with certainty is that on May 30, a Black teenager, thought to be nineteen years old, was employed in downtown Tulsa at a shoe-shining parlor.[63] With no available bathroom facilities on site, the white parlor owner planned for the African American employees to use the facilities within close proximity at the Drexel Building.[64] Since the facilities were on the building's top floor, Rowland stepped onto the elevator. What transpired next is uncertain. One narrative speculates that Rowland attacked Sarah Page, the seventeen-year-old white elevator operator, and then he ran out of the elevator. Another account, one that Ellsworth suggests is the most common, is that "Rowland accidentally stepped on page's foot in the elevator, causing her to lurch back, and when he grabbed her arm to keep her from falling, she screamed."[65] A third scenario suggests that page and Rowland knew each other and "had a lover's quarrel."[66] On Tuesday, May 31, Rowland was arrested. Learning of Rowland's arrest, the newspaper, the *Tulsa Tribune* scooped the story of the alleged incident for its afternoon edition.[67] In cloak-and-dagger journalistic fashion, the newspaper pages related to the Rowland arrest disappeared, including the article on the front page, in addition to the editorial page in its entirety. However, in 1946, Loren Gill, a graduate student wrote his master's thesis on the Tulsa Race Massacre, and discovered the missing article, which he concluded was "no less than inflammatory."[68] The headline read, "Nab Negro for Attacking Girl in Elevator."[69] Other copies of the article surfaced, but mysteriously vanished.[70] Adding insult to injury, a survivor recalls another headline in the *Tulsa Tribune* that read, "To Lynch Negro Tonight." Ellsworth believes that this headline very well could have been a headline on the missing editorial page.[71] After the paper appeared on the streets with talk of lynching, hundreds of white individuals gathered outside the courthouse where Rowland was being held, between 6 p.m. and 9 p.m., on May 31.

Although the Sheriff appeared to have the situation under control, having secured the safety of Rowland, some of the Black citizens were very concerned that Rowland could suffer a fate like that of Roy Belton—and he was white.[72] A small group of black men went to the courthouse to offer assistance in assuring Rowland's safety while detained, but their presence "electrified the white mob,"[73] which now totaled in the thousands. Having lost control of the mob, the situation deteriorated, and another group of Black citizens made their way towards the courthouse, "when a rumor began to circulate that the white mob was storming the courthouse."[74] The inflection point in this powder keg occurred around 10 p.m., when one of the white men tussled with one of the Black World War I veterans in an attempt to disarm him yelling out epithets, and then the gun went off.[75] Ellsworth quotes the Sheriff who said on the heels of this event, "the race-war was on and I was powerless to stop it."[76]

The violence intensified, and at the courthouse, white men and boys of the mob were deputized by the police, told by one officer to "get a gun and get a n**ger."[77] They looted the stores, grabbing guns and ammunition, making their way to the Black neighborhood.[78] The fires began to be set around 1 a.m. with scores of black owned business and homes ablaze by 4 a.m.[79] By around 6 a.m. June 1, "the wholesale burning and looting of black Tulsa began."[80] Martial law was declared at 11:29 a.m. on June 1.[81] By 8:00 p.m., the riot—for all intents and purposes—had run its course.[82] What was left? They torched the entire neighborhood, leaving it in ash and rubble, hundreds dead, many thrown unceremoniously into mass graves, arresting, interning the survivors, and leaving 10,000 citizens homeless.[83]

Although the Black citizens were charged with instigating the riot, no whites were imprisoned for murder or arson during the tragic 24-hour period.[84] And in another tragic and ironic twist, Sarah Page refused to file charges against Rowland, and he was exonerated of the alleged crime.[85]

In the speech, Biden says that common ground can only be achieved through repairing and rebuilding, a goal that resonates in the Jewish concept of "tikkun olam, which is steeped in the action of social justice."[86] Although not explicitly stated in the speech, a significant tenet of the deliberative/policy initiatives is reparations and the concomitant controversies surrounding them. Alfred Brophy is supportive of reparations based on four arguments.[87] First, he argues that Tulsa and the state of Oklahoma had culpability insofar as there probably would not have been a riot were it not for the collective misconduct and malfeasance of government officials.[88] Secondly, persons who are still alive, suffered direct harm.[89] Third, the reparations are chronologically and spatially bound, exhibiting limited but clear and legitimate parameters for reparations.[90] And lastly, even in the immediate aftermath, the city of Tulsa acknowledged the necessity of rebuilding the Greenwood neighborhood, and actually promised to do so.[91] As Brophy brilliantly summarizes:

> The riot represented the complete breakdown of the rule of law. It was the product of a failure of white Tulsans to uphold the law against lynching. The destruction was itself further evidence of the lack of the rule of law in Tulsa. The payment of reparations holds out the promise of allowing the rule of law to reign in the Tulsa riot, even if eighty years later.[92]

At the time of Brophy's writing, the Oklahoma legislature passed the 1921 Race Riot Reconciliation Act in Spring 2021,[93] but it excluded "direct payments to Tulsa riot survivors."[94] That situation changed May 2022, with Judge Caroline Woll's ruling that the plaintiffs' reparations lawsuit can move forward, which would "not only set the record straight on what took place between May 31 and June 1, 1921, but also create a special fund for survivors and descendants of the massacre that left at least 300 Black people dead and the once-booming neighborhood of Greenwood destroyed."[95] As a pastiche of sorts, the advocacy for reparations included the tagline, "No reconciliation without reparations,"[96] justified by the multi-generational loss of life, homes, businesses, cultural and financial legacies, and lives lived but rendered unfulfilled.[97] On September 1, 2020, Damario Solomon-Simmons filed a lawsuit, alleging that the defendants were profiting off of the massacre, by using the massacre to advance Tulsa's tourism, and at the expense of the reparations for the victims and their descendants.[98] Brilliantly, they used Oklahoma's "public nuisance" law. Because bona fide accountability had been circumvented by the defendants, and because the deleterious tragic outcome of the massacre still ensued, the Greenwood neighborhood, as argued by Solomon-Simmons, was, to this day, "a crime scene."[99]

In addition to the secular, fiduciary reparation provisions for which the government should be held responsible, the spiritual reparation provisions must be accounted for as well. Much work has been done and continues to be done to learn the truth about the hundreds of black citizens who were murdered and put in mass graves.

The exhumation of the profanely buried victims—as a fundamentally forensic act—exhibited both rancor and succor, as removing the souls from their state of rest, which is in more ways a state of unrest; and yet, in order for their souls to ultimately receive a sacred burial, the exhumation needs to occur on a spiritual level, as well as a forensic level, in order to literally and figuratively unearth the truth about the murdered victims of the Tulsa Race Massacre. The first excavation attempt began July 13, 2020, and ended July 22, 2020, since they found "zero evidence of a mass grave, or even of any individual burials."[100] A second dig occurred on September 14, 2020, providing no evidence of mass graves.[101] On October 20, 2020, several coffins were located, and on October 21, 2020, at Oaklawn Cemetery, a mass grave was discovered.[102] The excavating team continued their work in June, 2021, with human remains discovered in the area of the originally discovered mass grave.[103] The Tulsa Commission Report (2001) recommended that any remains identified as victims of the Tulsa Race Massacre, should not be reburied in Oaklawn Cemetery, which was the "final resting place of the prominent Tulsans who actively participated in the massacre,"[104] which included the Tulsa Police and Sheriff's Departments, the National Guard.[105]

As Reverend Turner witnessed the excavation October 2020, after failed attempts July 13–22, 2020, he knelt at the perimeter of the excavation site while placing his hands through the wrought-iron fence and prayed.[106] Reverend Turner expressed how important it was to provide a sacred burial:

> They are people, children of God, who were killed brutally, and they never had a funeral service. The ashes to ashes, dust to dust we say at the funeral is our symbolic way of releasing that person's soul to wherever it's going, and these people never had that... We have buried animals better than we handled the victims in Greenwood. We can do better.[107]

Deuteronomy 16:20, states, "Justice, justice, shall you pursue, that you may thrive and occupy the land that the Lord your God is giving you." Brophy states that "a primary goal of reparations is to do justice, to the extent that can be done."[108] Justice has legal tenets, some of which are retributive, some restitutive, but justice—as it engages righting a wrong, can be righting not only a "legal" wrong, but a moral wrong.

One policy was posited for achieving justice, resulting from the "inability of the residents to transfer their destroyed properties and wealth to future generations."[109] A restorative solution for "empowering stable wealth attainment and wealth transfer protected by estate planning and the rule of law"[110] is a theological and ancient proposal called "Replacement Theory."[111] The Jewish interpretation, based on the notion of "an eye for an eye" found in Exodus 2:24, is in contravention to its secular meaning. According to the biblical interpretation, as explained by the Aleph Institute, the phrase in Hebrew, literally translates as "eye for an eye," but in Hebrew, the word *tachas* means "in place of." Yes, justice demands "monetary compensation,"[112] but also demands the sensibility to "feel another's pain as if it were our own."[113]

As encouraging as the creation of the Tulsa Race Massacre Commission was, the Commission and Governor Stitt found themselves at cross-purposes with the passage of H.B. 1775 and its ramifications for teaching public school students in Oklahoma.[114] Seemingly not coincidental, Governor Stitt was removed from the Commission shortly after having signed H.B. 1775, which "prohibits instructors from teaching that 'one race or sex is inherently superior to another,' and that 'an individual, by virtue of his or her race or sex, is inherently racist, sexist or oppressive.'"[115] Although Stitt disavowed any connection between the mission of the Commission and the mandate of H.B. 1775, Phil Armstrong, the Centennial Commission project director would have none of it,[116] and claimed that the legislation "chills the ability of educators to teach students, of any age and will only serve to intimidate educators who seek to reveal and process our hidden history."[117]

Halfway through the speech, Biden addresses the deliberative aspects by foregrounding the inexpediency of a policy that ostensibly worked to ameliorate the post-massacre exigencies, but as Biden says, left much unresolved, and even in a worsened state. He then provides a series of six planks in a more global plan to achieve justice:

1. The first plank pursues "an aggressive effort to combat racial discrimination in housing."
2. In the second plank, the administration pledges "to increase the share of the dollars the federal government spends to small, disadvantaged business, including Black and Brown businesses."
3. Third, noting the importance of education, the recommendation is for every 3–4-year-old to have "access to school—not daycare, school."
4. Going hand in hand with the third plank, the administration proposes the infusion of more resources into Historically Black College and Universities (HBCUs), as a pathway to "creativity and innovation" and well-paying jobs.
5. Fifth, Biden touts the importance of improving the infrastructure, and ultimately, producing a safer environment.
6. The sixth plank, as part and parcel of a healthy environment and the promotion of a healthy lifestyle with all the attendant benefits, Biden wants to ensure access to clean water, clean air, healthcare, and accessible grocery store to militate against the ubiquity of food deserts for so many citizens lining in poorer areas of the country.[118]

Integral to the practicality section of this deliberative segment of the speech, Biden makes the argument that the above policies benefit all socio-economic strata, and can reverse the dearth of "generational wealth" brought about in no small way by the Tulsa Race Massacre.[119]

Biden allocates a substantial amount of time to the last two planks, with plank six stressing the foundational import of the right to vote, characterizing it as a "sacred right," which has been, and continues to be threatened. Repeating the words "overcome" and "overcame" six times, Biden is reinforcing the idea that, although the threats to voting and to democracy are ever looming, past efforts have not been insurmountable, and that the fight to protect these rights must endure.

In the peroration of the speech, Biden creates symmetry with the introduction by referencing Mother Fletcher, Mother Randle, and Mr. Van Ellis. Aristotle delineates the four parts of an epilogue (peroration) in this way: "make the audience well-disposed towards yourself and ill-disposed towards your opponent; magnify or minimize the leading facts; excite the required state of emotion in your hearers; [and] refresh their memories."[120] Biden expresses his profound gratitude to these three survivors, invoking the act of "overcoming," through a quote by the preeminent historian Dr. John Hope Franklin, whose father, Buck Colbert Franklin survived the Tulsa Race Massacre—a quote which reinforces the importance of goodwill, respect, and love:

> Whatever you do, it must be done in the spirit of goodwill and mutual respect and even love. How else can we overcome the past and be worthy of our forebearers and face the future with confidence and with hope?[121]

In highlighting the commemorative thrust of the speech, Biden characterizes June 1, 2021, as sacred and solemn, and the events of the past revivify that sense of hope. Biden links the future with hope, and in pursuit of that sentiment, he extols the virtues of the younger generations.

In stressing the advancement in racial equity, Biden provides a verifiable observation about the presence of people of color, including interracial couples in advertisements, an interesting corollary to the recent Citi ad referred to at the beginning of this analysis. Like many commemorative speeches, Biden cites and quotes from two literary artifacts: "An Essay on Man," by the eighteenth-century Enlightenment poet Alexander Pope, and Seamus Heaney's "The Cure at Troy." In Epistle I of "An Essay on Man," the iconic quotation, "hope springs eternal,"[122] quoted by Biden, reinforces the motif of hope throughout the speech. The penultimate statement in the speech—an inspirational passage from Heaney, forms a coalescence of history, hope and justice, reminiscent of Theodore Parker's iconic dictum, and its adaptation by Martin Luther King and other orators in the annals of American oratory.

The concept of justice is integral to memorable quotations in the history of oratory, one of the most familiar and oft quoted, delivered by Reverend Dr. Martin Luther King, Jr. The timetable for achieving justice spurred by the Tulsa Race massacre of 1921 has spanned over a century. In his speech "Remaining Awake

Through a Great Revolution," delivered on March 31, 1968, at the National Cathedral, King said, "We shall overcome because the arc of the moral universe is long, but it bends toward justice." In his speech on March 25, 1965, after the Selma March, on the steps of the Alabama State Capitol, King questions how long it will take for truth to reemerge, and King's self-retort is, "how long? Not long, because the arc of the moral universe is long, but it bends toward justice." The quote is memorable in the annals of American oratory and is a paraphrase of a passage penned by Theodore Parker, a nineteenth century abolitionist, Unitarian minister, and leading figure in the Transcendentalist movement. In "of Justice and the Conscience," his third sermon of his *Ten Sermons of Religion*, Parker says,

> Look at the facts of the world. You see a continual and progressive triumph of the right. I do not pretend to understand the moral universe, the arc is a long one, my eye reaches but little ways. I cannot calculate the curve and complete the figure by experience of sight; I can divine it by conscience. But from what I see I am sure it bends towards justice.[123]

In the National Cathedral speech, King prefaces the quote with the phrase, "We shall overcome," an iconic phrase used in protest speech and song during the civil rights movement of the 1960's. The creative provenance of the song is a musical composition (both music and lyrics), "I'll Overcome Some Day" by Charles Albert Tindley, one of the founders of American gospel and a Methodist minister.[124]

Lastly, Biden links the "hate and domestic terrorism" in Tulsa, Oklahoma in the Greenwood neighborhood in 1921, with the hate and domestic terrorism experienced today. Biden explicitly cites contemporary references like Charlottesville, Virginia in 2017, and speaks to the sentiments of Mother Fletcher, who bore witness to the events of 1921, and who compared the insurrection at the Capitol, January 6, 2021, to the events in Tulsa a century prior.

Each of the three survivors provided testimony to Congress's House Subcommittee on the Constitution, Civil Rights and Civil Liberties, May 19, 2021, and each testimony reinforces each genre's purpose. Mother Fletcher exhorted her country to acknowledge the tragedy of Tulsa and not to forget. Despite having been abandoned by her country in so many ways, Mother Fletcher did not abandon her patriotism, having worked in the California shipyards to support the war effort. She rebukes the Tulsa Centennial Commission for having raised thirty million dollars for tourist sites commemorating the Tulsa Race Massacre, while she remained in poverty. Most poignantly, Mother Fletcher demanded justice. Mr. Hughes Van Ellis, Mother Fletcher's 100-year-old brother rebukes the Oklahoma and federal courts for denying them the justice they so irrefutably deserved. Like his sister, Mr. Van Ellis highlights his patriotism and generosity to the country, serving in an all-black battalion in the Far East, but these virtues on his part were unreciprocated. Towards the end of his remarks, Van Ellis hopes for a time when they can be treated like first-class citizens, quoting the last five words of The Pledge of Allegiance: "liberty and justice for all." Mother Randle excoriates those people who perpetrated such a heinous act, attributing it to hate, saying, "It is disgusting that they hate us for no reason except that we are Black people."[125] The government at the city, county and state levels bears the responsibility for righting the grievous wrongs, and at the end of her remarks, Mother Randle pleads for "some justice."

In the concluding paragraph of her introductory essay for the 2022 Tulsa Race Massacre Symposium Issue of the Tulsa Law Review, Tamara A. Piety says,

> We worked so hard because we felt deeply that the events of these two days inflicted a wound that has continued to fester. The Massacre, and just as importantly, the actions and inactions which followed, represent a stain on the city and they undermine the moral standing of those who purport to lead it. Until there is compensation to the survivors' descendants, some meaningful and concrete atonement for the city's participation in the crime, peace, and real prosperity, for the city and for all its citizens will be out of reach—no matter how many memorials are built or apologies uttered. Justice is the best memorial.[126]

And although justice is not conventionally a part of the "built environment" as a brick and mortar edifice, it is inextricably bound to the forensic, deliberative, and commemorative genres, engendering a truly symbiotic relationship with potentially favorable outcomes.

CHAPTER 1: PART 2

Race, Gender, and Violence

The two different speech texts of this address are attributed the former slave woman who came to call herself Sojourner Truth. Truth delivered versions of the following transcribed speech text to the Woman's Right's Convention in Akron, Ohio on May 29, 1851. Evidence from newspaper accounts of both the *Anti-Slavery Bugle* and *The New York Tribune* reported that, Truth's rhetoric possessed a wit, skillful repartee, employed metaphors, alluded to women from the Bible, and that she confronted a hostile audience. Those closest to the event confirmed that Truth proclaimed, "I am a woman's rights" and that "she was a woman." The speech demonstrates a percussive performance that imbricates feminist and prophetic rhetorical discourse.

"ADDRESS AT THE WOMAN'S RIGHTS CONVENTION IN AKRON, OHIO"

Sojourner Truth

Akron, Ohio. May 29, 1851.

ROBINSON VERSION[1]

May I say a few words? I want to say a few words about this matter. I am a woman's rights. I have as much muscle as any man, and can do as much work as any man. I have plowed and reaped and husked and chopped and mowed, and can any man do more than that? I have heard much about the sexes being equal; I can carry as much as any man, and can eat as much too, if I can get it. I am as strong as any man that is now. As for intellect, all I can say is, if a woman have a pint and man a quart—why cant she have her little pint full? You need not be afraid to give us our rights for fear we will take too much,—for we cant take more than our pint'll hold. The poor men seem to be all in confusion, and dont know what to do. Why children, if you have woman's rights give it to her and you will feel better. You will have your own rights, and they wont be so much trouble. I cant read, but I can hear. I have heard the bible and have learned that Eve caused man to sin. Well if woman upset the world, do give her a chance to set it right side up again. The Lady has spoken about Jesus, how he never spurned woman from him, and she was right. When Lazarus died, Mary and Martha came to him with faith and love and besought him to raise their brother. And Jesus wept—and Lazarus came forth. And how came Jesus into the world? Through God who created him and woman who bore him. Man, where is your part? But the women are coming up blessed by God and a few of the men are coming up with them. But man is in a tight place, the poor slave is on him, woman is coming on him, and he is surely between a hawk and a buzzard.

GAGE VERSION[2]

Well, chillen, whardar's so much racket dar must be som'ting out o' kilter. I tinkdat, 'twixt the niggers of de South and de women at de Norf, all a-taking 'bout rights, de white men will be in a fix pretty soon. But what's all this here talking 'bout? Dat man ober dar say dat woman needs to be helped into carriages, and lifted over ditches, and to have de best place eberywhar. Nobody eber helps me into carriages, or ober mud-puddles, or gives me any best place; And ar'n't I a woman? Look at me. Look at my arm. I have plowed and planted and gathered into barns, and no man could head me—and ar'n't I a woman? I could work as much and eat as much as a man, (when I could get it,) and bear de lash as well—and ar'n't I a woman? I have borne thirteen chillen, and seen 'emmos' all sold off into slavery, and when I cried out with a mother's grief, none but Jesus heard—and ar'n't I a woman? Den deytalks 'bout dis ting in de head. What dis dey call it?" ["Intellect," whispered some one near.] "Dat's it, honey. What's dat got to do with woman's rights or niggers' rights? If my cup won't hold but a pint and yourn holds a quart, wouldn't ye be mean not to me have my little half-measure full? Den dat little man in black dar, he say woman can't have as much right as man 'cause Christ wa'n't a woman. *Whar did your Christ come from?*"

Whar did your Christ come from? From God and a woman. Man had noting to do with him. That if de fust woman God ever made was strong enough to turn de world upside down all her one lone, all dese togeder, ought to be able to turn it back and gitit right side up again, and now dey is asking to, de men better let 'em. 'Bleeged to ye for hearin' on me, and now old Sojourner ha'n't got nothin' more to say.

* * *

RHETORICAL ANALYSIS

Lucy Stone accurately characterized what the violence and the arrant horrors of slavery did to the woman Isabella, Isabelle, or Belle in employing the word "crushed."[3] Yet, ironically, such violence was converted into religious suffering, inducing a Burkean "exorcism by misnomer"[4] and endowed American eloquence with the abolitionist, suffragist, and prophetess Sojourner Truth. From the start of her oratorical career, Truth's slavery experience, womanism/feminism, and religion were inextricably yoked with her words. Even the content of posters promoting Truth lectures consistently included a conflation of "her experience as a slave mother and religious woman."[5] While Truth's conversion story and use of religious rhetoric are well documented,[6] it is a noteworthy reminder that as scholars of rhetorical history, Suzanne Pullon Fitch and Roseann M. Mandziuk observe, all accessible material about Sojourner Truth is always already filtered by other myth makers, including her biographical collaborator Olive Gilbert, who wrote *Narrative of Sojourner Truth, A Bondswoman of Olden Times*.[7] Even after Truth's freedom, slavery left an indelible lattice of painful scars on her body, mind, language, economic opportunity, religion, and our collective understanding of who she was.

Notwithstanding the freighted and fictive constructions of Truth,[8] her rhetorical hauntology enacts an inexpungible transcendence of her agency that defies dehistoricization.[9] Through the conceptual and critical imbrication of religious rhetoric's sacred succor/rancor interplay with violence, this chapter explicates how Truth addresses the central exigencies of her time—abolition and women's rights. To augment our analysis, we have elected to include both versions of the well-known "Woman's Rights Convention Address" at Akron in 1851.[10] In doing so, we widen the rich and exceptional rhetorical religious scholarship that claims Truth as a prophetic figure.[11] Extending the popular "black jeremiad" reading of Truth's religious rhetoric, we explore how Truth's prophetic persona of the suffering servant archetype,[12] replete with accounts of the rancorous violence of slavery, coalesce with her feminist arguments for equal rights, effectuating what we call the "sufferaging servant" motif. Through the rhetorical practice of *imitatio*, a familiar, yet distinctively inventive prophetic style emerges for Truth. She deftly integrates rancorous, eidetic depictions of the agony of slavery that produce not a hatred or vengeful thirst for redemptive violence, but a belying succor of phronesis, justice, conversion, and forgiveness in her address.

The rhetorical capacity of tragic suffering like that endured and recounted by Sojourner Truth is amplified when expressed through the heroic action of an orator of her aptitude. For as Kenneth Burke proclaims, "the suffered is the learned."[13] Truth's inventive use the tragic suffering of her own life inverts Burke's familiar aphorism and affirms that: "suffering is equipment for literature." Drawing on the poetic imagination of Aeschylus's depiction of tragic suffering, Nathan Crick explicates how the necessity of tragic suffering is pleached with acts of justice because it "shakes us awake" and moves witnesses to seeing with "moral clarity."[14] Crick expounds on of this rhetorical dynamic:

> For those who must undergo the brute force of necessity, tragic rhetoric provides the courage to endure suffering in the faith that the wisdom gained will compensate for the battles lost. For those who would witness this fate, rhetoric reveals the nature of *dikē* that appears through the suffering of others in the faith that coming possibility will be more just than the vanishing actuality.[15]

As we hope to demonstrate, Truth's pathos in bearing the evils of slavery and her public witness to its sinful pervasiveness embodies both the suffering and "sufferaging" servant tropes with the rhetorical intention of emptying America writ large of its acquisitive self with the aim of achieving civil rights for slaves and women.

Harry M. Orlinsky, in his Goldenson Lecture of 1964, defined the suffering servant as one "who…suffered vicariously in order that others, guilty of sin and hence deserving of punishment, might thereby be atoned and spared the punishment."[16] Fr. Matthew Carr describes the suffering servant as an enigmatic figure presented to us by the prophet Isaiah. The suffering servant is chosen by God to be a harbinger of justice; the servant will suffer for the sins of others and be "tortured for our iniquities; upon him was the chastisement that made us whole and by his blood drawn by the we whip we are healed" all so that others might have life.[17] Theophus H. Smith avows that the figure of the suffering servant in early Afro-American literature finds its locus in passage 53 from the book of the prophet Isaiah.[18] It should be noted here that, Smith's work provides a praxilogical nonviolent counter to René Girard's theory of religion as mimetic violence.

Early abolitionist rhetorics employed the suffering servant trope as a central figure in the Christian mimetic tradition. The aim in expressing slave suffering and victimization performed several rhetorical functions. First, in an effort to reconstitute the hegemonic discourse of moral conformity, servility, and nonresistance foisted on nineteenth-century Black Americans as well as women, William Whipper first advocated blacks interpolate themselves within the Christian typology of the "suffering servant."[19] Such undeserving suffering experienced by the slave was transformed through what Smith calls a Christological mode whereby the slave's suffering mimetically participates in Christ's own suffering.[20] Consequently, Wilson Jeremiah Moses infers, "by meditating on the bruised and battered Jesus…slaves were not only able to redeem their self-respect but share in the divinity of a masochistic God."[21] In short, such suffering made one "Christlike." While evidence exists that the suffering servant form within the antebellum epoch promoted the convention of "nonresistant slave stoicism,"[22] the suffering servant does in fact have redemptive and instrumental rhetorical benefits in addition to those Moses has outlined. Smith has identified the effective ends of the suffering servant trope with the salutary aim of transforming both the victim and the victimizer.[23]

The rhetorical potentiality and power of the suffering servant idiom lies in its hermeneutical polysemy and mimetic malleability. Since the meaning of the suffering servant has always been ambiguous, it could certainly be appropriated by a prophetess like Sojourner Truth. How does Truth embody and mimetically perform the suffering servant archetype? We present evidence from her life and rhetoric that correlates with the biblical prophecy of Isaiah.

As evidence to support the claim that Truth rhetorically models the suffering servant form, we begin with a linkage to and prefiguration of the words of the Old Testament, Hebrew prophet Isaiah, who is credited with the parturition of the archetype. In her characterization of "the lash's" violent and deleterious effects on Sojourner Truth, Lucy's Stone's choice of the word "crushed" is not inconsequential and, arguably and ironically, speaks to Truth's religious conversion and restoration as a suffering servant/reconciling messianic figure. Here one can substitute the pronouns "she" and "her" where he and him are found. As the prophet Isaiah wrote:

> But he was pierced for our transgressions, he was crushed for our iniquities...Yet it was the Lord's will to crush him and cause him to suffer, and although the Lord makes his life an offering for sin, he will see his offspring and prolong his days and the will of the Lord will prosper in his hands. After he has suffered, he will see the light of life and be satisfied, by his knowledge, my righteous servant will justify many, and he will bear their iniquities.[24]

Other translations specify the whip, a metonymical instrument of torture and substitution for the institution of slavery, "upon him the chastisement that made us whole and by his blood drawn by the whip we are healed." Fr. Mathew Carr denotes that Isaiah's words read like an eyewitness account of Christ's passion, but these words antecede the birth of Christ by hundreds of years.[25] Moreover, as further evidence for the relationship between Truth, the suffering servant and Isaiah's word "crushed," in an 1851 advertisement in the *Anti-Slavery Bugle* for Truth as speaker at the now famous Akron Women's Right's Convention Address, the announcement read, "Come give us your presence and counsel...Slavery, political, and personal, will crush humanity."[26]

The biblical description of the suffering servant depicted by Isaiah adumbrates historical and rhetorical evidence to establish our claim to Truth as a suffering servant for abolition and women's rights. Two significant incidents in the life of Sojourner Truth parallel the archetype. The first is Truth's traumatic and graphic account of being scourged. In Truth's 1856 speech to Michigan Friends, she portrayed the malice of a particular master who "tied [her] up in de barn and whipped [her]...'til blood run down on de floor."[27] Moreover, in Truth's 1853 sermon before the Congregational Church in Williamsburgh, New York, she is reported to have extended her use of *ekphrasis* and *enargia* in recounting the aforementioned violent episode:

> She related with tears in her eyes the manner in which she had been tied up in the barn, with her clothing stripped from her back and whipped until the blood stood in pools upon the floor, and scars upon her back were undeniable proofs of her assertion.[28]

The retelling of Truth's torturous suffering thereby fulfills the scriptural passages of Isaiah and constitutes her role as a suffering servant: "(s)he was pierced for our transgressions, crushed for our iniquities ... and caused ... to suffer."[29]

The second revelation of the suffering servant typology in Truth's life transpired around the illegal sale of her son Peter to a slaveholder in Alabama. Truth, in a brilliant navigation of forensic discourse, engaged in legal proceedings by entering a complaint to the Grand jury to retrieve her son. According to New York law after 1807, it was illegal to remove slaves from the state if the person taking them had not owned the slaves for ten years.[30] Truth was well informed of this statute and successfully worked within the judicial system and ultimately obtained a writ for the return of her son. Such an episode is in accordance with the Old

Testament words of Isaiah and the prophecy of the suffering servant, "(s)he will see [her] offspring and prolong her days...."[31]

A final instance of Truth's progeny in the sacred saga of salvation endured by the suffering servant prophecy occurs in Truth's reference to prominent women and mothers of the bible who all share the status of suffering servants and through their pain, grief, and loss, "will justify many." We will analyze each allusion to these biblical women in more detail. Eve is cited in both the Robinson and Gage versions of the 1851 Akron Convention Address. "That if de fust woman God ever made was strong enough to turn de world upside down all her one lone, all dese togeder, ought to be able to turn it back and git it right side up again, and now dey is asking to, de men better let 'em."[32] "Eve caused man to sin. Well if woman upset the world, do give her a chance to set it right side up again."[33]

Truth's allusion to Eve's transgressive strength is often understated or explained as an apologia made in the form of an *a fortiori* argument. However, the allusive analogy to Eve, when identified with the rhetorical idiom of the suffering servant, has deeper rhetorical significance. As a sacrificial punishment for she and Adam's offenses, Eve will experience the suffering of childbirth, a reality experienced by all mothers. Beyond this, Eve, as a mother, will suffer through the tragic violence of one son murdering the other resulting in his banishment. Historically, Eve bears the burdensome sobriquet of "Mother of the Fall," but also as a first mother, she is a matriarchal figure responsible for a long line of servant mothers who "will justify many."

Furthermore, drawing on the allusion to Eve, Truth offers a corrective to Eve's transgressions by transforming the darkness of sin and slavery experienced by the first woman into the light of freedom that comes with fighting for the socio-political causes of abolition and suffrage. The slavery of sin and the sin of slavery that deluded Adam and Eve into the hubris of thinking they were God is the same evil that slave masters harbor in the belief that they have the right to deny freedom to other human beings. The ineluctable eschatological freedom from sin and death earned by suffering servant mothers (like Eve), who, with God's aid, do see a son in Jesus conquer death by his eternal life. Finally, the metaphor of turning the world right side up underscores Christ's own social justice mission, which is always contrary to the normative order of things. Such a view reaffirms the transformative pharmakon of religion whereby the rancorous experience of suffering and enslavement can engender the redemptive succor of women "participating as full citizens to right spiritual and social wrongs."[34]

By 1851, Truth's take on the suffering servant coalesced with the early Suffragist movement. Truth prolonged the prophetic form of the suffering servant to include biblical female exemplars like Mary, the mother of Jesus, Eve, and Mary and Martha, the sisters of Lazarus. Truth then deftly grafted this cadre of religious representative anecdotes, of which she saw herself in union with, onto the early Women's Rights movement, thereby trussing the sacred with the secular in a concatenation of spiritual and political solidarity spanning from "The Fall" to Seneca Falls.

In employing a rhetorical synthesis of suffering servants with feminist activism, Truth invented a discursive form that we call the "suffraging servant." Truth's biblical and rhetorical knowledge demonstrated by her amplification of four sacred scions who share in a solidarity of suffering and service, thereby fulfilling Isaiah's scriptural foretelling "by [her] knowledge, my righteous servant will justify many." It is important to note that the knowledge Isaiah expresses here is knowledge edified by, and experienced through, suffering, and it is also salutary to remember Simone Weil's words, "justice is essentially non-active. It must either be transcendent or suffering."[35] In articulating an ancestry of servant advocates, women who clearly "justify many," Truth appeals to the Christian women of her audience and politically permits them to embrace suffrage without condemnation in an effort to "togeder...be able to turn it [the world] back and gitit right side up again."[36] But political and ethical reordering is only made possible by the suffering of those antecedent servants. Such a rhetorical and religious vision, which provides both eschatological as well as an egalitarian hope for women of nineteenth century America could not have been effectuated without violent suffering. How often do we forget the ransom and redemption paid by subaltern groups for the privilege of democracy. We now turn to an explication of the rhetorical labor of these other representative anecdotes that Truth highlights.

Mary the mother of Jesus was, too, a slave mother, who fled with a fugitive slave baby hunted by King Herod. Truth's grief-stricken testimony of the physical and psychological suffering endured by slave mothers when "none but Jesus heard" reveals a mimetic moment of Christ-like suffering and functioned as a potent pathos appeal with the aim of converting the hearts of slaveholders.[37] Truth emblemizes the worst malevolence of slavery, particularly when it came to her status as a mother. Her anguish reaches a tragic zenith in imagining the death of slave children. While Truth does not mention this directly in the Akron Address, Gilbert's account of Truth's slave narrative included her own version of the violent killings of slave children told to her by her father and a family friend.[38] Gilbert shared Truth's own painful reflection with the following authorial intrusion:

> Isabella found herself the mother of five children and she rejoiced in being permitted to be the instrument of increasing the property of her oppressors! Think, dear reader, without a blush, if you can for one moment, of a *mother* thus willingly with *pride*, laying her own children, the "flesh of her flesh," on the altar of slavery—a sacrifice to the bloody Moloch.[39]

In the Akron Address she states, "I have borne thirteen chilern, and see'em-mos all sold off to slavery, and when I cried out with my mother's grief, none but Jesus heard me!"[40] Hyperbole notwithstanding, the fictive increase in the number of her children subjected to the horrors of slavery is meant to amplify her suffering. Truth's motherhood parallels Mary's in that both saw their only sons torn from their arms and subjected to the violence of slavery and death. Jesus returned to Mary's arms after his death and crucifixion. Truth's son Peter is said to have died at sea. Yes, Truth took consolation and succor in knowing that the Lord hears the cry of the poor and Jesus listens to the grief and anguish of slave mothers because that's where he came from. However, in accordance with the suffering servant idiom, Truth and her children remained "abandoned to their enemies." With respect to this passage, both Karlyn Kohrs Campbell and Michael Phillips-Anderson adduce Truth presents an argument that through such suffering she has earned her rights as well as evidence that Jesus did not deny the humanity of women.[41]

By far the most powerful repudiation of the Christian misogynist tradition, the rhetorical locus at which the suffering and the suffraging archetypes surge in sermonic synthesis, transpires when Truth, based on Gage's interpolated narration of Truth's delivery, affords a rancorous rebuke with verve and aplomb to the charge from a minister that:

> "women can't have as much rights as a man, 'cause Christ wasn't a woman! Whar did your Christ come from?" *Rolling thunder couldn't have stilled the crowd, as did those deep, wonderful tones, as she stood there with outstretched arms and eyes of fire.* "Whar did your Christ come from? From God and a woman! Man had nothin' to do with Him!"[42]

Truth's use of *epiplexis* or rhetorical questions are meant to castigate rather than elicit responses is a rhetorical *pièce de résistance* in that it enthymematically engages her male Christian audience, who must confront a theological truth that they cannot reject while exposing their own hypocrisy in denying women rights on the grounds of that same religious faith. In many ways, just as the Lord used Mary, who willingly accepted the sacrifice of her only son for the salvation of all, Truth freely subjected herself to the horrors of slavery and the humiliation of being a black woman publicly crusading for the cause of abolition and suffrage. The hectoring, hostility, and bodily harm that Truth suffered even as a free woman speaking alongside the likes of Frederick Douglass, Elizabeth Cady Stanton, and Susan B. Anthony was courageously selfless and a repeated sacrificial act in knowing she fought for the empowerment of primarily white women.

The final instantiation of biblical suffering servants that Truth alludes to are the grief-stricken sisters Mary and Martha, who, due to Jesus's delay, have just buried their brother Lazarus. The Robinson version of the Akron Address remarks, "The Lady has spoken about Jesus, how he never spurned woman from him, and she was right. When Lazarus died, Mary and Martha came to him with faith and love and besought him to raise their brother. And Jesus wept—and Lazarus came forth." Fitch and Mandziuk contend Truth's reference to Mary and Martha are illustrative of the reciprocity of faith shared between Jesus and women. Mary and Martha are synecdoches for women's loyalty and devotion to God and thereby represent the spiritual fidelity of all women. This allusion conflates both natural rights with arguments by expedience, thereby declaring women's *sui generis* moral superiority to men and establishes their rights in accordance with their God given status.[43]

Phillips-Anderson asserts the Mary and Martha anecdote argues that women's voices are capable of constituting miracles. In briefly recounting the story, Philips-Anderson also notes that Jesus was persuaded by the aggressive logos of Martha, "If thou hadst been here, my brother had not died," as well as the pious pathos of Mary, who uttered the same words but wept as she repeated them.[44] Indeed, great transformation and reformation result from the advocacy of women. It was not Lazarus who asked to be healed when he was ill. Mary and Martha sought Jesus' help both before and after the agony of watching their brother die, even though Jesus got there too late, their faith did not falter. Both their suffering and their distinct stylistic appeals literally "gave rise" to their brother. "Jesus wept, and Lazarus came forth."[45]

Helane Androne and Leland G. Spencer explore how Truth's allusion to Mary and Martha completes the sacred cycle of birth, death, and transformation via resurrection, thereby reconciling Eve's transgression and affording her audience with yet another exemplum of women working together to set it [the world] right side up again.[46] Moreover, Androne and Spencer remark within the slave and antebellum society, Jesus was viewed as an iconoclast, whose gospel principles are antithetical to cultural norms. Truth's rhetorical adoption of Mary and Martha also "argued for socio-political transformation."[47] Pursuant of engaging speech texts from the critical framework of religious rhetoric's succor/rancor interplay, we read the representative anecdote of Martha and Mary as Martha providing the rancor and Mary the succor. Their respective rhetorical responses to Jesus and their suffering taken in concert are validated by the resurrection of their brother as well as Jesus's own catharsis catalyzed by the faith of women and their willingness to suffer in service to the Lord.

The analysis of this chapter explicates how Sojourner Truth calls her American Christian audience to witness the self-hood of slave women through the moral authority of Christ's compassionate relationship with women and his own violent agony. Truth's adoption of the suffering and "sufferaging" servant archetypes are not simply invitations to passive pity, but her narrative experiences implore her audience and broader America to purge what Jim Aune has called "the acquisitive self,"[48] of which slavery is an odious apotheosis and a dehumanizing practice of white, phallocratic, Christian misogyny, which relegates women and slaves to a reifying "I-It" relational status.[49]

Truth's rhetorical enactment of the suffering/suffraging servant, in recounting her own painful travails of slavery and similar misery shared by biblical women, demanded her audience confront the blasphemy of Christianity and slavery and misogyny and motherhood. What is most astounding about Truth's rhetorical life is her total commitment to fulfilling the suffering servant prophecy. In establishing her own humanity, argued through Christ's humanity, dependent as it on women, she readily empties that very self through a *kenosis* that inspires America to denounce its selfish desire to hold slaves and women as property. The prophetic words of Sojourner Truth exhibit a rare rhetorical and providential power, while simple, broken, and mundane are profoundly cogent and engender a Longinian sublimity of both rancor and succor, irony and truth, pain and promise, fulfilling and emptying. Truth's religious rhetoric offers succor for the violent brutality of slavery, instilling in her not a hatred of whites, but a logic of forgiveness.[50] She employs religion for reconciliation not retribution and demonstrates that abolition and suffrage offer counter narratives to policies that are neither sound in socio-political reality nor in theology. Fitch and Mandziuk note this reasoning in citing Truth's "Anti-Slavery" Convention Speech at Rochester, New York in which she inquired, "God will take care of the poor trampled slave, but where will the slaveholder be when eternity begins?"[51] Moreover, vivifying the violent victimhood of Truth constitutes her agency through adopting the persona of the suffering and sufferaging servant who comes to make right humanity's relationship with their neighbor, and thereby engenders what David A. Frank theorizes as acts of forgiveness with new beginnings.[52]

CHAPTER 2: PART I

LGBTQ and Violence

In 1978, Proposition 6, known as the Briggs Initiative was "the first attempt to restrict the rights of lesbian and gay Americans by popular referendum."[1] Councilman Harvey Milk was instrumental in his activism against Proposition 6 and for lesbian and gay rights. The rhetorical artifact examined here is the debate that took place on September 6, 1978 at New San Remo Restaurant in San Francisco.[2] The debate, between John Briggs and Harvey Milk, aired at 2:00 p.m., moderated by KPIX reporter Richard Hart and filmed by producer Bob Klein.[3] Although the edited 30-minute televised version is not extant, excerpts survive.[4] What makes this event unique resides in the ways that it introduces a variation of a subgenre under the rubric of "broadcast journalism and political communication."[5]

"HARVEY MILK VS. JOHN BRIGGS"[6]

A Televised Debate

San Francisco, California. September 6, 1978.

Briggs: I'll tell you what [Proposition] 6 does not do. It does not deny you the right to be a supervisor. It does not deny anybody in this room a right to have a job.

Milk: Yes, it does, it denies people the right to teach.

Briggs: But there are no teachers in this room.

Milk: But we don't know; there are some other people in this room.

Briggs: It does not deny anybody the right to a job. It does not deny anybody the right to rent or buy a house. All it does is say that parents —parents have the ultimate right as to who is going to teach their children.

Milk: Wait, wait, wait. Based on that—on that "ultimate right," at one time parents didn't want blacks to teach. At one time they didn't want women to teach. You know, the old Bible says women shouldn't be teachers, in the Old Testament. At one time. Because parents are locked in—they're afraid of something different. They're afraid of change. Because of fears and myths put into their heads. … One of those myths in this new ordinance is that you choose your sexuality. You don't choose your homosexuality. Like you don't choose blue eyes. Like you would choose your candidates …

Briggs: I care about this country. And I care about the family. And I really, sincerely, honestly, and truly believe from the bottom of my heart that homosexuality is a real threat to the survival of this country, if we continue to tolerate it and approve it and let it be raised to an equal level and standard of heterosexuality. That's what I truly believe.

Milk: That's the oldest game in the world! That's why I keep saying to you, study! I would be surprised what your next step is! … [Homosexuality] is not ever done because of an experience. It is determined before school age. And as every scientific study done says, it is not a choice. It is not a choice. That's the most fundamental mistake conservatives like Briggs bring up.

Briggs: But children learn by example. Children emulate. People need heroes. I said at the opening of the show that the reason you wanted to be elected to high office is so you can recruit and convert every young, adolescent homosexual. Those were your own words!

Milk: No, no, no. I said that one of the reasons of being elected is I'm a role model to young gay people. To young gay people. You see? You mis—turn things around like you turn everything else around.

Briggs: What about a teacher who's a role model?

Milk: A teacher to a [particular] sexual orientation? You see, Senator, you're turning things around. My statement was, I'm a role model to the young gay people. To people who have already established themselves as gay. Period. I didn't say— you're the one who keeps bringing up this phony recruitment. You know you're lying. You know you're changing the statements around. And you're doing that all the way around, just like you shifted the money around in your campaigns. And you talk about morality! And I question, what is your real motive behind it? What is your real ambition behind this? What are you really using this for? And stop this phony issue!

***

RHETORICAL ANALYSIS

On December 13, 2022, in her introductory remarks at the event where President Biden's signed H.R. 8404, the Respect for Marriage Act, Vice President Kamala Harris invoked some significant personal and historical reflections. V.P. Harris recalled the time in February 2004, when she performed some of the first same-sex marriages—the victory in striking down Proposition 8. which had made same-sex marriages unconstitutional in the state of California. When Proposition 8 was officially deemed unconstitutional by a Federal Court on June 26, 2013, Vice President Harris pronounced two of her friends legally betrothed on the Harvey Milk balcony, June 28, 2013. Clearly ecstatic about the passage of the most current Federal legislation, at the end of her remarks, Vice President Harris invoked Harvey Milk the person, after having already invoked the architecture (balcony) eponymously named for Milk, saying, "And as the great Harvey Milk once said, I quote, 'Rights are won only by those who make their voices heard.'" Harvey Milk was clearly prescient in appreciating the importance of dogged perseverance in achieving justice and equality.[7]

As uplifting, inspirational and sanguine as the December 13, 2022 event was, Vice President Harris expressed a potentially foreboding reality, articulated in Justice Clarence Thomas's concurring opinion in *Dobbs v. Jackson Women's Health Center*, decided some six month prior, overturning *Roe v. Wade*, eviscerating a woman's right to abortion and other reproductive and health care rights.[8] Although the SCOTUS majority opinion penned by Justice Samuel Alito argues for a distinction with a difference between abortion, which he argues is not a liberty protected by the Due Process Clause of the U.S. Constitution, and issues such as birth control, private consensual acts and same-sex marriage, as protected in the Supreme Court decisions of *Griswold v. Connecticut*, *Lawrence v. Texas*, and *Obergefell v. Hodges* respectively, Justice Thomas allows for the thin edge of the wedge in linking the excluded issues/cases in Justice Alito's opinion with abortion in the current case. Justice Thomas basically says that all of the above decisions characterized as "substantive due process precedents" are "demonstrably erroneous," and it is incumbent upon the Court to "correct the error." Vice

President Harris is incontrovertibly appreciative of the inexorable fallout of Justice Thomas's judicial "wish list" in his concurring opinion in saying, "The Dobbs decision reminds us that fundamental rights are interconnected, including the right to marry who you love, the right to access contraception, and the right to make decisions about your own body."[9] But Justice Thomas's concurrence in expressing the quiet "wish list" part out loud is matched, or really outmatched by Governor Ron DeSantis and his Republican State legislature with the passage of passed H.B. 1557, which took effect July 1, 2022, officially known as the "Parental Right in Education Act," but more familiarly and ominously known as the "Don't Say Gay" law. Tenets of the law include "prohibiting classroom discussion about sexual orientation or gender identity in certain grade levels or in a specified manner," and "classroom instruction by school personnel or third parties on sexual orientation or gender identity may not occur in kindergarten through grade 3 or in a manner that is not age-appropriate or developmentally appropriate for students in accordance with state standards."[10] Many school personnel and First Amendment scholars balked at the law heralded by DeSantis and the Republican legislators. Florida's law has been deemed vague and overbroad marred by ill-defined terms such as "age-appropriate" and "developmentally appropriate."[11] The academic freedom of both teacher and student could be jeopardized in a myriad of ways, including punishing artwork by a student drawing a picture of their family which includes gay parents.[12] Aggrieved parents could trigger investigations and lawsuits against school boards if they believe the statute was violated, notwithstanding the fact that H.B. 1557 "arguably runs afoul of the First Amendment's stringent prohibition on viewpoint discrimination and imposes an unconstitutional chilling effect on disfavored speech."[13] Some teachers even voiced concerns over having their family photos on their desks if those individuals in the photos would be perceived as outside of sexual orientation and gender identity norms.[14] Many educators found H.B. 1557 to be a solution for which there is really no problem, but the deleterious and potentially devastating effects of the law were clearly evident.

News outlets reported out even more draconian measures attached to H.B. 1557, taken by DeSantis and his administration, for which legislative approval was not necessary, and which was voted on April 19, 2023, by Florida's Board of Education, having been put on the table by Florida's Education Department.[15] Classroom instruction regarding sexual orientation and gender identity will now be *verboten* in grades K-12, "unless required by existing state standards or as part of reproductive health instruction that students can choose not to take."[16] Critics of the law in its amended form suspect "that the Parental Rights in Education Act was just a starting point for the DeSantis administration to erase the existence of queer people from teaching in Florida elementary, middle, and high schools."[17]

If the most recent policies seem like déjà vu, one need only hearken back to San Francisco, California, 1978, and the infamous Proposition 6, known as the Briggs Initiative. The Briggs Initiative possessed two cachets: it was "the first attempt to restrict the rights of lesbian and gay Americans by popular referendum,"[18] and "it was the first time voters had rejected an antigay measure,"[19] defeated by over 1,000,000 votes in a 58.4–41.6% victory, spearheaded by Harvey Milk.[20]

Harvey Milk is the most unlikely catalyst to embark on what appeared to be an ostensibly insurmountable mission to achieve something which enjoyed no precedent. Milk's professional pursuits prior to his political predilections gave no discernible hint of his historic role as a politician whose momentous work would be manifest forty-five years later in the rhetoric of succor with Vice President Harris, and forty-four years later with the rancorous intentions of Justice Clarence Thomas. Having only served 11 months before his assassination by Dan White on November 27, 1978,[21] and only weeks after the rejection of Proposition 6 by California voters, Milk solidified his status as an eminently consequential figure in the decades-long battles for gay rights.

Harvey Milk's politically persuasive heft was augmented and amplified when he teamed up with Sally Miller Gearhart. In June 1978. Milk and Gearhart joined forces with the United Fund to defeat the Briggs Initiative, and in her obituary, she is credited with collaborating in tandem with Milk to defeat Proposition 6.[22] As a faculty member at San Francisco State University (SFSU), Gearhart is noteworthy as one of the first uncloseted lesbians on tenure-track "at a major American university."[23]

In 1979, as Associate Professor of Speech Communication at SFSU, Gearhart published what is arguably, one of the most influential and significant pieces of scholarship, "The Womanization of Rhetoric." Gearhart vilifies the canonical, historical, and androcentric form of rhetoric *qua* persuasion, as a fundamentally eristic model and "an insidious form of violence."[24] What Gearhart finds most objectionable in its unilateral disposition, is imparting truth (or something else) to others bereft "of respect and openness."[25] She is not averse to the tools of rhetoric, but rather its *telos* of intent, where changing "people and things" is accepted and understood as *sine qua non*.[26] For Gearhart, this is a "conquest model of human interaction."[27] Communicative power is not simply instantiated in the one who speaks. Gearhart's metaphor describing a nonviolent and holistic model of human interaction is the matrix: "an atmosphere in which meanings are generated and nurtured."[28] This embodiment of co-creation, and eschewing the conquest/conversion model of persuasion and the "agonistic persuasion of violence" are evident in Wayne Booth's paradigm of rhetoric, with the key tenets of (1) "Rhetoric: the whole range of arts not only of persuasion but also of producing or reducing misunderstanding," (2) "Listening Rhetoric (LR): the whole range of communicative arts for reducing misunderstanding by paying full attention to opposing views," and (3) "Rhetorology: the deepest form of L.R., the systematic probing for 'common ground.'"[29]

In their brilliant essay, "Foresights from a Foremother: Sally Miller Gearhart," two preeminent scholars Cheryl Glenn and Andrea Lunsford reflect on Gearhart's "life and career," augmented by a three-hour conversation that Lunsford had with her, July 15, 2019, in Gearhart's cabin in a remote area near Willits, California.[30]

Gearhart's contribution was anything but tangential as documented in the Academy Award winning documentary *The Times of Harvey Milk*. On October 11, 1978, the PBS station, KQED TV, hosted a debate moderated by reporter Belva Davis, with John Briggs and Raymond Batema advocating for Proposition 6, and Milk and Gearhart opposing Proposition 6.[31] Faderman provides an excellent account of the debate which previewed the success of the Milk-Gearhart team.[32] As she observes, when Gearhart interjected, she was "cool and composed…aimed with real figures and facts instead of Briggs's nonsensical math."[33] In the highlight of the debate, Briggs argues that if gay teachers were banned from schools, the incidence of molestation would drop precipitously, with Milk articulating an obvious contradiction to what Briggs had previously claimed.[34] In what has to be one of the most quintessential rhetorical takedowns, Briggs claims that 90–95% of child molesters are gay. After several lively volleys with Milk, Gearhart—having sat patiently, listening to Briggs's fallacious reasoning, telegraphed her desire to speak with a subtle movement of her hand, and landed the winning response, bereft of the manipulation and the spoken "sleight-of-hand" that many ethical speakers find objectionable. Gearhart's primary telos was to respond to Briggs's statements with objectively verifiable data. Her retort to Briggs's outrageous claim is: "Why take out the homosexual group when it is more than, you know, overwhelmingly—it is true that it is the heterosexual men I might add who are the child molesters."[35] When Briggs questions her claim and the evidence to substantiate that claim, Gearhart, looking at her notes, cites the FBI, the National Council on Family Relations, the Santa Clara County Child Sexual Abuse Treatment Center in corroboration of her claim.[36] Briggs and Batema seemingly appear to have been caught flat-footed, and visibly flustered.[37] And in this pivotal encounter, just 27 days before the election, Faderman concludes that "Harvey Milk dominated the debate from the start."[38] Milk provides a salvo of interrogatives directed at Briggs, along with a biting retort to Briggs's inane contention that, gay teachers' most important pedagogical mission is indoctrination and grooming—i.e., "to teach their students to be homosexual," and Milk counters with, "How do you teach homosexuality? Like you teach French?"[39]

With some contradiction, Deborah Craig observes that Gearhart "was a master debater who rejected persuasion and rhetoric as violence and sought more equitable and mutually respectful forms of communication."[40] Upon first blush, Gearhart's skill sets and success with Milk might appear to run afoul of her thesis in "The Womanization of Rhetoric," but the issue is really one of intent and degree and does not warrant a wholesale jettisoning of rhetoric—one of the three foundational liberal arts within the trivium. In the spirit application of Booth, Gearhart clearly practiced Rhetorology and LR.

The evisceration of LGBTQ rights continues to this day, with states such as Arkansas, Tennessee, and most imminently, Texas, enacting state laws prohibiting cities from the enactment of LGBTQ protections, particularly in the realm of employment,[41] noteworthy as a deleterious sequel to Anita Bryant's handiwork. Harvey Milk's advocacy militated against a Dade County-like ordinance, with the failure of Proposition 6. Milk's legacy is incontrovertibly being channeled, even in Florida today. Alyssa Marano, a former math teacher who resigned from the Hernando School district, expressed her consternation and dismay at a recent and highly contentious school board meeting regarding anti-LGBTQ school policies across the state, and responded to particularly rancorous allegations with the following retort: "no one is teaching your kids to be gay!…Sometimes they just are gay. I have math to teach. I literally don't have time to teach your kids to be gay."[42]

Proposition 6 was the diabolically inspired handiwork of John Briggs, who, in turn was inspired by Anita Bryant. In 1977, the provenance of what we are currently seeing in the scores of homophobic and transphobic laws across the country, began in earnest in Dade County, Florida, where Anita Bryant founded Save Our Children, the organization whose mission it was to repeal Dade County's anti-discrimination ordinance. The upended anti-gay ordinance had banned discrimination "in employment, housing, and public accommodations."[43] As a milestone piece of legislation, "the ordinance marked the first time any southern city had passed a gay rights law."[44] Bryant and her organizational efforts were successful, and the ordinance was repealed.[45] Likened to current justifications, Bryant and her ilk were obsessed with the ill-conceived and false allegation of recruitment.[46] Bryant succeeded in placing the initiative on the ballot, undoing Dade County's LGBT gay rights ordinance.[47] The election, held on June 7, 1977 was a drubbing, with 385 out of 446 precincts voting to repeal the gay rights ordinance.[48] As the spokesperson for the Florida Citrus commission, this grim milestone was dubbed "Orange Tuesday" by LGBT citizens.[49] On the night of Bryant's victory press conference, Briggs was present, and exclaimed "We won, we won."[50] At the time, he was running as a candidate for Republican governor in California, and on the heels of Bryant's victory, Briggs found his ideological platform, with the hopes of notching a political win—tantamount to—maybe even paramount to Bryant's.[51]

A California state legislator, Briggs's Proposition 6, more commonly known as the Briggs Initiative, was "the first attempt to restrict the rights of lesbian and gay Americans by popular referendum."[52] Section 44837.5 was added to Section 1 of the education Code; Section 44837.6 was added to Section 2 of the Education Code; and Section 44933.5 was added to Section 3 of the Education Code. The emendations to the three sections of the proposed law express the duty of the government in California to provide accepted role models for whom they deem "impressionable" students in the schools, and employing school personnel who might be engaged in a same sex activity is incommensurate with that duty. The words, action or conduct do not even have to be codified as constituting a crime, as long as it is neither discreet nor practiced within a private realm. The slippery slope of being deemed "unfit for service" is inescapable, insofar as "public homosexual conduct means the advocating, soliciting, imposing, encouraging, or promoting of private or public homosexual activity directed at or likely to come to the attention of school children and or other employees."[53]

Harvey Milk's peripatetic professional life traverses a diverse and interesting range of pursuits, which, according to Emery, all contributed to his ultimate success as a politician, with his "grab-bag of occupations" instilling important skills engendering an impressive synergy.[54] Emery credits Milk's strengths of "connecting, persuading and leading the troop" to his success in the political arena.[55]

Harvey Milk was born on May 22, 1930 to Jewish parents on Long Island in Woodmere, New York.[56] Prior to his political career, Emery characterizes Milk's career trajectory as "the first eight lives of Harvey Milk."[57] He worked as a retail clerk beginning in his teenage years.[58] After graduating college in 1951 with a history major and a mathematics minor, he enlisted in the U.S. Navy and served as a deep-sea diving officer and a deep-sea diving instructor.[59] Schooled in college as a teacher, he then taught tenth and eleventh grade math. Milk then had a short stint as an actuarial statistician, and then as a securities research analyst.[60] Milk then worked in the theatre, collaborating with the director Tom O'Horgan on several successful plays, including *Hair*, *Jesus Christ Superstar* and *Lenny*.[61]

In 1973, Milk opened a camera store called Castro Camera, which served as a local meeting place, and with that venue, Milk received the moniker the "Mayor of Castro Street."[62] Milk was also a prolific writer in a variety of venues on a variety of topics, including sports, business, theatre, and gay liberation.[63] In terms of his political aspirations, Milk's first three attempts at getting elected were unsuccessful: November 6, 1973, November 4, 1975 and June 8, 1976. The fourth time was indeed the charm, with his election on November 8, 1977 to District 5 of the Board of Supervisors, and officially sworn in January 9, 1978.[64]

Although Harvey Milk's corporeal life was not marked by longevity, his accomplishments are. Commemoratively, he was a posthumous awardee of the Presidential Medal of Freedom in 2009.[65] Harvey Milk Day was proclaimed an annual event the same year. In 2014, the U.S. Postal Service issued a commemorative stamp in honor of Milk.[66] On May 22, 2014, the Deputy Postmaster General Ronald Stroman dedicated the Harvey Milk postage stamp at a White House ceremony. In his dedication, the Deputy Postmaster said, "Let this stamp inspire a new generation to continue Harvey Milk's legacy—to keep working toward a world where prejudice gives way to acceptance, where division gives way to unity and where fear gives way to hope."[67] And how appropriate that this stamp is a "Forever" stamp! In 2021, the U.S. Navy launched and christened the USS Harvey Milk. The Secretary of the Navy Carlos Del Tora commented that, "leaders like Harvey Milk taught us that diversity of backgrounds and experiences helps contribute to the strength and resolve of our nation. There is no doubt that the future Sailors aboard this ship will be inspired by Milk's life and legacy."[68]

Harvey Milk's life and life after death are distinguished by powerful visual and discursive rhetoric, contributing to his augmented legacy.

When the GLBT History Museum opened in San Francisco, 2003—"the first American museum dedicated to gay, lesbian, bisexual and transgender history," its opening piece, called "Saint Harvey—The Life and Afterlife of a Modern Gay Martyr," Krutzsch describes the exhibit as,

> [A] massive cross made from the blood-soaked suit Harvey Milk wore when he was shot to death in 1978…With Milk's bullet-punctured suit displayed as a ross, the GLBT History Museum depicted Milk's assassination, like Christ's crucifixion, as an event of transformative and salvific significance.[69]

Although Krutzsch acknowledges Milk's Judaism, "in death the GLBT History Museum memorialized him with widely recognizable Christian imagery to enshrine him as the gay movement's most venerated political martyr."[70] Gilders describes Susan Stryker's intention, the exhibit's curator in the following way: "to make use of religious cultural forms to express the status accorded to Milk by LGBTQ people. Most strikingly, she displayed Milk's clothing in a cruciform arrangement, identifying Milk with Christianity's suffering savior and paradigmatic martyr."[71] In an updated version of the exhibit, changes include displaying the clothing,

> Flat, only partially unfolded, as if just removed from its storage box. It is behind a mesh screen, obscured to view, except when a button is pushed that turns on a light—as well as a holographic image of Milk's face, projected onto the museum floor, and the sound of Milk's voice from his recorded political testament. Milk's disembodied voice comes to the ears, while the eyes can take in the clothing.[72]

Gilders observes that the aspects of the Milk exhibit, especially the ones less beholden to multimedia components, can be likened to museum exhibits of the

Holocaust.⁷³ With his posthumous stature as a "hero-martyr," in 2008, the periodical *The Advocate* dubbed Milk as the "Gay M.L.K."⁷⁴

In gaining strength and leverage in the Jewish community, Congregation Sha'ar Zahav (CSZ) helped set the stage, with its founding by a trio of Jewish gay men in San Francisco, 1977.⁷⁵ At its first Rosh Hashanah service, the congregation published a newsletter referencing Anita Bryant's Save Our Children campaign, which succeeded in repealing LGBT protections in Florida's Dade County, in June 1977.⁷⁶

On the evening of November 18, 1977, ten days after his successful election, he made three tapes as his "political wills" and testament. Milk left one tape with his attorney John Wahl, another with his friend Frank Robinson, which includes a prophetic and oft-quoted passage: "If a bullet should enter my brain, let that bullet destroy every closet door."⁷⁷ And the third tape was left with Walter Caplan, containing a passage which clarifies his wishes for memorial services for him, and the fraudulent succor and the genuine rancor that Milk finds so abhorrent in religion:

> I hope there are no religious services. I would hope there are no services of any type, but I know some people are into that and you can't prevent it from happening, but, my God, nothing religious. Until the churches speak out against the Anita Bryants who have been playing gymnastics with the Bible, the churches which remain so quiet have the guts to speat in the name of Judaism or Christianity or whatever they profess to be for in words but not action and deeds. God—and that's the irony. God—churches don't even know what it's about. I would turn over in my grave if there was any kind of religious ceremony. And it's not a disbelief in God—it's a disbelief and disgust of what most churches are about. How many leaders got up on their pulpits and went to Miami and said, 'Anita, you're playing gymnastics with the bible—you're desecrating the bible'? How many of them said it? How many of them hid and walked away? Ducked their heads in the name of Christianity and talked about love and brotherhood.⁷⁸

He made this statement, contemplating—quite prophetically—his assassination in 1978 after his election to District 5 of the San Francisco Board of Supervisors in 1977.⁷⁹

After his death, which shocked and stunned the community, Rabbi Martin Weiner officiated a service at the Gay Community Center, and Congregation Sha'ar Zahave led a service in a rented auditorium with an overflow crowd, officiated by Rabbi Bennett.⁸⁰ The official Jewish service took place at Temple Emanu-El, the largest synagogue in San Francisco, which also happened to be Acting Mayor Dianne Feinstein's synagogue, and officiated by Rabbi Joseph Asher. Although Rabbi Asher was active in fighting for civil rights across the country, "he was not a proponent" of LGBTQ rights and was not really supportive of Rabbi Bennett, who was "the only openly gay Rabbi in San Francisco giving the eulogy."⁸¹ But Rabbi Asher allowed Rabbi Bennett to participate, and in her reflection on this part of the narrative, Faderman states that Harvey "would have liked that at the podium of stuffy Temple Emanu-El an openly gay Rabbi talked about Harvey Milk's pride in his Jewishness."[82] In October 1978, Milk attended High Holiday services on Rosh Hashanah and Yom Kippur, and told Rabbi Bennett after the Yom Kippur service, "how good it is to 'be home' with his Jewishness."[83] Milk, irrefutably, embodied gay pride and Jewish pride.

Milk's closest friends embarked on the schooner Lady Free, sailed into the open sea, passing under the Golden Gate Bridge, and dropped his ashes into the ocean.[84]

Milk's relationship to his Jewish faith, distinguished by ostensible paradoxes, was by far, the preeminent influence, and specifically, "the Holocaust became a major metaphor in the speeches he gave and the editorials he wrote."[85] Milk "analogizes Nazi persecution of Jews to discrimination against gays in America, one of his frequently employed tropes."[86]

Milk not only did not leave his Jewish identity behind or render it opaque, but was transparent about all facets of his Jewishness, from cooking dishes like matzo brei, telling Jewish jokes, and hanging a picture of himself in his camera store, as a Bar Mitzvah boy.[87]

Krutzch's treatment of Milk's Jewishness and its role in his legacy as a gay activist and advocate is curious and somewhat off-putting. Knowing what we know about Milk's relationship to Judaism, which was admittedly conflicted on many levels, Krutzsch argues that Milk earned and garnered respect "by eliding not only his sexual practices, but also his Jewish identity."[88] Krutzsch is to be commended for providing an inclusive biography of Milk, including many interesting details about his Jewish ancestry, and when he resided in San Francisco, he enjoyed interspersing conversation with Yiddishisms, and spent Passover with a friend, Walter Caplan.[89] Krutzsch concedes that "Milk explicitly campaigned as a Jew," and in campaigning, ensured that people "knew he was a 'Jewish Democrat,'" and "to both friends and the broader community, Milk regularly presented his Jewishness as constitutive of his identity and actions."[90] Krutzsch observes that many of the artifacts (name them) that cemented Milk's legacy, merely invoked his Jewishness as obiter dicta, if at all, although the opera *Harvey Milk* "highlights Milk's Jewish identity and Christianizes him," and represented Milk "as a resurrected savior-prophet."[91] But Krutzsch's conclusion that "the erasure of Milk's Jewishness in *Milk* and elsewhere allows him to function better as a gay American everyman,"[92] is a disservice to the life that Milk lived, and which served all people, not in spite of his Jewishness, but arguably, because of it, championing a cross-section of citizens from workers to women, to people of color, seniors, and the those with disabilities.[93] He counted himself "as part of an ultraliberal Jewish tradition that fought for the oppressed of all stripes."[94]

Krutzsch's conclusion regarding Milk's legacy are somewhat eyebrow raising, when he says,

> By veiling Milk's Jewish identity, white Christian Americans find a man who seems less foreign. The Warsaw-ghetto referencing, Yiddish speaking, secular Jew is not a universal relatable figure; his Jewish particularities reinforce his multiple differences from the dominant Christian society...In death he could be made to pass as a universally relatable rather than specifically Jewish American.[95]

What a staggering conclusion that Milk's identity had to be contorted and his Jewishness effaced for a "particular"—albeit "hegemonic" Christian constituency—a uniquely Protestant constituency, since his full identity could jeopardize and imperil his cause as a gay rights activist and politician. In order for Milk to garner respect as a gay man, his Judaism had to be jettisoned in his memorialization, ultimately, an act of infidelity to Milk's lived life. Milk's martyrdom relied on the unadulterated Christianization of a Jewish man.[96] Inferring, based on the artistic decisions made in both fictive and non-fictive artifacts made by their creators, that downplaying of Milk's Judaism rendered him more favorably disposed to a larger, more Christian and heteronormative swath of the public, was a consummately flawed conclusion conceived by proxy, on behalf of Harvey Milk.

In his brilliant work, *The Rule of Metaphor*, Paul Ricœur credits Aristotle with the first discussion of metaphor in the works of the *Rhetoric* and the *Poetics*, and preliminarily, Ricœur defines metaphor as "a trope of resemblance."[97] In the *Poetics*, metaphor "is the application of an alien name by transference either from genus to species, or from species to genus, or from species to species, or by analogy, that is proportion."[98] In expounding upon the meaning of analogy, Aristotle states that "when the second term is to the first as the fourth to the third, we may then use the fourth for the second, or the second for the fourth."[99] Ricœur observes that although poetics and rhetoric engage qualitatively different goals, whereas rhetoric employs argumentation for purposes of locating proofs and proving something within more of a historical sphere within the confines of the three genres of deliberative, forensic, and epideictic poetry's purpose is mimesis—"an essential representation of human action,"[100] and speaking to universal truths through fiction within the tragic drama in order to achieve catharsis, and the arousal of the emotional states of fear and pity.[101] Aristotle defines tragedy as "an imitation of an action that is serious, complete, and of a certain magnitude."[102] As Ricœur states,

> ...Poetry and oratory mark out two distinct universes of discourse. Metaphor, however, has a foot in each domain. With respect to structure, it can really consist in just one unique operation, the transfer of meanings of words; but with respect to function, it follows the divergent destinies of oratory and tragedy. Metaphor will therefore have a unique structure but two *functions*: a rhetorical function and a poetic function.[103]

In her brilliant article, "Whose Memory? Whose Victimhood? Contests For the Holocaust Frame in Recent Social Movement Discourse," Arlene Stein examines the "two types of Holocaust rhetoric" used in the lesbian and gay movement, beginning in the 1970's and subsequently, in the Christian right movement.[104] Stein questions whether these movements typify unethical appropriations of the Holocaust, in their uses of the "Holocaust frame."[105] In exploring this question, Stein examines the two types of appropriation the movements utilize: "*revisionism* (efforts to rewrite the history of the Holocaust) which makes claims about a historical event," and "*metaphor creation* (efforts to compare present events or experiences to those of the Holocaust)."[106] Within this framework, the movements promulgate victimhood through the Aristotelian tragic drama lens of the victim as "protagonist" and the enemy, perpetrating the genocide, as the "antagonist."[107] In the earliest rhetorical phase of the gay/lesbian movement, Stein claims that "gay activists have sought to revise the historical record to reflect the extent of gay victimhood during the Nazi period."[108] In Shilts' superb biography, *The Mayor of Castro Street*, he claims that approximately 220,000 gay people were exterminated by the Nazis, the next highest cohort killed after the Jews.[109]

In his speech "That's What America is," delivered by Milk on June 25, 1978, at the Gay Freedom Day Parade, he introduces himself, then states the need to fight for the preservation of democracy against Briggs and Bryant, and then says,

> We are not going to allow that to happen. We are not going to sit back in silence as 300,00 of our gay brothers and sisters did in Nazi Germany. We are not going to allow our rights to be taken away and then march with bowed heads to the gas chambers.[110]

According to the *Holocaust Encyclopedia*, Paragraph 175, part of Germany's criminal code, introduced in 1871, and not entirely removed until 1994, criminalized sexual relations between men.[111] From 1933–1945, 5,000–15,000 men were sent to concentration camps, with possibly 10,000 having perished.[112] Jewish men who were also gay were persecuted and murdered, but the number has to date not been ascertained.[113] Regarding the employment of revisionism as a rhetorical strategy, the gay movement modified the quantitative date and the extensiveness of the persecution of homosexuals by the Nazis.[114] Milk employed a multifunctional, historical frame with his effective use of the metaphor. The revisionism purports to strengthen the historical relationship between the two atavistic events in pursuing the analogous metaphorical construct. As Faderman says, "Milk became aware of the Holocaust and the 'destruction of European Jewry,' in his childhood, and this knowledge had a profound influence on his entire life."[115] For Milk, the Holocaust functioned as a foundational metaphor for his rhetoric in opposition to Proposition 6.[116] When speaking to Jewish groups, "the metaphor poured out of him in a torrent of emotion."[117] Milk analogized Proposition 6 as banning gays from teaching in the public schools in California, to the German laws which prohibited Jews "from teaching or holding any other civil service positions."[118]

When the Nazis arrested gay people under Paragraph 175 and put them in concentration camps, they were forced to wear the Pink Triangle.[119] A controversial exhortation was issued in the 1970's when gay people were encouraged to wear the pink triangle, for, then "everyone would, as a gay man, be recognized, discovered, discriminated against, and oppressed."[120] This approach seems ostensibly contraindicative and counterintuitive from gay men's perspective. The rationale is that "only then would these liberated gays truly realize the homophobia that surrounded them."[121] One activist explained the artifactual analogy, in that adorning the pink triangle is comparable to being attired in drag, since that would be an effective way to "stand up for myself and not deny who I am."[122]

In his "That's What America Is" speech, Milk spoke to a crowd of between 250,000 and 375,000 people, and said the following to them:

> Gay people, we will not win their rights by staying quietly in our closets...We are coming out! We are coming out to fight the lies, the myths, the distortions! We are coming out to tell the truth about gays![123]

And later in the speech, Milk with a series of jussive statements, says,

> Gay brothers and sisters, what are you going to do about it? You must come out. Come out...To your parents...I know that it is hard and will hurt them but think about how they will hurt you in the voting booth! Come out...to your relatives. I know that it is hard and will upset them but think of how they will upset you in the voting booth. Come out to your friends. Come out to your neighbors...to your fellow workers...To the people who work where you eat and shop. Come out only to the people you know, and who know you. Not to anyone else. But one and for all, break down the myths, destroy the lies and distortions. For your sake. For their sake. For the sake of the youngsters who are becoming scared by the votes from Dade to Eugene.[124]

Unlike the nonverbal communication of the pink triangle, Milk promotes a more discerning, selective group of receivers for the "coming out" message.

For Milk, a sub-Holocaust metaphor was the Warsaw Ghetto Uprising: its meaning and object lesson. In furthering gay rights and advocating fighting the good fight, the Warsaw Ghetto Uprising served as an inspirational motif.[125] Black and Morris claim that "Milk's deeper political inclinations may be attributable, by his own accounting, to the 1943 Jewish uprising in the Warsaw Ghetto."[126] The Warsaw Ghetto was a cautionary tale for gay people, that defeating one's enemies is the only viable option for survival.[127] For a teenage Harvey, the threat was contemporaneous and perceived as closer than a continent away, given that antisemitism pervaded his own hometown of Woodmere, Long Island.[128] Milk recognized the bravery of the fighters in the Warsaw Ghetto, and even in the face of inescapable defeat, they forged onward. Of the uprising in the Ghetto, Milk reflected that, "When something evil descends on the world, you have to fight, even when it's hopeless."[129]

Stein's critique of the use of the Holocaust metaphor is worth noting. Through the appropriation, "lesbians and gays position themselves as heirs to the homosexuals who perished through the Nazi genocide, or as Jews on the brink of destruction."[130] For both the gay movement and the Christian right, each of their uses of the Holocaust metaphor engaged "hyperbole to appeal to the 'emotional predispositions' of the public."[131] This rhetorical cooptation is seen as a "trivialization" of the Holocaust and a diminution of its "uniqueness" as a tragic event nonpareil in the annals of history.[132] In analogizing the Holocaust, not only is history, in an objectively verifiable way, revised (i.e., "historical revisionism"), but also de-Judaicize[d] the Holocaust.[133] Stein concedes, however, that the Holocaust functions characteristically as both "unique and comparable," sharing in both Jewish history and "human history."[134] But unlike the use of the metaphor with the Christian right, Stein affords more magnanimity to the lesbian and gay movement in its use of the Holocaust metaphor:

> The lesbian and gay movement has appropriated the Holocaust as metaphor to dramatize its plight as a marginalized group in American society; it has also engaged in revisionism, attempting to correct the historical record to reflect the extent of gay victimhood.[135]

Although proportionality and degree are misaligned and incommensurate, Stein does concede that gays and lesbians have been the victims of homophobia and hate, paralleling the antisemitism and hate directed towards Jews, so plausibility and intellectual sincerity are inherent in the uses of these rhetorical strategies.[136]

The rhetorical artifact which is the focus here is the debate that took place on September 6, 1978 at New San Remo Restaurant in San Francisco.[137] The venue was a particularly interesting one with the artifactual ambiance and trappings more likened to a cordial meal among friends than a contentious debate between two politicians opposed to each other on a highly consequential issue to be voted on two months later by the people of California, November 7, 1978. If Milk's rhetorical strength was in his artistry, instantiated in his poetic use of the metaphor, as we previously discussed, his rhetorical aptitudes demonstrated an equal adeptness in effectuating a confluence of argument and performance, in his speeches, as well as within the interactive, interpersonal framework of the news/panel interview and the news debate. According to Emery, the cachet of this debate is the fact that it was "one of the first," and "one of the liveliest."[138] And that it was! The debate aired at 2:00 p.m., moderated by KPIX reporter Richard Hart and filmed by producer Bob Klein.[139] Although the edited 30-minute televised version is not extant, excerpts survive.[140] What makes this event unique resides in the ways that it introduces a variation of a subgenre under the rubric of "broadcast journalism and political communication."[141] Clayman and Heritage delineate the various subgenres within broadcast media, including talk shows, panel discussions, debates, and the news interview.[142] The news interview holds a vaunted place within that sphere insofar as it is a key tool for "gathering and disseminating information," and essential in furtherance of providing information to the citizenry in sustaining democracy.[143]

Although Emery's volume is titled *The Harvey Milk Interviews*, he concedes that the televised dialogues between Milk and Briggs were more commensurate with the debate rather than the interview genre. In his blurb introducing the September 6, 1978 "event," Emery says, "the debates between Milk and Briggs are not exactly interviews, but they are more interactive than strictly prepared speeches."[144] As a televised event, "the news interview is plainly a vehicle for communicating to a mass audience, but it is, at the same time, a form of interpersonal communication between interviewer and interviewee."[145]

In this "hybridized genre," Milk and Briggs speak on a newsworthy topic, "ideologically opposed to one another, and informally debating the issue."[146] A panel interview, like a debate, invariably has an interviewer in the former and a moderator in the latter, but what makes the Briggs-Milk debate unique is the tangential—almost nonexistent role that the interviewer/reporter, Richard Hart plays—from the textual and broadcast documentation available to us. Clearly, with Briggs and Milk, each takes on an "adversarial role vis-à-vis one another," and "the interviewer is removed from the heat of battle and is free to act as a disinterested catalyst," with a much more attenuated role.[147] As Clayman and Heritage state, "in the panel interview format, there is interplay, not only between interviewers and interviewees, but also-directly or indirectly—between the interviewees themselves,"[148] and the latter, direct interaction between Briggs and Milk is outsized, but not inappropriate, and compelling as a televised event. Clayman and Heritage do caution when the journalist's role is marginalized, and where the emphasis is on "conflict and confrontation."[149] They worry of the danger in "generating more heat than light. When disagreement intensifies to the level of a shouting match, when the participants become unable to develop their points without interruption, when they have difficulty being heard above the din, then it can be said that entertainment value has overwhelmed informational substance."[150] With these characteristics, Clayman and Heritage classify this subgenre as the "debate interview," but the "trappings" do not really manifest themselves in negative ways in the Briggs-Milk debate. Although Clayman and Heritage are not specifically referencing the Briggs-Milk event, you have "a lively sparring match between thoroughly committed adversaries."[151]

This analysis applies two methodological approaches to a particularly lively section of this debate which raises important points. Communication Analysis

(CA), a methodology introduced in the field of sociology in the 1960's and its use expanded to many other academic disciplines, including communication, "stresses the basically social nature of language use in human interaction…"[152] Conversational interactions with others in a wide array of contexts, in a multitude of ways, constitute the "primary forms of social action."[153] CA's foci of describing communication include "turn-taking (the allocation of opportunities to speak among participants), the organization of conversational sequences, the internal structuring of turns at talk and the formation of actions, the organization of repair (dealing with difficulties in speaking, hearing and understanding talk), storytelling and narrative, prosody, and body behavior," and "forming the technical bedrock on which people build their social lives, and construct their sense of sociality with one another."[154] Clayman and Heritage note that the use of conversation analysis in studying human interaction, involves "the direct observation of naturally occurring interaction as captured on audio and video recordings,"[155] with the added benefit of possessing it for posterity, allowing for greater scrutiny, and potentially, of discovering newly found verbal and nonverbal behaviors that heretofore, might not have been perceived.

Lauerbach argues that argumentation theory is a fruitful complement to conversation analysis, in not only describing the interaction, but in assessing its cogency in the subgenre of political talk show interviews.[156] This methodological approach is especially advantageous when analyzing interviews engaging "claims and counterclaims…heated debate and biting rhetoric."[157] The argumentation theory paradigm "is an essentially dialogic discourse practice using Stephen Toulmin's argument structure of the categories of claim, data, warrant, backing, qualification, and conditions of rebuttal."[158] Argumentation theory—in evaluating "discourse practices," strengthens the description of discourse analysis, employing the critical apparatus of the enthymeme (the truncated syllogism) and discernment of fallacious reasoning.[159]

For this analysis, we utilized three artifacts: the texts of the September 6, 1978 in *An Archive of Hope* and *The Harvey Milk Interviews*, in addition to the excerpts from the KPIX televised broadcast.[160] The available broadcast is 2 minutes and 54 seconds, and we looked at a section of the broadcast, beginning with Briggs's statement at 1:14, bookended with Milk's last statement at the end of the debate at 2:52, immediately preceding Hart's final comment. With the benefit of the tape, and its documented use as the preferred and optimal documentation for Conversation Analysis, the tape serves as the primary artifact, and we engaged in a reconciliation of the two texts with the tape. The taped broadcast offers a channel richness with the availability of edifying characteristics within the "performative" realm including paralinguistics and nonverbal dimensions of the individuals and the environs.

The format of this event shares characteristics with the drama, combining monological arguments subsumed within dialogical arguments, with each interviewee/interlocutor speaking for longer stretches, as is evident in Briggs's opening and Milk's closing.[161]

Briggs: "I care about this country. And I care about the family. And I really, sincerely, honestly, and truly believe from the bottom of my heart that homosexuality is a real threat to the survival of this country, if we continue to tolerate it and approve it and let it be raised to an equal level and standard of heterosexuality. That's what I truly believe."

Milk: A teacher to a [particular] sexual orientation? You see, Senator, you're turning things around. My statement was, I'm a role model to the young gay people. To people who have already established themselves as gay. Period. I didn't say—you're the one who keeps bringing up this phony recruitment. You know you're lying. You know you're changing the statements around. And you're doing that all the way around, just like you shifted the money around in your campaigns. And you talk about morality! And I question, what is your real motive behind it? What is your real ambition behind this? What are you really using this for? And stop this phony issue!

This section of dialogue follows Briggs' speech stated above.

Milk:	...the oldest game in the world. That's why I keep saying to you <u>study</u>. I wouldn't be surprised what your <u>next step</u> is because you...always. It is not ever done because of experience.
Hart:	Purely determined before school age?
Milk:	Determined before school age, that is every scientific study, and I say
Milk:	(something) is not a choice. It is not a choice. That's the most fundamental mistake in Senator Briggs' argument
Briggs:	Children learn by <u>example</u>. Children <u>emulate</u>. People need <u>heroes</u>.
Milk:	Okay, okay
Briggs:	[I said if—the reason you wanted to be elected is so you can recruit and convert every young adolescent
Milk:	((Laughs))
Briggs:	Those were your own words
Milk:	No
Briggs:	I read it in the Chronicle
Hart:	[Did you say that?]
Milk:	[No]

This section is a particularly trenchant example of what Clayman and Heritage refer to as "partisan interviewees playing the role of adversary vis-à-vis one another," and where we can observe the interviewer (Hart) "removed from the heat of battle and is free to act as an impartial moderator and catalyst."[162] Clearly, the interviewees "escalate their disagreements by departing from the question-answer turn-taking system, with its mediated pattern of interaction, so as to deliver their objections with greater immediacy and directness." Hart's role is ancillary with the most minimal direct interaction between himself and the interviewees. As Milk and Briggs speak directly to another, their "disagreement is plainly intensified and becomes more confrontational."[163] We can also observe that this section reflects an important point made by Greatbatch, in that, with a co-interviewee's turn, "IEs may initiate a disagreement interruptively, as an on-the-spot response to statements in a yet-to-be completed co IE's turn."[164]

In Milk's closing statement, he seems to be attacking Briggs' supposed fallacious reasoning, which to Milk, smacks of a red herring argument. Milk calls Briggs' fundamental attack a "phony issue," and then proceeds to cast aspersions on Briggs' by accusing him of lying and questioning his morality related to alleged mishandling of campaign monies.

In the case of Harvey Milk, succor and rancor are manifest in his rhetoric, in ways that might seem like confounding and inexplicable antinomies. His success as a persuader, his masterful use of the rhetorical canons, might be construed as belying mastery of his craft, but that would be a simplistic reading. Milk's rhetorical strategy militated against mutual exclusivity, engaging a more confluent and entropic instantiation of succor and rancor. The paradoxes are noteworthy and *sine qua non* in appreciating and understanding Milk's rhetorical efficacy. As Black and Morris observe, "Milk quelled violence even as he wasted no time in escalating his bellicose rhetoric so as to frame Dade's outrage as a catalyst for intensified activism."[165] They also note that,

> Harvey Milk's words, too, teach us that successful activists speak locally, that the art of activist eloquence should be measured by the singularity of each ordinary persuasive opportunity, quotidian audience or fleeting performance. Milk's purple passages and stump cliches teach us that hope's discourse, at close hearing by real people, is by turns and toil both sublime and hackneyed in situ. And with each of those hit-or-miss moments of rhetorical invention and embodiment, with each handshake, with each overbearing exchange, shameless flirtation, corny joke, and lump in the throat moment when he was on a roll, Milk brought the GLBTQ folk of San Francisco to sexual justice and freedom, to gay rights.[166]

Milk was deferent to and had reverence for logical reasoning (*logos*), emotion (*pathos*), and character/goodwill/charisma (*ethos*), and the inextricable, oftentimes elusive relationship among these modes of proof (*pisteis*). Milk employed and harmonized these, achieving fortuitous ends. Maybe his methods were sometimes steeped in rancor, but his was a *telos* where one could affirm that the ends surely justified the means, and violence was never a tenet of that rancorous part of his rhetorical disposition.

With an eclectic constellation of life experiences, Faderman opines that, for Milk,

> Each 'life' represented some genuine (if contradictory) aspect of Harvey Milk—and in each transformation, he thought for a while that he had found himself. But it as only in his final life, as an openly gay politician, that he discovered who had had wanted to be all along. In the five years he had left to live, as he grew into becoming that person, he made a coherent whole out of the many parts of himself.[167]

Milk did not fit into neat categories.[168] He could call himself an atheist and also a New York Jew; he was not an observant Jew but never renounced his Jewish heritage, history, culture or identity; and in one of his recorded wills, he expressed belief in God.

In Aristotle's *Rhetoric*, the concept of virtue is comprised of justice, courage, temperance, magnificence, magnanimity, liberality, gentleness, prudence, and wisdom.[169] Virtue is defined as "faculty of providing and preserving good things; or a faculty of conferring many great benefits, and benefits of all kinds on all occasions."[170] These forms of virtue are beneficent in that they provide an essential utility to others.[171] To keep the movement alive, he advocated all to come out, and called out the institutions of religion to at least be faithful to the tenets of love and humanity. Harvey Milk's life of advocacy and activism are exemplified in an iconic line spoken by Polonius Act I, scene 3 of Shakespeare's *Hamlet*: "To thine own self be true." And as Harvey Milk was true to himself with all of the potential and realized solipsism, he was ultimately a quintessential facilitator in bettering the lives of all people with the loftiest intentions—and no better operationalization of succor could be found.

CHAPTER 2: PART 2

LGBTQ and Violence

One month after of the tragic killing of Matthew Shepard, the literary luminary Tony Kushner wrote a piece titled, *Matthew's Passion* which appeared in *The Nation* on November 11, 1998. In this text, Kushner adopts the persona of an indignant gay prophet and views the murder of Matthew Shepard as a crisis juncture to excoriate the Religious Right, who remained silent after the violent lynching of Shepard. Kushner's missive sought to call out the hypocrisy, moral turpitude, and apostasy of American political and Christian leadership.

"MATTHEW'S PASSION"[1]

Tony Kushner

From *The Nation*. November 9, 1998

When Trent Lott heard the news about the murder of Matthew Shepard, the first thoughts that flashed through his mind were all about spin. Trent Lott worried about how to keep his promise to the religious right, to speak out against the homosexual agenda, without seeming to endorse murder. Trent Lott endorses murder, of course; his party endorses murder, his party endorses discrimination against homosexuals and in doing so, it endorses the ritual slaughter of homosexuals.

Democracy is a bloody business, demanding blood sacrifice. Every advance American democracy has made toward fulfilling the social contract, toward justice and equality and true liberty, every step forward has required offerings of pain and death. The American people demand this, we need to see the burnt bodies of the four little black girls, or their sad small coffins; we need to see the battered, disfigured face of the beaten housewife; we need to see the gay man literally crucified on a fence. We see the carnage and think, Oh, I guess things are still tough out there, for those people. We daydream a little: What does that feel like, to burn? To have your face smashed by your husband's fist? To be raped? To be dragged behind a truck till your body falls to pieces? To freeze, tied to a fence on the Wyoming prairie, for eighteen hours, with the back of your head staved in? Americans perfected the horror film, let's not kid ourselves: These acts of butchery titillate, we glean the news to savor the unsavory details.

And then, after we've drawn a few skin-prickling breaths of the aromas of torture and agony and madness, we shift a little in our comfortable chairs, a little embarrassed to have caught ourselves in the act of prurient sadism, a little worried that God has seen us also, a little worried that we have lazily misplaced our humanity, a little sad for the victims: Oh, gee, I guess I sort of think that shouldn't happen out there to those people, and something should be done. As long as I don't have to do it.

And having thought as much, having, in fact, been edified, changed a very little bit by the suffering we have seen, our humanity as well as our skin having been pricked, we turn our back on Matthew Shepard's crucifixion and return to our legitimate entertainments. When next the enfranchisement of homosexuals is discussed, Matthew Shepard's name will probably be invoked, and the murder of gay people will be deplored by decent people, straight and gay; and when the religious right shrills viciously about how the murder doesn't matter, as it has been doing since his death, decent people everywhere will find the religious right lacking human kindness, will find these Gary Bauers and Paul Weyrichs and Pat Robertsons un-Christian, repulsive, in fact. And a very minute increment toward decency will have been secured. But poor Matthew Shepard. Jesus, what a price!

Trent Lott endorses murder. He knows that discrimination kills. Pope John Paul II endorses murder. He, too, knows the price of discrimination, having declared anti-Semitism a sin, having just canonized a Jewish-born nun who died in Auschwitz. He knows that discrimination kills. But when the Pope heard the news about Matthew Shepard, he too worried about spin. And so, on the subject of gay-bashing, the Pope and his cardinals, and his bishops, and priests maintain their cynical political silence. Rigorously denouncing the abuse and murder of homosexuals would be a big sin against spin; denouncing the murder of homosexuals in such a way that it received even one-thousandth of the coverage his and his church's attacks on homosexuals routinely receive, this would be an act of decency the Pope can't afford, for the Pope knows: Behind this one murdered kid stand legions of kids whose lives are scarred by the bigotry this Pope defends as sanctioned by God. None of these kids will ever be allowed to marry the person she or he loves, not while the Pope and his church can prevent it; all of these kids are told, by the Holy Catholic Church, and by the Episcopalians and Lutherans and Baptists and Orthodox Jews: Your love is cursed by God.

To speak out against murdering those who are discriminated against is to speak out against discrimination. To remain silent is to endorse murder.

A lot of people worry these days about the death of civil discourse. The Pope, in his new encyclical, Fides et Ratio (Faith and Reason), laments the death of civil discourse and cites "ancient philosophers who proposed friendship as one of the most appropriate contexts for sound philosophical inquiry." It's more than faintly ludicrous, this plea for friendship coming from the selfsame Pope who has tried so relentlessly to stamp out dissent in churches and Catholic universities, but let's follow the lead of the crazies who killed Matthew Shepard and take the Pope at his word.

Friendship is the proper context for discussion. Fine and good. Take the gun away from the head, Your Holiness, and we can discuss the merits of homosexual sex, of homosexual marriage, of homosexual love, of monogamy versus promiscuity, of lesbian or gay couples raising kids, of condom distribution in the schools, of confidential counseling for teenagers, of sex education that addresses more than abstinence. We can discuss abortion, we can discuss anything you like. Just promise me two things, friend: First, you won't beat my brains out with a pistol butt and leave me to die by the side of the road. Second, if someone else, someone a little less sane than you, feeling entitled to commit these terrible things against me because they understood you a little too literally, or were more willing than you to take your distaste for me and what I do to its most full-blooded conclusion, if someone else does violence against me, friend, won't you please make it your business to make a big public fuss about how badly I was treated? Won't you please make a point, friend, you who call yourself, and who are called, by millions of people, the Vicar on Earth of the very gentle Jesus, won't you please in the name of friendship announce that, no one who deliberately inflicts suffering, whether by violence or by prejudice, on another human being, can be said to be acting in God's name? And announce it so that it is very clear that you include homosexuals when you refer to "human beings," and announce it so that the world hears you, really hears you, so that your announcement makes the news, as you are capable of doing when it suits your purposes? Won't you make this your purpose too? And if you won't, if you won't take responsibility for the consequences of your militant promotion of discrimination, won't you excuse me if I think you are not a friend at all but rather a homicidal liar whose claim to spiritual and moral leadership is fatally compromised, is worth nothing more than…well, worth nothing more than the disgusting, opportunistic leadership of Trent Lott.

A lot of people worry these days about the death of civil discourse, and would say that I ought not call the Pope a homicidal liar, nor (to be ecumenical about it) the orthodox rabbinate homicidal liars, nor Trent Lott a disgusting opportunistic hatemonger. But I worry a lot less about the death of civil discourse than I worry about being killed if, visiting the wrong town with my boyfriend, we forget ourselves so much as to betray, at the wrong moment in front of the wrong people, that we love one another. I worry much more about the recent death of the Maine antidiscrimination bill, and about the death of the New York hate crimes bill, which will not pass because it includes sexual orientation. I worry more about the death of civil rights than civil discourse. I worry much more about the irreversible soul-deaths of lesbian, gay, bisexual, transgendered children growing up deliberately, malevolently isolated by the likes of Trent Lott and Newt Gingrich than I worry about the death of civil discourse. I mourn Matthew Shepard's actual death, caused by the unimpeachably civil "we hate the sin, not the sinner" hypocrisy of the religious right, endorsed by the political right, much more than I mourn the lost chance to be civil with someone who does not consider me fully a citizen, nor fully human. I mourn that cruel death more than the chance to be civil with those who sit idly by while theocrats, bullies, panderers and hatemongers, and their crazed murderous children, destroy democracy and our civic life. Civic, not civil, discourse is what matters, and civic discourse mandates the assigning of blame.

If you are lesbian, gay, transgendered, bi, reading this, here's one good place to assign blame: The Human Rights Campaign's appalling, post-Shepard endorsement of Al D'Amato dedicates our resources to the perpetuation of a Republican majority in Congress. The HRC, ostensibly our voice in Washington, is in cahoots with fag-bashers and worse. If you are a heterosexual person, and you are reading this: Yeah yeah yeah, you've heard it all before, but if you have not called your Congressperson to demand passage of a hate crimes bill that includes sexual orientation, and e-mailed every Congressperson, if you have not gotten up out of your comfortable chair to campaign for homosexual and all civil rights—campaign, not just passively support—may you think about this crucified man, and may you support—may you think about this crucified man, and may you mourn, and may you burn with a moral citizen's shame. As one civilized person to another: Matthew Shepard shouldn't have died. We should all burn with shame.
Tony Kushner

*　*　*

RHETORICAL ANALYSIS

The traumatic and reprehensible murder of Matthew Shepard, a twenty-one-year-old, gay University of Wyoming student at the hands of Russel Henderson and Aaron McKinney is a tragic touchstone of American, anti-gay violence; it became the Burkean perfection of homophobia's "cult of the kill."[2] As the media framed the details of the grisly lynching and Matthew Shepard's funeral garnered more and more attention, so, too, did the religious rhetoric. Several news media accounts and secular LGBTQ publications depicted Shepard as a Christ figure.[3] Moreover, eschatological questions over Matthew Shepard and his sexuality formed the discursive battlegrounds of a culture war that would continue to play out after Matthew's death. The ill-famed, defrocked pastor of Westboro Baptist Church, Fred Phelps, known for his notorious motto "God Hates Fags" and gay funeral protests, vowed to demonstrate at Shepard's funeral in Casper, Wyoming. Phelps failed to appear. However, in April of 1999, at Russel Henderson's court hearing in Laramie, Phelps and fellow protesters were on site replete with children holding signs that read "Fags Die God Laughs," "No Tears for Queers," and Phelps himself flaunted an over-sized photograph of Matthew Shepard, which read "Matt in Hell."[4]

The counter-protest comprised LGBTA students from the University of Wyoming and other protesters from Denver; they rallied under the appropriate agonistic appellation "angel action." Dozens of "angels," inspired by Matthew Shepard's cherubic countenance, donned halos and strategically positioned themselves in front of Phelps and his brood. By spreading their vast, seven-foot high, white sheeted wings they effectively encumbered Phelps' malicious messages. Beth Loffreda depicted the event as "a witty repossession of the sacred by the very people Phelps deems profane and damned."[5] The rhetorical inflections of religious reflection in Loffreda's own words are purposeful and demonstrate the consubstantiality between rhetoric and religion. In the preface of her book, Loffreda also observes that even before Shepard died, he "underwent a strange American transubstantiation...filtered and fixed as an icon by national news media," no doubt influenced by the factious politics of sexuality.[6] Reviewing cultural and academic analyses of the Mathew Shepard murder, one would be hard pressed to not find religious conceptions abiding in the discourse. Words like Loffreda's "transubstantiation," "sacrifice," "ritual," "repossession," "guilt," "scapegoat," "sacred," "redemption," "martyr," "crucifixion," and "resurrection" abound.

Scholars and critics have examined the rhetoric of the Matthew Shepard murder articulated in various media outlets, protest events, and Christian responses.[7] Moreover, the relationship between religious rhetoric, violence, and homosexuality is a thorny one entangled within a thicket of cultural ideology and discursive formations. In his exceptional book, *God Hates Fags: Rhetorics of Religious Violence*,

Michael Cobb analyzes the deep implications that conservative Christian appeals for religious intolerance and violence against homosexuals ("the last safe group to hate") have on American society.[8]

LGBTQ people have long been seen as aberrations, scapegoated by a "Christian society." Cobb argues such views are distinctively expressed by religious authorities through the rhetorical form of "the jeremiad," a sermonic discourse aimed at community of backsliders rife with spiritual declension and decay.[9] Beyond this, evangelical Christians regularly depict themselves as a persecuted people, rhetorically constructing a narrative of victimhood; they claim to be besieged by a depraved secular world of homosexuality, hell bent on destroying humanity. Such a religious rhetoric, which finds its telos in the hate speech of "Fags Die God Laughs," demands purgation of the homosexual threat and thereby provides succor for a disquieting Christian majority desiring to reestablish order. In an effort to address this prevailing religious discourse, Cobb's book inventively theorizes a "queering of conservative religious hate speech about queers," and how "religious hate language becomes a language through which queers strategically mediate conventional structures of national belonging."[10] Cobb's focus shares an affinity with our claims about the homeopathic functions of religious rhetoric, whereby a sacred succor/rancor, tonic/toxin cause/cure provide a theriac resource available to rhetors.

Through a kind of jeremiadic inversion, Cobb aims to turn the venom-filled fangs of religious discourse, poised to scapegoat homosexual people and a larger polity, back on itself. Cobb's project intends to demonstrate how queers can utilize the very antipathy they experience as a strategic antidote and through the form of a national jeremiad can carve out a sustainable place for them. Concomitantly, the significance of Matthew Shepard's gay sacrificial death and why it mattered to a Christian nation are elucidated by religious scholar Brett Krutzsch. In his book *Dying to be Normal*, Krutzsch examines how gay activists truss the death of Matthew Shepard to Christian concepts of crucifixion, sacrifice, and martyrdom. Such discourse foments gay political activism by depicting Shepard, a "pious Protestant," and gays as "compatible with culturally resonant Christian narratives."[11] In portraying Shepard's murder as sacrificial, gay rights advocates inventively situate Shepard's death within a Christian armature. Rhetorical parallels to Jesus Christ's own crucifixion, death, and resurrection were elucidated.

The central rhetorical text featured in this chapter is award-winning playwright Tony Kushner's piece titled *Matthew's Passion* which appeared in *The Nation* on November 11, 1998, one month after Mathew's Shepard murder. Similar to Cobb and Krutzsch, we want to argue that Kushner, adopting the persona of an indignant gay prophet, views the murder of Matthew Shepard as an inflection point to castigate the Religious Right, who have remained silent in the wake of a tragic violent lynching and thereby expose the hypocrisy, moral turpitude, and apostasy of Christian leadership. As Krutzsch observes, Kushner does not condemn McKinney and Henderson for Shepard's murder. Rather, he indicts Republicans and the Religious Right, cast as Pharisees. The Pharisees were, according to the synoptic Gospels, a conclave of doctrinaire Jewish leaders who actively crusaded to eradicate Jesus from the community.[12]

While comparisons to Matthew Shepard's and Jesus's deaths abound, we interpret Kushner's rhetoric as an instance of jeremiadic inversion in which the admonishment is ironically troped back on religious leadership. Kushner's article reads as an apostolic epistle penned by an improbable and indignant prophet.[13] As we have witnessed, religious rhetoric is often deployed after tragic violence to provide succor for a suffering polity. As Kenneth Burke argues in *Proletariat Literature in the United States*, "religion and politics are matters of welfare."[14] Burke went on to remark that religious rhetoric is "produced for purposes of comfort, as part of the *consolatio philosophiae*. It is undertaken as equipment for living, as a ritualistic way of arming us to confront perplexities and risks."[15]

However, as other situational perplexities and ambiguities reveal, succor can be blinkered and leave rhetors and audiences implacable. Both René Girard and Danielle Allen acknowledge that ritual sacrifice is *sine qua non* for communities and democracies.[16] Nevertheless, in the wake of tragic violence, extending solace for habitual sacrifice is not always a fitting response to such an exigence. Religious rhetoric with succor as its aim often fails to soothe an audience, especially persecuted groups who are relentlessly the subject of ritual sacrifices. As Allen states, "The hard truth of democracy is that some citizens are always giving things up [including their lives] for others."[17] Using Ralph Ellison's *Invisible Man* and his conception of the "critical knife," Allen argues the marginalized have a responsibility to criticize the dominators of society for the failure of reciprocal sacrifice.[18] Kushner fulfills this role of the "knife carrier," wielding what Martin Luther King Jr. called the "sword that heals"[19] through his sharp and pointed criticism of the hypocoristic discourse of both the religious and political right who seek to preserves authority by failing to denounce the murder of Matthew Shepard.

Kushner's words take the shape of a rancorous mocking, whereby lambasting augments lament. Sacred succor and rancor are conflated and operate as a productive paradox of virtuous invective where what is conventionally seen as vice, derision, and caustic ad hominem attacks becomes vulnerary. Vituperative venting can be cathartic; a justifying salve washes over the wielder and those they represent when the slings and arrows of kairotic anger hit their mark.

The primary impetus of Kushner's poignant response attacks conversative politicians and religious leaders for indifferent silence which "endorses the ritual slaughter of homosexuals."[20] On one hand Kushner begrudgingly sees Matthew Shepard's violent martyrdom for what it is, a bloody sacrifice offered in the name of advancing equality, justice, and liberty. Disturbingly, Shepard's death is part and parcel of an American rite for rights. While this may be a painful historical and socio-political reality, such atrocities should always elicit outrage and condemnation especially from a nation's moral leaders. Thus, Kushner's true ardor and ire are aimed at the Christian Right's inscrutable inaction in spurning discrimination and murder. Kushner's rhetorical weapons are manifold and analyzing them is no sinecure. However, we examine several discursive strategies housed in Kushner's broader quiver of honorable objurgation, designed to desecrate normative political conventions and expose hypocrisy; they are: *engergia*, *epiplexis*, apostrophe, and *a fortiori* argument.

In titling his piece *Matthew's Passion*, Kushner presents Shepard as an archetypal "Christ figure," thereby inviting readers to interpret the violence endured by Matthew Shepard through analogical resemblance to the "suffering" (the Latin word for "passion") of Jesus Christ and the anguish and torture that Matthew Shepard underwent. Kushner employs the word "crucifixion" several times in his article, and, as we hope to demonstrate, functions as a terministic screen of reappropriation. From the opening of the essay, Kushner straightaway declares Trent Lott, then the Majority Leader of the United States Senate, complicit in the murder of Matthew Shepard. Kushner reasons Lott, due to his political imbroglio with the religious right, refused to condemn violence fomented and perpetrated by homophobia and heteronormative discrimination. Lott seems to have "washed his hands" of Matthew's crucifixion and is symbolic of Pontius Pilate. His indifference instantiates his culpability in the "ritual slaughter of homosexuals."[21]

Kushner expands the reach of indictment to include America writ large, noting that democracy is a "bloody business." Carnage becomes spectacle for Americans; voyeuristic pleasure satiates our craving for sacrifice. Kushner likens his American audience to horror film viewers and underscores our pathological fixation with the visual and sensorial violence that "we need to see."

> The burnt bodies of the four little black girls, or their sad small coffins; we need to see the battered, disfigured face of the beaten housewife; we need to see the gay man literally crucified on a fence…We daydream a little: What does that feel like to burn? To have your face smashed by your husband's fist, To be raped? To be dragged behind a truck till your body falls to pieces? To freeze, tied to a fence on the Wyoming prairie, for eighteen hours, with the back of your head staved in?[22]

Kushner argues that the American public confronts such violence only in a detached and daydream like spectacle, affirming "how tough it is out there for those people," yet refusing to get our hands dirty in fighting the injustice. To cure this selfish isolation and ersatz empathy, Kushner stylistically interweaves the tropes of *accumulatio* and *energeia* within the armature of *epiplexis*, or rhetorical question by rebuke. Kushner employs the Aristotelian figure of *energeia*, or a vivid visualization/actualization, "bringing-before-the-eyes" of an audience.[23] Kushner reinforces his claim by graphically depicting the very violence he indicts America for fetishizing. In doing so, his persona is that as a prophet and a *parrhesiastes*, speaking hard truths to power by infusing his prose with two drops of Gorgon blood, one venom and the other vivacity.

Decrying the depravity of America's "needing to see" cruel sacrifice, evoked by the violent visuals of hatred and prejudice, Kushner intensifies his derision with a sensorial shift. Reprising the antecedent violent episodes, but this time readers experience them through the visceral sensation of feeling, framed by rhetorical questions (*epiplexis*). Kushner amplifies the poignance, presence, pain, and the prophetic blame. He acknowledges there does exist some feeling of "skin-prickling" chagrin or worry that "God has seen" the audience reveling in "the aromas of torture and agony," but not enough to unmoor us from our "comfortable chairs" and do something about it. The figure of *accumulatio*, "heaping up" trussed with *epiplexis*, or rhetorical questions meant to castigate rather than elicit answers pile more than enough evidence to convict. "What does it feel like to burn? To have your face smashed by your husband's fist? To be raped? To be dragged behind a truck until you're your body falls to pieces, To freeze…?" *Epiplexis* comports with Kushner's persona of an admonishing prophet whose own outsider identity is judged immoral in the eyes of the Religious Right (and subject to the same violence of Matthew Shepard).

After admonishing Trent Lott and constructing him as a political synecdoche representing a party that discriminates against homosexuals and approves of gay murder, Kushner identifies Pope John Paul II as the religious counterpart to Trent Lott. Depicting the pontiff as hypocritically representing an institution indifferent to discrimination, and complicit in the murder, of homosexuals. Citing the Pope's recent canonization of a Jewish born nun who died in Auschwitz, Kushner remarks that, "the Pope knows discrimination kills. But when he heard the news about Matthew Shepard, he too (like Trent Lott) worried about spin." Kushner surmises the Pope's "cynical political silence" in denouncing the murder of homosexuals is because the Pope, too, must defend a God that "hates fags."

Moreover, Kushner emphasizes the egregious incongruity of JPII's promotion of the philosophy of friendship and civil discourse penned in his encyclical, *Fides et Ratio* (Faith and Reason 1998) in the face of heinous violence against Matthew Shepard. Employing the apostrophic form or *prosopopoeia*, Kushner pens an imaginary encounter with the Pope.

> Take the gun away from the head, Your Holiness, and we can discuss the merits of homosexual sex…Just promise me two things, friend: First, you won't beat my brains out with a pistol butt and leave me to die by the side of the road. Second if someone else…feeling entitled to commit these terrible things against me because they understood you a little too literally…if someone else does violence against me, friend…Won't you please, friend, you who call yourself…the Vicar on Earth of very gentle Jesus, won't you please in the

name of friendship announce that no one who inflicts suffering, whether by violence or prejudice, on another human being, can be acting in God's name? And announce…that you include homosexuals when you refer to "human beings," and announce it so that the world hears you, really hears you, so your announcement makes the news as you are capable of doing when it suits your purposes? Won't you make this your purpose too? And if you won't, if you won't take responsibility for the consequences of your militant promotion of discrimination, won't you excuse me if I think you are not a friend at all but rather a homicidal liar whose claim to spiritual and moral leadership is fatally compromised, is worth nothing more than…the disgusting opportunistic leadership of Trent Lott.[24]

Apostrophe, "the act of turning oneself away," "calling upon," or today we might say "calling out" is a sudden averting in a speech by which one pivots from one audience to address another, real or imagined, absent or present.[25] Quintilian remarked on apostrophe's effect of turning on one's adversary. According to Cicero, the apostrophe (*exclamatio*) is a figure that expresses animus or indignation by addressing some man or city or place or object. Cicero contends apostrophe, when used adroitly by the orator, can instill in the audience as much indignation as desired.[26] Laurent Pernot provides excellent examples for apostrophe's use, "to blame the troops, one turns to the general, to reprimand students, one speaks in front of them to their teacher."[27] Following this figural logic, Kushner assails the supreme authority of the Catholic Church, Pope John Paul II.

Kushner engenders a striking incongruity in referring to the Pope with the venerable sobriquets of "friend" "Your Holiness," "Vicar on Earth of the very gentle Jesus" immediately followed by the image of a pistol pointing pontiff malevolently intent on inflicting violence and suffering. The apostrophic form affords Kushner a fictive audience with the Pope in which he takes full rhetorical advantage.[28] Imagine calling someone whose silence endorses violence and prejudice against a group of people in which you identify with as "a friend." The verbal irony of this erroneous "friendship" reaches an absurd apex when Kushner, indicting the pope for refusing to denounce the consequences of violent discrimination, invectively states, "I think you are not a friend at all but rather a homicidal liar whose claim to spiritual and moral leadership is fatally compromised."[29] Kushner manifests directly what the figured sarcasm intends to illuminate; it is not the death of civil discourse that the Pope should be worried about, but the death of his own "fatally compromised" moral authority.

Moreover, Kushner ironically and intentionally violates the call for civil friendship through a juxtaposing ad hominem affront that characterizes the Pope (now a canonized saint of the Catholic Church) as a "homicidal liar." Figured sarcasm typically resides under the rubric of "ironic praise." For example, as Pernot notes, to say to a coward, "You're a veritable Hercules." But since the prophet's errand is to turn structures, material and linguistic, on their heads the inverse would work as well. Imagine the incongruity of telling Hercules, the epitome of

Greek mytho-poetic valor, that's "he is a coward." This is the same critical "disease" that Kushner invites his readers to experience through the inconceivable conflation of Pope John Paul II with "homicidal liar."

Such searing slurs and vituperation set up a further incongruity that Kushner attends to in the next paragraph. His kariotically deployed ad hominem attack purposefully vitiates the civil political discourse the Pope has called for thereby elucidating the hamartia in the Pope's position. In other words, why are moral authorities preoccupied with civility when homosexuals are being murdered? Kushner drives this criticism home with the use of an *a fortiori* argument. *A fortiori* argument, from the Latin meaning, "from the stronger" is essentially a literal analogy used when drawing a conclusion that is even more obvious or convincing than the one just drawn. While the Pope is not wrong to advocate political friendship and civil discourse, but vis-à-vis the murder of Matthew Shepard, Kushner demonstrates *a fortiori* (with even stronger reason) why tragic violence and a refusal to condemn it far surpasses calls for civil discourse. The first line of Kushner's penultimate paragraph sarcastically replays an ad populum fallacy interlaced with the figure of paralepsis. "A lot of people worry these days about the death the civil discourse and would say I ought not call the Pope a homicidal liar." Then, framed as an *a fortiori* argument, Kushner counters with:

> But I worry a lot less about the death of civil discourse than I worry about being killed if, visiting the wrong town with my boyfriend...I worry much more about the irreversible soul-death of lesbian, gay, bisexual, transgendered children growing up deliberately, malevolently isolated by the likes of Trent Lott and Newt Gingrich...I mourn Matthew Shepard's actual death, caused by the unimpeachably civil "we hate the sin, not the sinner," hypocrisy of the religious right, endorsed by the political right much more than I mourn the lost chance to be civil with someone who does not consider me fully a citizen, nor fully human. I mourn the cruel death more than the chance to be civil with those who sit idly by while theocrats, bullies, panders, and hatemongers, and their crazed murderous children, destroy democracy...[30]

Kushner's worry transforms into mourning over unspeakable actualities and displays of monumental inhumanity that must supersede apocryphal anxieties over impolite speech. One does not negotiate with hate or courteously converse with lynch mobs.

The conclusion of Kushner's piece advocates for civic action on passing hate crime legislation, anti-discrimination bills, and participation in larger civil rights campaigns. In an effort to inspire such action, Kushner, encourages his readers to "think about this crucified man" proclaiming that "we should all burn with shame."[31] Kushner leaves readers with the central symbol of Christianity, the crucifixion, but not Christ's, Matthew Shepard's. Appropriating the religious icon of crucifixion and resignifying it with Shepard's martyrdom, Kushner's rhetoric enacts the role of an ironic but indignant prophet, whose reproach reminds citizens and religious adherents not of salvation, but of their sinful culpability in the murderous sacrificing of those deemed as aberrant to America's Christian moral vision. Thus, in our failure to realize this and repent, we are left not with the soothing succor of hope, but with the stinging rancor of shame. Tony Kushner's *Matthew's Passion* is paradigmatic of religious rhetoric's sacred succor/rancor antimony that functions to cure a polity infected by the disease of discrimination and violence with accountability, mortification, atonement, and just action where Christian and political leadership betrays.

CHAPTER 3

Geopolitics, Violence, and Remembrance

Pope Francis visited the 9/11 Memorial and Museum on his first trip to the United States and participated in what was deemed an "Interfaith Peace Gathering." Through a healing hermeneutical depiction of the memorial's visual-spatial rhetoric, Pope Francis delivered a powerfully, prayerful panegyric conjoining religious consolation with public commemoration. Additional participants in the interreligious prayer service included Rabbi Elliot Cosgrove of the Park Avenue Synagogue in Manhattan and Imam Khalid, Executive Director, and Chaplain at New York University Islamic Center Latif. The September 25, 2015, event provides an opportunity for a microcosm of the world's religions through their representatives, to come together in prayer at the site of the fallen World Trade Center Towers, the inhabitants of the Towers who died, and the first responders who died saving lives on September 11, 2001.

"INTERFAITH MEETING WITH POPE FRANCIS AT SEPTEMBER 11 MEMORIAL AND MUSEUM"[1]

Pope Francis

New York City, New York. September 25, 2015.

Archbishop Timothy M. Dolan (00:00:28): Papa Francesco, on behalf of this very distinguished group representatives of the Hindu, Buddhist, Jain, Sikh, Native American, Jewish, Islamic, civic and public officials, and the board of the September 11th Memorial Foundation, I renew to you our welcome and our joy at your visit. Welcome, Holy Father. [applause]. Now I can tell you, Papa Francesco, we, in New York, are sinners. We are sinners. We have many flaws. We make many mistakes. But one of the things we do very well is sincere and fruitful inter-religious friendship. Our ancestors came here for religious freedom, and they found, in New York City, an atmosphere of respect and appreciation for religious diversity of which you just spoke at the United Nations. We, who have the honor of pastoring our people, work together, we pray together, we meet together, we talk to one another, and we try to serve as one the city we are proud to call our earthly home while awaiting our true and eternal residence in heaven. So very often do we recall the faith of the Psalmist, "God is in the midst of the city." Your prayer, presence, and words this morning inspire us, so thank you for being here. [applause].

***

Imam Khalid Latif (3:46): You may be seated.
Rabbi Elijah Cosgrove: In this place, where horrendous violence was committed falsely in the name of God, we representatives of the world religions, in this great city of New York, gather to offer words of comfort and prayer. With love and affection, we recall the victims of the 9/11 attacks. We pray that their souls, and the souls of all those serving the first responders are forever remembered for an eternal blessing. Today and every day, may we understand our shared mission to be, in the words of Pope Francis, "a field hospital after battle to heal the wounds and warm the hearts of a humanity in so desperate need of comfort."
Latif: Intolerance and ignorance fueled those who attacked this place. The courage of today's gathering distinguishes us from the opponents of religious freedom as we stand together as brothers and sisters to condemn their horrific acts of violence, and honor each life that was lost unconditionally. As read in the Koran, "one life lost is like all mankind," and "one life saved is like all mankind." To God all life is sacred and precious. Where others fail, let us be the peaceful reminders of that notion to His creation.

Cosgrove: The Book of Psalms teaches us that we should love peach and we should pursue peace. Let us honor those killed in this place by becoming, in the words of St. Francis, "instruments of peace." Where there is hatred, let us sow love. Where there is injury, pardon. Where there is doubt, faith. Where there is despair, hope. Where there is darkness, light. And where there is sadness, joy.

Latif: Men and women from all walks of life ran to this place in hopes of saving lives. The soul intent of those first responders was the protection of others, regardless of the cost to them as individuals. As the worst of humanity sought to take life, they exemplified the best of humanity through their selflessness, willing to give their entire life in hopes of saving another. Their story is one that each of us should carry forward with us, both in thought and in action, as we move forward from this place. The Koran Declares that "Allah is with those who are righteous, and those who do good." Let us embody their unconditional love, their continued strength, their unwavering hope, and their pursuit of good, as we seek to build a much needed peace.

Cosgrove: Let us learn to share this "big apple" we call home, in all its diversity and flavor. Through friendship and dialogue, may the timbre and tonality of each of our faith traditions be heard in the great symphony of our city and nation. On this, in the historic anniversary of Nostra Aetate, let us celebrate, affirm, and build on our shared commitment to interreligious dialogue. In the words of Pope Francis, "may we respect and love one another as brothers and sisters. May we learn to understand the sufferings of others." May we live to see the day, as envisioned by the Prophet Micah, that "everyone will sit under their own vine and under their own fig tree and no one shall make them afraid, for the Lord Almighty has spoken."

Latif: The Koran states, "Oh mankind, we have created you from a male and a female and made you into nations and tribes so that you might know one another." We have gathered here today, as men and women who seek to meet ignorance with understanding, through our knowing of each other today. Let us move beyond a mere toleration of our differences and work towards a much-needed celebration of them. Let us be bold enough to build partnerships with new friends and allies, and together be the reason that people have hope in this world, and not the reason that people dread it.

***

Pope Francis (9:35–13:46): Oh God of love, compassion, and healing, look on us, people of many different faiths and religious traditions, who gather today in this hallowed ground, the scene of unspeakable violence and pain. We ask you, in your goodness, to give eternal light and peace to all who died here—the heroic first-responders, our fire fighters, police officers, emergency service workers, and port authority personnel, along with all the innocent men and women who were victims of this tragedy simply because their work or service brought them here on

September 11. We ask you, in your compassion, to bring healing to those who, because of their presence here 14 years ago, continue to suffer from injuries and illness. Heal, too, the pain of still-grieving families, and all who lost loved ones in this tragedy. Give them strength to continue their lives with courage and hope. We are mindful as well of those who suffered death, injury, and loss on the same day at the Pentagon and in Shanksville, Pennsylvania. Our hearts are one with theirs as our prayer embraces their pain and suffering. God of peace, bring your peace to our violent world, peace in the hearts of all men and women, and peace among the nations of the earth. Turn to your way of love those, whose hearts and minds are consumed with hatred and who justify killing in the name of religion. God of understanding, overwhelmed by the magnitude of this tragedy, we seek your light and guidance as we confront such terrible events. Grant that those whose lives were spared may live so that the lives lost here may not have been lost in vain. Comfort and console us, strengthen us in hope, and give us the wisdom and courage to work tirelessly for a world where true peace and love reign among nations and in the hearts of all.

***

Cantor Azi Schwartz (22:28–28:00): [Recites the Prayer for the Fallen, *El Malei Rachamim*, in Hebrew.] Exalted, compassionate God, grant infinite rest in Your sheltering presence, among the holy and pure, to the souls of all our beloved who have gone to their eternal home. Merciful One, we ask that our loved ones find perfect peace in Your tender embrace, their memory enduring as inspiration for commitment to their ideals and integrity in our lives. May their souls thus be bound up in the bond of life. May they rest in peace. And let us say: Amen.

***

Pope Francis (29:34–44:23): Dear Friends, excuse myself for not speaking English. I cannot. [laughter]. I feel many different emotions standing here at Ground Zero, where thousands of lives were taken in a senseless act of destruction. Here grief is palpable. The water we see flowing towards that empty pit reminds us of all those lives which fell prey to those who think that destruction is the only way to settle conflicts. It is the silent cry of those who were victims of a logic which knows only violence, hatred, and revenge. A logic which can only cause pain, suffering, destruction, and tears.

The flowing water is also a symbol of our tears. Tears shed at so much devastation and ruin, past and present. This is a place where we weep, we weep out of a sense of helplessness in the face of injustice, murder, and the failure to settle our differences through dialogue. Here we mourn the wrongful and senseless loss of innocent lives because of the inability to find solutions which respect the common good. It is flowing water reminds us of yesterday's tears, but also of all the tears still being shed today.

A few moments ago, I met some of the families of the fallen first responders. Meeting them made me see once again how acts of destruction are never impersonal, abstract or merely material. They always have a face, a concrete story, and names. In those family members, we see the face of pain, a pain which still touches us and cries out to heaven.

At the same time, those family members showed me the other face of this attack, the other face of their grief: the power of love and remembrance. A remembrance that does not leave us empty and withdrawn. The names of so many loved ones are written around the towers' footprints. We can see them, we can touch them, and we can never forget them.

Here, amid pain and grief, we also have a palpable sense of the heroic goodness which people are capable of, those hidden reserves of strength from which we can draw. In the depths of pain and suffering, you also witnessed the heights of generosity and service. Hands reached out, lives were given. In a metropolis which might seem impersonal, faceless, lonely, you demonstrated the powerful solidarity born of mutual support, love, and self-sacrifice. No one thought about race, nationality, neighborhoods, religion, or politics. It was all about solidarity, meeting immediate needs, brotherhood. It was about being brothers and sisters. New York City firemen walked into the crumbling towers, with no concern for their own wellbeing. Many succumbed; their sacrifice enabled great numbers to be saved.

This place of death became a place of life too, a place of saved lives, a hymn to the triumph of life over the prophets of destruction and death, to goodness over evil, to reconciliation and unity over hatred and division.

It is a source of great hope that in this place of sorrow and remembrance I can join with leaders representing the many religious traditions which enrich the life of this great city. I trust that our presence together will be a powerful sign of our shared desire to be a force for reconciliation, peace and justice in this community and throughout the world. For all our differences and disagreements, we can live in a world of peace. In opposing every attempt to create a rigid uniformity, we can and must build unity on the basis of our diversity of languages, cultures and religions, and lift our voices against everything which would stand in the way of such unity. Together we are called to say "no" to every attempt to impose uniformity and "yes" to a diversity accepted and reconciled.

This can only happen if we uproot from our hearts all feelings of hatred, vengeance and resentment. We know that that is only possible as a gift from heaven. Here, in this place of remembrance, I would ask everyone together, each in his or her own way, to spend a moment in silence and prayer. Let us implore from on high the gift of commitment to the cause of peace. Peace in our homes, our families, our schools and our communities. Peace in all those places where war never seems to end. Peace for those faces which have known nothing but pain. Peace throughout this world which God has given us as the home of all and a home for all. Simply peace.

In this way, the lives of our dear ones will not be lives which will one day be forgotten. Instead, they will be present whenever we strive to be prophets not of tearing down but of building up, prophets of reconciliation, prophets of peace.

***

A THEOLOGICAL RESPONSE TO A GEOPOLITICAL EXIGENCE

As cataclysmic as were the bombings of the World Trade Center, February 26, 1993, by foreign terrorists, and the Alfred P. Murrah Federal Building in Oklahoma City on April 19, 1995 by domestic terrorists, the events of September 11, 2001 brought the consequences of terrorism to tragic heights, as the four aircraft fell from the skies, crashing into the field in Shanksville, Pennsylvania, the Pentagon, and the North and South Towers of the World Trade Center, bringing the Stendhalian twin edifices, with their inspiring verticality, to ground level, in contortions of twisted metal, heaps of rubble, and incalculable loss of life.[2] Walker observes that the bombings of the World Trade Center and the Murrah building showed, beyond a doubt, that the United States faced a serious problem with terrorism at home and abroad.[3] The events that galvanized the world exemplified the worst in us and the best in us.

Michael Bloomberg, former mayor of New York City, 2002–2013, and Chair of the National September 11 Memorial & Museum, said that the Memorial & Museum's mission "helps us fulfill the pledge and honor the memories of all those who were killed in the World Trade Center, at the Pentagon, and aboard Flight 93 on that fateful morning, as well as the lives lost in the attacks on February 26, 1993."[4]

A total of nineteen terrorists, members of Al-Qaeda, boarded the four, ill-fated aircraft in coordinated hijackings, all originating on the East Coast, for destinations in California, which would not be reached. The death toll reached 2,977 with thousands injured.[5]

September 11, 2001 began as another uneventful Tuesday with calm skies as the end of the summer solstice was fast approaching. But the tranquility was short-lived as the skies trembled with violence and impending doom. American Airlines Flight 11 departed Boston's Logan International Airport for Los Angeles at 7:59 a.m. and crashed into the North Tower of the World Trade Center at 8:46:40.[6] United Airlines Flight 175 departed Logan International Airport at 8:14 a.m., also bound for Los Angeles.[7] At 9:03:11, UA 175 crashed into the South Tower of the World Trade Center.[8] American Airlines Flight 77 departed Washington's Dulles International Airport at 8:20 a.m., and at 9:37:46, it crashed into the Pentagon.[9] United Airlines Flight 93 departed Newark International Airport at 8:42 a.m. bound for San Francisco.[10] The hijackers' intention was to crash into the U.S. Capitol or the White House,[11] and although the passengers bravely and courageously foiled the plan to reach one of those two destinations, they were unable to gain control of the aircraft, and it plummeted 580 miles per hour, crashing into a field in Shanksville, Pennsylvania at 10:03:11.[12]

The September 11 attacks were conceived and executed by the terrorist organization Al-Qaeda, under the direction of Osama bin Laden, originally organized in 1989.[13] Khalid Sheikh Mohammed was the tactical "on site" commander presenting the skeletal plan for the 9/11 attacks in 1996, which bin Laden approved, leaving the actual implementation to Mohammed and those under his command.[14] Al-Qaeda's mission was "to serve as an incitement to Muslims to join a defensive jihad against the West and against tyrannical secular Muslim regimes," including training participants in their cause.[15] According to bin Laden, the jihad or the struggle was irrefutably binary between "the global Crusader alliance with the Zionist Jews, led by America, Britain and Israel, and the other side is the Islamic world."[16]

The 9/11 Memorial and Museum's press release for Pope Francis's historic visit was touted as "Pope to Pay Tribute to 9/11 Victims and Lead Interfaith Peace Gathering in Museum."[17] An interreligious service can be precarious for persons of identified faiths with concern over "the appearance of syncretism, the merging and muddying of religions."[18] The challenge of such a service, according to Bishop James Massa of the Brooklyn Diocese is to "do it in a way that is respectful of individual religious identity."[19] However, Bishop Massa's subsequent statement seems to undermine the full embrace of an interreligious service in saying that "it's not praying together but being in the presence of the other praying. That's the distinction we make—being in the presence of, with great respect and great appreciation for the other."[20] In an essay on interfaith dialogue, Hacker Daniels has said that interfaith dialogue in not about "affiliation with," but rather "affinity for."[21] An interfaith service—arguably more than interfaith dialogue—seems to contract that distance despite a perceived fear of vitiating the tenets of a unique, autonomous religion.

According to A. James Rudin, the interreligious golden age began with *Nostra Aetate* (In Our Time), the Declaration on the Relation of the Church to Non-Christian Religions, proclaimed by Pope Paul VI, October 28, 1965.[22] One of the main goals of the document was to foster genuine dialogue between Christians and those of other faiths, including Hinduism, Buddhism, Judaism and Islam. As stated in *Nostra Aetate*,

> the Catholic Church rejects nothing that is true and holy in these religions. She regards with sincere reverence those ways of conduct and of life, those principles and teachings which, through differing in many aspects from the ones she holds and sets forth, nonetheless often reflect a ray of that Truth which enlightens all men.[23]

In the three Abrahamic faiths, one can certainly locate opprobrious ideas within each religion towards the other(s), nonetheless *Nostra Aetate* was an effort at reconciliation. However, the events of September 11, 2001, jeopardized rather delicate and fragile interfaith relations, particularly between Christians and Muslims, and Muslims and Jews.[24] In *Nostra Aetate*, the Church "decries hatred, persecutions, displays of anti-Semitism, directed against Jews at any time and by anyone."[25] In his brilliant work, *The Rhetoric of Antisemitism*, Amos Kiewe credits *Nostra Aetate* "as the single and most profound statement on the origin and longevity of Christian-Catholic antisemitism, [and] was a watershed Christian-Jewish relationship. This document took out one of the most hurtful causes of antisemitism—the charge that all Jews are to be considered Christ-killers at any place and time."[26]

Although *Nostra Aetate* favors the absolution for Jews of eternal guilt, the absolution for deicide (the death of Christ), is more ambiguously articulated.[27] Articulated in *Nostra Aetate*, a series of interrogatives purport to locate the connective tissue—notwithstanding differences—between and among the religions of the world:

> Men expect from the various religions answers to the unsolved riddles of the human condition, which today, even as in former times, deeply stir the hearts of men: What is man? What is the meaning, the aim of our life? What is moral good, what is sin? Whence suffering and what purpose does it serve? Which is the road to true happiness? What are death, judgment and retribution after death? What, finally, is that ultimate inexpressible mystery which encompasses our existence: whence do we come, and where are we going?[28]

September 11, 2001, catapulted the exigencies surrounding the already devolving relations, and augmented misconceptions of one religion towards the others, fomenting xenophobia, hatred and violence.[29] Interfaith dialogue seemed to provide a salutary response in pursuit of rehabilitating and possibly ameliorating the less than positive relations among the religions of the world. As Daniel Brown states in *A Communication Perspective on Interfaith Dialogue*, "As Jews and Christians advanced their relationship, the attacks of 9/11 highlighted the glaring lack of relational dynamism that existed with the third Abrahamic faith, Islam."[30] For various and sundry reasons, many well-intentioned persons, who would like to break the seemingly irrefragable chains of intolerance and animus, are hesitant to do so, for fear of appearing "disloyal" to the tenets of their faith, contributing to a syncretism which could potentially and arguably, vitiate the essence of the religion. Edelmayer provides a very illuminating discussion of the development of interfaith dialogue, and seemingly conventional wisdom would suggest that the discipline of communication studies and rhetoric would play a uniquely outsized role in the development of interfaith dialogue both in theory and *praxis*. For many scholars and practitioners, the sub area of interfaith dialogue arrived later than other disciplinary areas, but when it did, it brought important theories and applications to the enterprise of interfaith dialogue.[31]

The publication of Nostra Aetate in 1965 exerted a profound influence on the use of the term "interreligious," as more representative of the intention of engaging in "dialogue with those who represent a specific religious tradition."[32]

The events of 9/11 posed unique challenges for interfaith dialogue, wherein major aspects of our lives were altered as a way of averting tragedies comparable to that of 9/11. As Jonathan Magonet reflects on the predominant incentive for his volume, *Talking to the Other*, he says:

> The immediate trigger for finally writing this book is the event that shattered our understanding throughout the world about how life needs to be conducted between peoples of different religious faiths in this new millennium. The attack on the World Trade Center in New York on 11 September 2001 brought home the horror of terrorism as never before. But it also revealed the depth of our ignorance of one another, and hence the mistrust and often hostility between different faith communities…The language of "jihad", used almost cynically by the supporters of terror to summon Muslims to a holy war against the demon America, and used uncritically by our own media, fed Western fears and fantasies about the nature of Islam. There is a massive task of education and rethinking that needs to be done alongside the actions taken at least to curtail the power of those who practice terror. Part of that task is also to attempt to eliminate the injustices, poverty and despair that breed the desperation that leads to terror.[33]

Bronstein, Cahill, and Elmirzana also recognize the events of September 11, 2001 as engendering interest in and curiosity about the religions of others, particularly the Abrahamic faiths.[34] Eugene J. Fisher conceives of September 11, 2001 as having "inaugurated a world of fear and terrorism on the one hand, but it also prompted innumerable people of goodwill—Jews, Christians and Muslims—to turn toward one another in dialogue and deepen and intensify efforts at outreach across the permeable boundaries of our three faiths. Sometimes, good can be wrung out of evil."[35] Khaleel Mohammed reflects that, "September 11 exemplifies the worst and the best in people."[36] "While one of the worst manifestations of suffering caused by hate, it has propelled people of righteousness to work harder at promoting interreligious discussion in the noble quest for understanding and respect, with particular emphasis on the major three Abrahamic faiths."[37] In his very personal essay, "Transformation Through Dialogue of a Muslim Scholar's Search for Identity," Muhammad Shafiq reflects on September 11's impacts on the Muslim community in fostering a "greater commitment on the part of the entire Muslim American community to interfaith dialogue."[38]

The constellation of tragic events surrounding September 11, 2001 certainly precipitated the exigence as one which had at its core, the rancorous relationship among religions, particularly the three Abrahamic faiths. Sunggu A. Yang offers a paradigm for a multireligious prayer service, based on the service held September 25, 2015 with Pope Francis and the other religious leaders at the 9/11 Memorial and Museum, conceding that this type of service "is very hard to imagine and practice."[39] Kathleen Mary Black delineates the occasions that warrant interfaith and interreligious prayer services, including one where "the nation gathers people from every religion and no religious affiliation to lament and mourn the deaths of those killed in the 9/11 attacks in the United States."[40] As Bronstein, Cahill and Syafa'atun observe, in the wake of September 11, 2001, "clearly the 'children of Abraham' are becoming interested in each other's unique religious and cultural heritage and are desirous of discovering where and how these traditions intersect."[41]

Interfaith services are not intended to create a new religion nor to be a substitute for the regular pattern of prayer of any faith community. Rather they are special occasions which both acknowledge the rich diversity of humankind's spiritual traditions and affirm the unity of the "human family."[42]

Although interfaith and interreligious are understood synonymously, the World Council of Churches parses an important distinction, which is the definitional inclusion in the term "interfaith" of "ideologies and systems of belief which transcend specific religious identification," in contrast with "interreligious," which exists within the purview of "established religions."[43]

Pope Francis visited the 9/11 Memorial and Museum on his first trip to the United States, and participated in what was deemed an "Interfaith Peace Gathering."[44] The Memorial opened in 2011 on the ten year anniversary of the September 11, 2001 attacks, and the museum opened to the public on May 21, 2014.[45] The former mayor of New York and the 9/11 Memorial Chairman Michael Bloomberg said of the venue, "now it is a beautiful and inspiring place, a symbol of our rebirth and resilience that is full of life, and that honors the victims of the attacks and tells their stories to the world."[46]

As important as interfaith dialogue is in cultivating and enriching an augmented understanding among people of different religions, tragic events have warranted the necessity to cultivate a heightened genre of communication—interreligious or multireligious prayer.[47] In 1972, the World Congress of Faiths became a "pioneer of 'All Faith Services.'"[48] In Britain, Commonwealth Day is observed at Westminster Abbey, with people of many faiths participating.[49] Lewis notes the five recent themes of Commonwealth Day: "care for the natural world; the dignity and worth of the human person; the need to establish justice and peace; the supremacy of love; service and sacrifice for the common good."[50] The practice goes as far back as 1893, where the first "modern interfaith activity was held at the World's Parliament of Religions" in Chicago, Illinois.[51] The Fellowship of Reconciliation, created in 1914, brought together people of different faiths with the aim of promoting peace.[52] In the aftermath of the cataclysm of World War II, the Fellowship in prayer "was established in the belief that unified prayer would bridge theological differences between the world's faiths."[53] As Lewis says, "much work has been done in trying to give an answer in the general field of dialogue between faiths, but there has been less work when it comes to the special case of worship and prayer."[54] Clearly, there exists a delicate balance in achieving religious pluralism in welcoming other religions—especially in a prayer context—while at once respecting the distinctness and theological autonomy of each religion.[55] Lewis and other scholars remind us, that, although interreligious prayer is not without its pitfalls, this type of prayer engagement can engender that which can be consummately elusive in many contexts: common ground.[56]

The 9/11 memorial service venue was not "identified" by a particular faith. The representation of different religions was heard and seen through prayers, expressed in their original languages and translations, in addition to the artifactual communication of the cultural garb, enhancing the distinctiveness of each, while haptics as observed through handshakes and embraces helped position the sense of the unity of the prayer service. The macrocosmic raison d'être for the 9/11 interreligious service was the promotion of peace.

The scholarship on inter/religious prayer provides edifying ways in which the somewhat perilous terrain can be traversed in the journey from interfaith/interreligious dialogue to interreligious/multireligious prayer.

Braybrooke recognizes two subclassifications of interreligious prayer: multireligious prayer and united interreligious prayer.[57] In multireligious prayer, each religion is unadulteratedly distinct in offering prayers with no entrée "into the spirituality of the other," although a downside is a cachet of distinctness from the other devolving into a distance from the other.[58] In united interreligious prayer, the service is ordered "with some prayers or affirmations said together," amounting to praying together.[59]

Marianne Moyaert classifies two major types of interreligious ritual participation: "outer-facing and inner-facing."[60] With outer-facing, "believers belonging to various faith traditions come together for prayer, celebration or worship in *response* to some external event or challenge (e.g., war prompting a prayer for peace), or to commemorate and mourn the victims of a national calamity (e.g., religious leaders standing shoulder to shoulder to remember the victims of 9/11)..."[61]

In her superb, edited volume, *Interreligious Relations and the Negotiation of Ritual Boundaries,* she applies interrituality "to the way[s] that interreligious encounters are concretized in the performance of embodied ritualized practices."[62] These rituals occur "in the space between people who believe and practice differently."[63] The venues for these rituals are variegated, occurring in "sacred spaces (e.g., mosques, temples, churches) or in secular or quasi-secular spaces (e.g. schools, hospitals.),", and unlike the 9/11 event, the event can be steeped in succor, "with friendly intentions," or rancor, with "antagonistic intentions."[64]

As initiated in 1986 by Pope John Paul II for the World Day of Prayer for Peace in Assisi, with continuation by Pope Benedict XVI and Pope Francis I in subsequent years, this outer-facing event brought "religious leaders [together] from all over the world to pray in their own way"…with the goal of demonstrating that "violence in the name of religion is never justified, and that all religions, despite their undeniable differences, together intend to bring peace and harmony to the world."[65]

According to Black, the terms multifaith and multireligious are used to characterize "ritual gatherings," of people of various religions, commensurate with the meaning of 'interfaith,' convening for "deeper understanding and fostering peace."[66] For Black, the term "prayer" is preferred to the term "worship," as the former is more appropriately applicable to a wider range of religion, connoting a more "common usage and multivalent nature," than worship, which is seen as more aligned with Christianity.[67]

AN EXEMPLAR FOR CONDUCTING AN INTERRELIGIOUS PRAYER SERVICE

The 9/11 prayer service seems to partake of characteristics of three models of interreligious prayer as delineated by Black. The 9/11 service, on the fourteenth anniversary, paid tribute to the victims and those who helped save lives, and led by Pope Francis on his first trip to the United States, exhibited aspects of the guest/host model.[68] In addition, the guest/host model was augmented by Archbishop Timothy M. Dolan's introductory comment, where he welcomed everyone to the service and previewed key themes of the service.[69] In the second model, "serial interfaith prayer, people gather to offer texts, songs/chants, prayers, symbolic artifacts, and actions from their own religion in the presence of persons from other religions," representative of "coming together to pray."[70] This model avoids the perceived peril of syncretism, insofar as each religious tradition maintains its autonomy and is recognized as such, but at the same time, appreciating and respecting other religious traditions.[71] The key characteristic in this model is the recognition that people are "coming together to pray, not praying together."[72] The third model is known as inter-riting, united interreligious prayer, interreligious prayer, and integrative religious prayer. This model purports to distinguish the event as one where "people come to pray together rather than coming together to pray."[73] The goal here is inclusiveness and participation, but can be construed as achieving the "highest common denominator" with mutual affirmation, or the least common denominator, insofar as the latter can occur with the possible dilution of each religion's traditions, rendering each, not only unrecognizable, but can engender deleterious effects, including misappropriation,[74] disrespect,[75] a misalignment/incommensurability between truth and ritual,[76] and inauthenticity.[77]

The forty-eight-minute service included participants from the three Abrahamic faiths, as well as Hinduism, Buddhism, Sikhism and Greek Orthodox, and serves as an exemplar of interreligious prayer.

After greeting each other, Cardinal Timothy Dolan made introductory remarks. In his introduction, Cardinal Dolan concedes that, although New Yorkers are sinners, they are adept at participating in "sincere and fruitful interreligious friendship."[78] He then extols the virtues of New York which was a place where the persecuted from around the world found "religious freedom" and "an atmosphere of respect and appreciation for religious diversity."[79] This sentiment is substantiated by Tony Carnes in providing the data that New York City "is the most ethnically diverse place on the globe,"[80] and as Richard John Neuhaus observes, it is "a city of many cities, a world of many worlds."[81] The service foregrounds the three Abrahamic faiths, for as Berger states, "Judaism, Christianity, and Islam remain in the forefront of the contemporary discussion about how to achieve what Judaism terms *tikkun ha-'olam*, repair or restoration of the world."[82]

The first two participants in the prayer service, Rabbi Elliot Cosgrove and Imam Khalid Latif, function dyadically, approaching their respective lecterns downstage, left and right. Rabbi Cosgrove of the Park Avenue Synagogue in Manhattan offers succor with words spoken by Pope Francis.[83] Imam Khalid Latif, Executive Director and Chaplain at New York University Islamic Center, speaks to the causes of the 9/11 attacks, as attributable to "intolerance and ignorance." While the violent acts are anathema to the precepts of religious freedom, Imam Latif cites the Quran Surah 5:32, in punctuating the point about the preciousness of each life and our responsibility to each other with "one life lost is like all mankind," and "one life saved is like all mankind."[84] This same sentiment is expressed in the Jewish Tractate Sanhedrin 37a: "For this reason was man created alone, to teach thee that whosoever destroys a single soul of Israel, scripture imputes [guilt] to him as though he had destroyed a complete world; and whosoever preserves a single soul of Israel, scripture ascribes merit to him as though he had preserved a complete world." The Mishnah Sanhedrin 4:9, states, "…Whosoever destroys a soul, to teach you that whosoever destroys a single soul, Scripture considers that personas though they had destroyed a complete world; and whosoever preserves a single soul, Scripture ascribes [merit] to that person as though they had preserved a complete world."[85]

The themes of peace and the sacredness of life revert to Rabbi Cosgrove with a paraphrased passage from Psalms 34:14, exhorting us to "love peace and pursue peace," and transforming the hatred in acts of violence, invoking the passage from St. Francis of Assisi's Peace Prayer.[86] Imam Latif then extols the virtues of the first responders in their sacrifice and selflessness to save lives in the face of violence, hatred, and peril. He references the Quran 24:55, articulating the benefits to those who are righteous and engage in good deeds.[87] Rabbi Cosgrove hearkens back to the special venue of New York City, using the rhetorical device of antonomasia, with "The Big Apple," then quoting Pope Francis, followed by a passage from the prophet Micah, 4:4. Immediately preceding this passage from Micah, is one of the most iconic scriptural passages regarding war and peace:

> And they shall beat their swords into plowshares. And their spears into pruning hooks, nation shall not take up sword against nation; They shall never again know war.[88]

In concluding this responsive section of the service, Imam Latif reinforces the importance of rapprochement with a passage from the Quran, Sura 49:13, and in the spirit of interfaith/interreligious life, we should participate in a celebration, rather than a revulsion of differences, ultimately achieving an extirpation of hatred.

The holy father began with a brief prayer of healing for the pain, suffering, and trauma wrought by the odious terrorist attacks of September 11, 2001. After Pope Francis's brief prayer of healing, a prayer is offered in Hindi and English, reinforcing peace, with the repetition of the word "peace" in English and Hindi (shanti). Following the Hindu prayer is a Buddhist prayer, chanted in Pali or one of the vernacular languages, extolling the virtue of truth which is "above everything."[89] The next prayer is Sikh, also extolling the virtues of "truthful living."[90] The Greek Orthodox Priest provides a reading from the Greek text of the gospel of Matthew,[91] followed by its translation in English, which includes the canonical teachings of Jesus in the Sermon on the Mount.[92] This section of the service concludes with the words of the prophet Muhammad,[93] recited by Imam Latif in Arabic, again emphasizing the theme of peace.

The attendees are politely asked to stand for the Jewish prayer *El Malei Rachamim* (Prayer for the Fallen), chanted by Azi Schwartz, Cantor and Music Director at the Park Avenue Synagogue in Manhattan. This prayer is the only one in the service that is not translated into English. *El Malei Rachamim* is an important prayer in the Jewish liturgy, chanted at funeral services, at grave sites, on anniversaries of deaths, and other rituals.[94] In the Jewish prayer book, there are two versions of the prayer: one in memory of the six million who died in the Holocaust, and one in memory of all of those who have died, and Cantor Schwartz adapts the latter to the tragedy surrounding September 11, 2001.[95] Immediately after *El Malei Rachamim*, Cantor Schwartz chants the last line of the Mourner's

Kaddish in Hebrew, the first three words of which, *oseh shalom bimromov*, are from Job 25:2, and as Cantor Schwartz begins, you can hear attendees at the service chanting it in Hebrew with him. Cantor Schwartz chants two versions. The English translation of the first version is: "May the one who brings peace to His universe bring peace to us and to all Israel. And let us say Amen."[96] Upon repeating the verse, Cantor Schwartz replaces the phrase *v'al kol Yisrael*, which means "to all Israel" with *v'alkol yoshvei tevel*, which means "all of the inhabitants of the earth"—a phrase that is added in prayer services in promulgating peace.[97]

A "large makeshift cross, which was made out of steel beams found at the site," is a part of the hall where the service was held.[98] Ferrone quotes Bishop Massa, who stated—as we have previously noted—that they are not praying together, but rather "in the presence of the other praying."[99] But Ferrone sees it differently, as others do as well. In the lead to her *Atlantic* article, "Pope Francis Assembles a Squad to Fight Religious Extremism," Emma Green states the following: "Two days after Yom Kippur, Pope Francis stood behind a Jewish cantor and listened to him pray. At least one priest chanted along as Azi Schwartz sang *oseh shalom* at the 9/11 memorial in New York City…"[100] What was so remarkable about this moment was, not only the Cardinal's chanting of the prayer, but doing so in Hebrew, synchronously, with Cantor Schwartz.[101] Cantor Schwartz's participation did not go unnoticed by Christopher Purdy of NPR News, WOSU 89.7, in "The Pope and the Cantor at Ground Zero," when he declared, "this Irishman from Boston can be forgiven for suggesting that the Pope, who began foremost in everyone's mind, lost center stage when this young man got up to sing and pray."[102] But the issue is not that Cantor Schwartz, or any of the other participants upstaged Pope Francis, but rather that the Cardinal's participation and Purdy's observation comport with the genuine meaning of a prayer service that achieves a profound and meaningful espousal of the three models.[103] This part of the service highlights the third model in an affirming way without devolving into syncretism. Lewis in fact argues that a more flexible approach to interfaith prayer engagement need not ineluctably lead to syncretism but can actually solidify one's own religious beliefs.[104] After Cantor Schwartz's prayer, Pope Francis delivers his major speech in Spanish, for which a translation is provided.

As an interreligious service, Lewis reflects on the "opportunity for interfaith worship and prayer to provide a means for mutual support and to be a real power-house for change."[105] He augments the exigence by saying, "there are theological grounds for joining fully in worship, to which is added the urgency of the issues that surround us: the fragile state of our own world, the cry of the suffering, the longing for peace."[106] Although predicated on a tragic event, the 9/11 memorial interfaith event exemplifies the "interreligious event within the public sphere, the goals of which are to foster conciliation and inclusiveness."[107]

RHETORICAL ANALYSIS OF POPE FRANCIS'S SPEECHES AT THE 9/11 MEMORIAL

In conjunction with his historic 2015 apostolic sojourn to the United States, Pope Francis visited the National September 11 Memorial and Museum. There he spent time praying in silence before the memorial pools, met with families of fallen first responders, and led an interfaith prayer meeting. After several other representatives of omnifarious religious traditions offered prayers, chants, songs, and other forms of inter-riting, Francis again rose to the pulpit with more prolonged words that activated a sacred succor, speaking on the conceits of grief, remembrance, and unity through diversity while integrating references to architectural and aesthetic features of the material memorial into his speech. Ever the Catholic orator, cognizant of *prep on* and *kairos*, Francis met the moment with the purpose of honoring the victims and renewing the spirit of religious diversity dedicated to unity and remembrance that enveloped the *mise-en-scène*.

Rhetorical scholars who study the public memory of memorials and museums have recently produced edifying readings of the 9/11 Memorial and Museum itself. In contradistinction to the conventional reading of the National September 11 Memorial and Museum as a reverential commemoration that aids visitors in coping with collective trauma and personal mourning, Nicholas S. Paliewicz and Marouf Hasian, Jr. examine the memorial and museum as a darker "thanatopolitical site" that commemorates "melancholia by evoking an amalgamative, polysemic sense of loss, grief, and sadness [which] occurs through a dialectic of absence and presence...that leads to trauma and a lingering presence of grief."[108] In this way, like Derrida suggests in *Specters of Marx*, "we learn to live with ghosts."[109]

Yet, Kenneth Burke reminds us that the tents of rhetoric's field hospital are always pitched in the soil and the soiled to assoil; it is well stocked with homeopathic and hauntological medicine. Appropriating Milton's preamble to *Samson Agonistes* to reflect on the genre of tragedy, Burke quotes, "for so, in physic, things of melancholic hue and quality are used against melancholy, sour against sour, salt to remove salt humors."[110] Memorials are then "terminstic scenes" of discomfort, convalescence, and demands for peace and justice. For instance, in a future article, Paliewicz shifted his focus on the "brighter visual symbolicity" of museum artifacts and explicated how such objects evoked feeling of resilience, nationalism, and collective unity.[111]

In a 2014 *New York Times* video entitled *The Keepers of 9/11*, New York State Museum Director Mark Schaming observed that in the early days of the 9/11 Memorial and Museum exhibition visitors would openly weep at viewing the simplest of artifacts, but he then claimed, after a few years of the exhibit's opening, a performative "shift from the sacred to the historical" occurred.[112] Schaming provides scant, anecdotal evidence to support this claim. Has such a shift actually transpired? What would enable an encounter with the memorial that evoked spiritual catharsis to shift to one of mere archival record? Is it chronological duration, or temporal disjunction that has precipitated this transformation of the space's public memory from a sanctifying experience to one of secular historicity? Why do the performative experiences have to be mutually exclusive? What is it about the memorial space and visitors' engagement with it that constitutes it as "sacred?"

Related to these questions, an exposition of Pope Francis's rhetorical situation, and in particular some of the paradoxical constraints endemic to his exigence, problematizes the interfaith event further. For example, as the supreme leader of one of the world's dominant religious traditions, what can Francis say considering the fact the terrorist attacks of 9/11 were rationalized in the name of religion? How can the violence engendered by a rancorous discourse of distorted religious patterns eventuating in the horrors of 9/11 be commemorated, exorcised, or converted? At this "scene of unspeakable violence and pain," what can be said? How can a rhetor stir the susurrations of remembrance of historic tragedy in a way that is authentic and does not resign the audience to emptiness, detachment, or a state of *alaston penthos* or perpetual mourning?[113] Memorials and museums are never merely places that mark geographical location or record historical events. Rather they are sites of symbolic action that function as a mode of rhetorical *heuresis* and persuasive argument. Couple such spaces with prayer, an epideictic variant of situated rhetorical performance that facilitates invention and argument through the cultural and spiritual practice of remembrance and memorial, and rhetors can provide sacred succor for memories stained by violence and tragedy.[114]

In addition to exploring an exemplar of interreligious prayer service, this chapter also aims to address these aforementioned questions by examining the prayerful address delivered by Pope Francis during the 2015 Interfaith Meeting at the 9/11 Memorial and Museum. Given the polysemy evoked by the 9/11 Memorial and Museum, we argue a sacred hermeneutic can be employed to reveal a meaningful analysis adduced by a coalescence of sacre-tropological (tropes performing a sacred function) and topological (spatial) rhetoric. Employing our critical armature of religious rhetoric's sacred succor/rancor dialectic we explore the role such prayerful rhetoric plays in confronting, comforting, and commemorating sites of tragic violence. Francis's words invite a healing panegyric that sanctifies the 9/11 memorial, a painful site of public remembrance, through a *consolatito theologica*.[115]

Antecedent to our formal analysis of Francis's prayer-based textual and spatio-visual rhetoric, a word on the relationship between rhetoric and prayer is necessary. William Fitzgerald's book *Spiritual Modalities* argues for an interdependence between rhetoric and prayer. "Prayer is part of rhetoric, a particular use of language for thoroughly persuasive ends; it extends practices of communication among human beings to communication between humans and divine beings."[116] Fitzgerald continues, "prayer is first of all, an art of situation: It is situated and situating discourse that speaks both from and to the condition that gives rise to its occasion as utterance."[117] In terms of examining Pope Francis interfaith prayer address and the 9/11 memorial, Fitzgerald reminds us, "the persistence of prayer across diverse spiritual habitats and diverse manifestations are a testament to the 'felt' need for reverence in responding to situations."[118]

Paliewicz, whose reading of the 9/11 memorial extends beyond the reverential, acknowledges the rhetorical salience of affect. "Feeling public memory is just as important as knowing it."[119] Pope Francis's pious reflections at the 9/11 memorial interfaith meeting are presented in a situation in which prayer is an expected and rhetorical performance, manifesting a "felt" sense of grief endemic to the memorial. Francis's words and gestures cohere with Fitzgerald's assertion that prayer can be understood as an alternative space of performance. Prayer ineluctably activates the sacred in hallowed spaces. Apropos of specific commemorative contexts like memorials and museums, Fitzgerald's words have significant resonance, "Prayer operates at the intersection between communicative and cultural memory."[120] Moreover, he intones, "Prayer is the primary vehicle of commemoration, mediating the past to serve the present."[121]

In several ways, our analysis draws on and melds the works of both Fitzgerald and rhetorical theorist Allison Prasch, who contends that "place can be felt when it is enacted through the rhetorical event itself."[122] As a complement to close textual analysis, Prasch desires to understand how, "oratorical texts activate... within and speak through their contexts."[123] Her theory of the *deixis* is instructive here for such a rhetorical display "allows the critic to identify where and how the speaker uses language to activate the scenic or situational elements of immediate historical and sociopolitical [and we would add religious] contexts for his or her purposes."[124] Our analysis of Francis's *figurae causae* reveals how prayer as a form of commemorative rhetoric relies on the deictic dynamics of his situated discourse and its material means of persuasion.

One of the most striking rhetorical observations of Francis's remarks is what was absent, what was not said. Any reference to specific biblical passages and Francis's familiar tactic of exegetical application to enlighten his audience of his *topos* and their shared, present context is conspicuously absent in his discourse. Instead, in a pious effort to comport with the decorum of an interfaith meeting, Francis paints with more universal, archetypal, and inclusive hues, thematically expressed in terms of pain, healing, remembrance, peace, and unity. Francis addressed his audience as "Dear Friends" and incessantly used the pronouns "our" and "we," and employs the memorial's material feature of the flowing reflective pools as the central locus of his sacred rhetoric.

The words of Francis's opening prayer are illustrative of the contradictory contours that constrain his rhetorical situation. "Oh, God of love, compassion, and healing, look on us, people of many different faiths and religious traditions, who gather today in this hallowed ground, the scene of unspeakable violence and pain."[125] Critically drawing an analog to Lincoln's rhetorical situation at Gettysburg, one may ask how Francis can hallow ground that has already been consecrated by "all who died here?" Recall that Ground Zero is the final resting place for many victims of the 9/11 terrorist attacks whose bodies were never recovered. Relatedly, how can Francis continue speaking after constituting the scene as one of "unspeakable violence and pain?" Moreover, a short while later in his more extended prayer, Francis publicly begs pardon for "not speaking English." Despite having spoken English just moments ago, Francis does not address the audience in English; he says it is because, "I cannot." We read Francis's negation more as commentary on the ineffability of his rhetorical situation as he confronts the gravity of 9/11's memorial space than on his fluency of the English language. How does Francis respond to this paradox? If the rancorous pain and inexpressible sorrow autochthonous to the 9/11 memorial are to be expiated, they must first be named and felt through means other than linguistic.

The emotional magnitude of the occasion seems to overwhelm Francis, rendering him unable and unsure of how to communicate. Joshua Gunn defines the ineffable as how people use and abuse signs and symbols to negotiate ineffability, that which cannot be expressed or described in language.[126] Ineffable communication, represented in considerable poetic and religious forms of signification, can extend beyond the capacity of words to convey the inarticulate. For example, Kenneth Burke's *Rhetoric of Religion* explores how symbol systems attempt to describe the indescribable. Burke affords such instances as how "The Almighty" is depicted in sacred scriptures. Burke cites such descriptions of God synecdochically through the anthropomorphic body parts of ears, eyes, hands, and singular emotions like love, wrath, envy, melancholia, and pleasure. Consistent with Paliewicz's and Hasian's reading of the spatial features of the 9/11 memorial evoking mourning, absence, and melancholia, it is noteworthy that Francis, emphasizes the emotional experience of grief. "Here grief is palpable."[127] In an attempt defy the ineffability of this moment, Francis chooses to foreground the existentiality of the space as if to say, "here at the 9/11 memorial grief expresses itself." One just feels its inescapable recognition. This occurs rhetorically by inventively transposing signification via a sensorial surrogate. Such a discursive maneuver functions like a visual metonymy, a spatial or material substitution for verbal or linguistic expression. Francis's sensorial alchemy commences in his subsequent utterance, where he materializes grief by directing his audience's memory to the memorial's reflective pools above. What do they mean? How do they emote grief?[128]

> The water we see flowing towards that empty pit reminds us of all those lives which fell prey to those who think that destruction is the only way to settle conflicts. It is the silent cry of those who were victims of a logic which knows only violence, hatred, and revenge. A logic which can only cause pain, suffering, destruction, and tears.[129]

The unutterable emptiness of grief manifests extra-rhetorically in the sensorial transposition to the material reality (sight, sound, and touch) of the memorial pools. Since pronouncement of the ineffable is itself paradoxical, Francis elucidates the memorial's central feature of the cataract, paradoxically, as the "silent cry" of the victims, thereby providing prayerful and sublime visual, aural, and haptic instantiations of grief's ineffability. It is one thing to say that grief is palpable, it is another to physically experience it. Concomitantly, grief is an archetypal corollary of absence, loss, death, and emptiness. Visually the cascading water pools confront viewers with another set of antimonies, "absence made visible" and suffusing emptiness. The expansive "footprints" where the Twin Towers anteceded are now acre-sized reflective pools, encased by bronze parapets with the names of nearly three thousand victims engraved in them. From the margins of each pool, the water ebbs to the center of each footprint towards a massive drain 30 feet below. Plummeting an additional 20 feet, the water forcefully spills into an unseen cavity where the process recurses. Optically, the pools dramatize the inverse of Derrida's trace, displaying a presence of absence.[130] According to architect, Michael Arad, who titled the flowing water memorials "Reflective Absence," "the pools represent absence made visible."[131] While not using the word grief or mourning, Arad enthymematically infers the loss and emptiness of presence, "although water flows into the voids, they can never be filled."[132]

The rancorous experience of grief has been named and felt through the immensity and profundity of memorial pools' spatial aesthetic, which Francis poetically compares to an "empty pit" and the "silent cry" of victims. However, in a 2011 *Huffington Post* review of the 9/11 memorial, G. Roger Denson claimed the pools produce a therapeutic tranquility, and engender the "calm necessary for contemplation and spirituality."[133] The pools "reflect" a "harmony with nature," similar to Daoist tenets, the experience "embodies…the gravity to which all earthly things, animate and inanimate, must submit."[134] Comporting with the propriety of Francis's interfaith meeting, we highlight that Paliewicz and Hasian Jr. note the archetypal meaning of water, its Christian sacramental understanding, as well as water's role in ritual washing connected with Hinduism, Buddhism, Sikhism, Judaism, Shinto, Taoism, and Islam.[135] Paliewicz and Hasian Jr. also acknowledge the public memorial's inductive inference flowing from the general to the specific, present to past, the "soothing rhetorical effects [of water] as we think back to the fires and dust of that tragic day."[136]

Continuing to draw on metaphorical construct of mourning via the memorial pools Francis states,

> The flowing water is also a symbol of our tears. Tears shed at so much devastation and ruin, past and present. This place is a place where we weep, we weep out of a sense of helplessness in the face of injustice, murder, and the failure to settle our differences through dialogue. Here we mourn the wrongful and senseless loss of innocent lives because of inability to find solutions which respect the common good. It is flowing water reminds us of yesterday's tears, but also of all the tears still being shed today.[137]

Hearing Francis's moving interpretation of the incessantly flowing water as "tears," one might draw parallels to the Old Testament matriarch Rachel and her inconsolable lamentation at the death of her children. "Rachel's wells," as the pools might be called, emblematize the perpetual depth, not only of the physical flowing pools, but the prodigious depth of ever-lingering, inconsolable pain and rancor the victims' families and collective America still feel.

Yet, the imagery of tears reveals a cathartic dynamism; such a trope recurs in Pope Francis's religious rhetoric.[138] So much so that, Cardinal Luis Antonio G. Tagle, archbishop of Manila, Philippines, theorizes Francis's frequently used crying trope as a "theology of tears" through which Francis teaches the "Gospel of tears."[139] Tagle further notes that, for Francis, "words without tears cause more pain."[140] This sentiment supports Francis's description of the Reflective Absence memorial as a "silent cry". No words, only tears can militate against inflicting any more pain, tears as both tributary and salutary. Notice, too, Francis shifts perspective from victims to visitors (or pilgrims), from past to present, and from bitter bewailing in the face of senseless injustice and murder, to, as he will instruct, "another face of love and remembrance"[141] born out of his intention to comfort. Tears, as Tagle asserts, "deepen our relationship with Jesus, and they open paths for our mission of mercy and solidarity." "Tears" even function as a synecdoche, a partial emotional response, depicting the whole of grieving and mourning.

Francis's rhetorical prayer glides from his visual-spatial engagement with the material memorial and its palpable anguish to a comforting purgation, from nefarious logics of violence and hatred, to acts of heroic goodness, and from empty suffering to the fullness of self-sacrifice and the common good. "No one thought about race, nationality neighborhoods, religion or politics. It was all about solidarity, meeting immediate needs, brotherhood."[142] Solidarity is a central tenet of Catholic Social teaching. Solidarity is beyond a feeling of vague compassion; it is a moral virtue and commitment to our responsibility for the fragility of others as we strive to build a common future. Solidarity is a social covenant, that recognizes our interconnectedness; we are relational beings with duties toward one another other and are all called to embrace the "reality that we are bound by the bonds of reciprocity."[143] Solidarity was wholly enacted by first responders on 9/11.

Moreover, given that an ethical and religious sense of solidarity speaks to seeing human existence predicated on interdependent relationships where separate, individual parts indeed represent unifying wholes brought and held together by our mutual responsibility to one another, the ideal trope for rhetorically constituting, communicating, and performing solidarity is synecdoche.

The concept of synecdoche can be explained in both simple and more complex terms. Richard Lanham defines synecdoche as "the substitution of part for whole, genus for species, or vice versa: 'All hands on deck.'"[144] As Burke observes of synecdoche in his "Four Master Tropes," "We might say that representation (synecdoche) stresses a relationship or connectedness between two sides of an equation, a connectedness that, like a road, extends in either direction."[145] Recall, Fitzgerald affirms memory in prayer is manifested…in our capacity to bring things into relationship (parts for wholes). David Tell argues that synecdoche converts upward and "'induces' an audience to overcome the limitations of language."[146] Therefore, synecdoche as a unifying and transcendent trope supports the function of memory in rhetorical prayer, aids in expressing the ineffable, and promotes the social justice principles of solidarity and the common good.

Francis's rhetoric moves auditors and viewers through a series of synecdoches of solidarity that aim to build unity on the basis of diversity in order to bring about hope and peace in our world. We briefly examine how Francis unifying synecdoches of "hearts," "faces," "hands," and "names" progressively interanimate and culminate with encountering the memorial space where "names" of victims who died on September 11, and in the 1993 World Trade Center Bombing are preserved. As we will soon see, Francis, again, interlards the visual memorial into his verbal discourse. Francis amplifies the relational solidarity through the visual and tactile exergue where the names of the nearly 3000 lives lost are engraved on the parapets that envelope the reflecting pools.

Francis's first synecdoche of "hearts" is straightforward and does not necessitate the depth of analysis that other part for whole transactions will. Mindful of all who suffered death, Francis entreats, "Our hearts are one with theirs…God of peace bring your peace to our violent world, peace in the hearts of all men and women…peace and love…in the hearts of all."[147]

Next, Francis states, "A few moments ago, I met some of the families of the fallen first responders. Meeting them made me see once again how acts of destruction are never impersonal, abstract, or merely material. They always have a face, a concrete story, names."[148] Francis professes these words in the presence and proximity of "The Last Column" memorial erected at the center of the 9/11 Memorial Museum's Foundation Hall. The Last Column memorial exhibits and reinforces the phenomenological and empirical truth that the very faces, stories, and names which Francis references are de facto, "concrete," and real humans who gave their lives in the spirit of service and solidarity. The Last Column is a monument of remembrance and perseverance, a resolute remnant of the collapsing towers that "fireman walked into with no concern for their own wellbeing."[149] Elsewhere, Pope Francis has remarked that "Solidarity finds concrete expression in service."[150] In providing service "individuals learn to set aside their own wishes and desires…before the concrete gaze of those who are most vulnerable. Service always looks to their faces, touches their flesh, senses their closeness, even in some cases [like 9/11] suffers that closeness and tries to help them."[151] Francis's synecdoches remind his audience those parts, faces, and names, always maintain an interconnected and wholistic human story. The photos and messages, synecdochic representations of the missing many, are preserved, plastered on this prodigious beam that symbolizes the lives of first responders, sacrificial "pillars," who perished at ground zero.[152]

Employing another interrelated synecdoche, Francis intones, "Hands reached out, lives were given."[153] Reminding his audience that the heroic efforts of first responders and rescue workers, synecdochicially expressed as "hands," are connected to complete, whole human lives, many whose faces and names appear on The Last Column referenced earlier. Like the antecedent strategic textual and syntactical arrangement, Francis employs isocolonic parallelism again to cement an elegant and forceful density, trussing and balancing the synecdochic equation of "hands" with "lives" and "reaching out," a metonymy for duty and service, with "given," synonymous for surrendered or sacrificed. Additionally, the rhetorical artistry of the isocolonic structure's rhythm produces a sublime momentum that makes the message seem ineluctable. Finally, the finality of the heroes' deaths is amplified temporally by the past tense expressed in the passive voice, yet enacts universal and unifying anonymity in that first responders' sense of sacrificial duty was ubiquitous and their service indiscriminate.

The title of Stephen Foley's piece after the opening of the 9/11 memorial, taken from the words of a visitor who lost her nephew there, captures the rhetorical relationship between style and affect, figure and feeling. "We are able to put a hand on him, feel part of him. We're at peace now."[154] Such testimony provides a compelling case for the rhetorical and affective functions of memorializing and the consolation synecdoche provides. Grief while, perhaps, never completely eliminated, through the spark of synecdoche aids in remembrance and peace for those who have lost family members to violent tragedy. While it is unclear precisely what aspect of the memorial the visitor references, but one wonders if it was the experience of touching the engraved name.

In a final instance where the pontiff's stylistic deployment of synecdoche, solidarity, and sensorial remembrance amalgamates transpires in his reference to the "name of so many loved ones written around the towers' footprint." "We can see them, we can touch them, and we can never forget them."[155] Exhibited as grapholectal graves, the names enact a tributary remembrance of the ontological whole of human existence, personal loss, and collective mourning. Writing about the encountering the bronze parapets that house the engraved names of all those who died on September 11 and in the 1993 World Trade Center bombing, Paliewicz observes, "Visitors are provided space to privately take in the individuality of loss and the collectivity of mourning."[156]

Through the rhetorical form of public prayer, the names immuring the reflective pools perform a haunting reminder that the antimony of Derrida's metaphysics of presence is absence. Furthermore, the assemblage of names is not arbitrary and reinforces the strength of solidarity. According to the 9/11 memorial website, the names are arranged in a system of "meaningful adjacencies."[157]

> Friends and colleagues appear together, as well as the crews of each of the four flights and first responder agencies and units. Additionally, during the Memorial's development, victims' next of kin were invited to request that their loved ones' names be inscribed alongside specific others. In this way, those who were connected in life reside together on the Memorial.[158]

Each name is a synecdochic instantiation comprising networks of communal friendship, representing powerful paradigms of solidarity: "mutual support, love, and self-sacrifice."[159]

The physical, sensorial experience of encountering the names amplifies remembrance with Francis's compressed tricolonic parallelism of "see them," "touch them," "and never forget them." Comforting harmony and sacred faith in the ritual of remembrance are organically felt through the rhetorical and extra-rhetorical process of "seeing," "touching," and the superlatively placed, "never forget." Emphasizing the names, where and how they are memorialized, is a creative culmination attained through a vivid concatenation of mnemonic vivacity aesthetically produced by the synecdoches of faces, hearts, hands, seeing, touching, bound up in a shared solidarity that performs a percussive religious rhetoric of remembrance and healing.

Pope Francis's discursive healing through harmonizing content and form provides a final application of *decitic* rhetoric. In a prayerful shift from the inescapable rancorous grief and mourning felt at the 9/11 memorial to a feeling of hallowed succor, Pope Francis activates what we refer to as allopathic antistochon. Antistochon is a subspecies of antithesis involving the counterbalancing of oppositional statements and conceptions.

> This place of death became a place of life too, a place of saved lives, a hymn to the triumph of life over the prophets of destruction and death, to goodness over evil, to reconciliation and unity over hatred and division.[160]

Comporting with the inclusivity of an interfaith meeting and as a genuflection to previous speakers, Pope Francis's antistochon reverberates spiritual themes shared in the Prayer of St. Francis intoned by Rabbi Cosgrove. Life overcomes death by the solidarity of self-sacrificing service, evil while physically manifest in the destructive carnage of 9/11, will not triumph over goodness, and reconciliation and unity are countervailing forces necessary for healing hatred and division, and immense sorrow is allayed by commemorative remembrance. Leading this interfaith meeting and speaking at a former site of devastation, now a place of profound public memory, Francis offered additional expressions of allopathic antistochon, stating, "we can and must build unity on the basis of our diversity of languages, cultures, and religions. Together we are called to say 'no' to every attempt to impose uniformity and 'yes' to a diversity accepted and reconciled." It is worth observing by the end of Francis's remarks, at the place where, when he began, he could find no words. Now, his vocal negation of dogmatic, homogeneous fundamentalism and his affirmation for a reconciling diversity of acceptance and peace resounds. Such a discursive transformation enacts the aims of the interfaith meeting commemorating 9/11.

As we have witnessed, Pope Francis accomplishes his rhetorical purposes in three significant ways: First, by ironically conveying the ineffable sense of pain, grief, and remembrance by embracing the emotional palpability of scene through sensorial transposition that stylistically amplified invites auditors and viewers to experience the discursive density and convergence of emotive interplay between: text and context, verbal and nonverbal (visual), and syntactical and spatial dimensions. This is effectuated specifically through Francis's reference to the reflective pools. Next, in conjunction with the presence of The Last Column and names surrounding the reflective pools, Francis's religious rhetorical use of synecdoches of solidarity reinforced his message of unity among diversity and oneness through varying parts of "holistic" help, healing, and hope for the future. Finally, through a seriatim of allopathic antisagoge, or compensatory antithesis, Francis enacts a prayerful and palliative strategy that engenders rhetorical and empirical balance and harmony, ultimately leaving the audience with a sense of comfort and peace. The physical, visual, and spatial rhetoric of the Interfaith Meeting at the 9/11 memorial site voices itself in a healing heteroglossia that marked the significance of the event. Black extols the sacred virtues that interfaith prayer gatherings "encourage us to cross boundaries, develop community, even friendships with those often deemed 'the other.'"[161] These prayer services, "build bridges that help us navigate difficult terrain so that those long separated may be able to come together to pray and come to pray together."[162]

CHAPTER 4

Gun Violence and the Historic Tragedy of Sandy Hook

The Sandy Hook Interfaith prayer vigil provided an opportunity for the community and the nation to offer spiritual consolation after one of the deadliest school shootings in our nation's history. The vigil took place on Sunday, December 16, 2012, just two days after the school shooting at Sandy Hook Elementary School in Newtown, Connecticut. The prayer vigil was held in the Newtown High School auditorium and was initiated by the Newtown Interfaith Clergy Association. Reverend Matt Crebbin, Senior Pastor of the Newtown Congregational Church provided opening remarks, followed by a panoply of representative voices from Newtown's diverse religious communities. One of the central speakers of the interfaith prayer vigil was President Barack Obama. Obama provided a compassionate eulogy that articulated a parental theology of political responsibility.

"INTERFAITH PRAYER VIGIL ADDRESS AT NEWTOWN HIGH SCHOOL"[1]

Barack Obama

Newtown, Connecticut. December 16, 2012

Rabbi Shaul Praver: I offer you this prayer from my heart to your heart, on behalf of all your children and all your loved ones, the Hebrew memorial prayer. [In

Hebrew] Oh God exalted and full of compassion, grant perfect peace among the holy and the pure to the souls of all of our ones that perished on that horrible day. They have gone to their eternal home, master of mercy, we beseech you. Remember all of their worthy and righteous deeds that they performed in the land of the living. May their souls be bound up in the bond of life eternal. There is no death, just transformation. May they rest in peace. Let us say amen.

Jason Graves: In the name of God, the compassionate and the merciful, the Muslim community at the al-Hedaya Islamic Center in Newtown, in Connecticut and throughout the nation joins with our fellow Americans grieving for those who died in this senseless tragedy and praying for them and their families. We ask God to grant those lost a special place in paradise, and we ask their families to be granted the strength to endure the unendurable. It is in such times of almost unbearable loss that we seek the comfort with our Creator, and that artificial divisions of faith fall away to reveal a nation of mothers and fathers, brothers and sisters, sons and daughters, all united in a desire to bring healing and renewed hope. The Koran, Islam's revealed text, tells us that God's mercy and compassion are without limit and always available for those who ask. God says, "when my servants question you about me, tell them that I am near. I answer the Prayer of every person who calls on me," Chapter 2 Verse 186. In the Koran, God also says give glad tidings to those who endure with patience, who when afflicted with calamity say, "we belong to God and to him we shall return. Such are the people on whom there are blessings and mercy from God." Chapter 2 Verse 155–157. So let us all of every faith, of everything background pray for God's comfort at this time of heart-breaking tragedy. "Barely, with every difficulty there is ease. Barley, with every difficult there is ease." Chapter 94 Verse 4–6. Amin.

President Barack Obama: Thank you. (Applause.) Thank you, Governor. To all the families, first responders, to the community of Newtown, clergy, guests—Scripture tells us: "…do not lose heart. Though outwardly we are wasting away… inwardly we are being renewed day by day."

For our light and momentary troubles are achieving for us an eternal glory that far outweighs them all. So we fix our eyes not on what is seen, but on what is unseen, since what is seen is temporary, but what is unseen is eternal. For we know that if the earthly tent we live in is destroyed, we have a building from God, "an eternal house in heaven, not built by human hands."

We gather here in memory of twenty beautiful children and six remarkable adults. They lost their lives in a school that could have been any school; in a quiet town full of good and decent people that could be any town in America.

Here in Newtown, I come to offer the love and prayers of a nation. I am very mindful that mere words cannot match the depths of your sorrow, nor can they heal your wounded hearts. I can only hope it helps for you to know that you're not alone in your grief; that our world too has been torn apart; that all across this land of ours, we have wept with you, we've pulled our children tight. And you must know that whatever measure of comfort we can provide, we will provide; whatever portion of sadness that we can share with you to ease this heavy load, we will gladly bear it. Newtown – you are not alone.

As these difficult days have unfolded, you've also inspired us with stories of strength and resolve and sacrifice. We know that when danger arrived in the halls of Sandy Hook Elementary, the school's staff did not flinch, they did not hesitate. Dawn Hochsprung and Mary Sherlach, Vicki Soto, Lauren Rousseau, Rachel Davino and Anne Marie Murphy – they responded as we all hope we might respond in such terrifying circumstances – with courage and with love, giving their lives to protect the children in their care.

We know that there were other teachers who barricaded themselves inside classrooms, and kept steady through it all, and reassured their students by saying "wait for the good guys, they're coming"; "show me your smile."

And we know that good guys came. The first responders who raced to the scene, helping to guide those in harm's way to safety, and comfort those in need, holding at bay their own shock and trauma because they had a job to do, and others needed them more.

And then there were the scenes of the schoolchildren, helping one another, holding each other, dutifully following instructions in the way that young children sometimes do; one child even trying to encourage a grown-up by saying, "I know karate. So it's okay. I'll lead the way out." (Laughter.)

As a community, you've inspired us, Newtown. In the face of indescribable violence, in the face of unconscionable evil, you've looked out for each other, and you've cared for one another, and you've loved one another. This is how Newtown will be remembered. And with time, and God's grace, that love will see you through.

But we, as a nation, we are left with some hard questions. Someone once described the joy and anxiety of parenthood as the equivalent of having your heart outside of your body all the time, walking around. With their very first cry, this most precious, vital part of ourselves – our child – is suddenly exposed to the world, to possible mishap or malice. And every parent knows there is nothing we will not do to shield our children from harm. And yet, we also know that with that child's very first step, and each step after that, they are separating from us; that we won't – that we can't always be there for them. They'll suffer sickness and setbacks and broken hearts and disappointments. And we learn that our most important job is to give them what they need to become self-reliant and capable and resilient, ready to face the world without fear. And we know we can't do this by ourselves. It comes as a shock at a certain point where you realize, no matter how much you love these kids, you can't do it by yourself. That this job of keeping our children safe, and teaching them well, is something we can only do together, with the help of friends and neighbors, the help of a community, and the help of a nation. And in that way, we come to realize that we bear a responsibility for every child because we're counting on everybody else to help look after ours; that we're all parents; that they're all our children. This is our first task – caring for our children. It's our first job. If we don't get that right, we don't get anything right. That's how, as a society, we will be judged.

And by that measure, can we truly say, as a nation, that we are meeting our obligations? Can we honestly say that we're doing enough to keep our children – all of them – safe from harm? Can we claim, as a nation, that we're all together there, letting them know that they are loved, and teaching them to love in return? Can we say that we're truly doing enough to give all the children of this country the chance they deserve to live out their lives in happiness and with purpose?

I've been reflecting on this the last few days, and if we're honest with ourselves, the answer is no. We're not doing enough. And we will have to change. Since I've been President, this is the fourth time we have come together to comfort a grieving community torn apart by a mass shooting. The fourth time we've hugged survivors. The fourth time we've consoled the families of victims. And in between, there have been an endless series of deadly shootings across the country, almost daily reports of victims, many of them children, in small towns and big cities all across America – victims whose – much of the time, their only fault was being in the wrong place at the wrong time.

We can't tolerate this anymore. These tragedies must end. And to end them, we must change. We will be told that the causes of such violence are complex, and that is true. No single law – no set of laws can eliminate evil from the world, or prevent every senseless act of violence in our society.

But that can't be an excuse for inaction. Surely, we can do better than this. If there is even one step we can take to save another child, or another parent, or another town, from the grief that has visited Tucson, and Aurora, and Oak Creek, and Newtown, and communities from Columbine to Blacksburg before that – then surely we have an obligation to try. In the coming weeks, I will use whatever power this office holds to engage my fellow citizens – from law enforcement to mental health professionals to parents and educators – in an effort aimed at preventing more tragedies like this. Because what choice do we have? We can't accept events like this as routine. Are we really prepared to say that we're powerless in the face of such carnage, that the politics are too hard? Are we prepared to say that such violence visited on our children year after year after year is somehow the price of our freedom?

All the world's religions – so many of them represented here today – start with a simple question: Why are we here? What gives our life meaning? What gives our acts purpose? We know our time on this Earth is fleeting. We know that we will each have our share of pleasure and pain; that even after we chase after some earthly goal, whether it's wealth or power or fame, or just simple comfort, we will, in some fashion, fall short of what we had hoped. We know that no matter how good our intentions, we will all stumble sometimes, in some way. We will make mistakes, we will experience hardships. And even when we're trying to do the right thing, we know that much of our time will be spent groping through the darkness, so often unable to discern God's heavenly plans.

There's only one thing we can be sure of, and that is the love that we have – for our children, for our families, for each other. The warmth of a small child's embrace – that is true. The memories we have of them, the joy that they bring, the wonder we see through their eyes, that fierce and boundless love we feel for them, a love that takes us out of ourselves, and binds us to something larger – we know that's what matters. We know we're always doing right when we're taking care of them, when we're teaching them well, when we're showing acts of kindness. We don't go wrong when we do that. That's what we can be sure of. And that's what you, the people of Newtown, have reminded us. That's how you've inspired us. You remind us what matters. And that's what should drive us forward in everything we do, for as long as God sees fit to keep us on this Earth.

"Let the little children come to me," Jesus said, "and do not hinder them – for to such belongs the kingdom of heaven."

Charlotte. Daniel. Olivia. Josephine. Ana. Dylan. Madeleine. Catherine. Chase. Jesse. James. Grace. Emilie. Jack. Noah. Caroline. Jessica. Benjamin. Avielle. Allison.

God has called them all home. For those of us who remain, let us find the strength to carry on, and make our country worthy of their memory.

May God bless and keep those we've lost in His heavenly place. May He grace those we still have with His holy comfort. And may He bless and watch over this community, and the United States of America. (Applause.)

***

RHETORICAL ANALYSIS

On Friday morning, December 14, 2012, 20-year-old Adam Lanza, having already murdered his mother Nancy Lanza, at the home he shared with her, took her car and drove to Sandy Hook Elementary School. There, attired with paraphernalia, including a utility vest, Lanza prepared to kill with a Glock 10 mm handgun, a Sig Sauer 9 mm, and a Bushmaster AR-15 style rifle on his person. He gunned down 26 individuals: 20 children and 6 adult school personnel.[2] After the massacre, Lanza was found dead in classroom 10 from a self-inflicted gunshot with the Glock 10 mm handgun.³ Of the 20 children killed, 18 were pronounced dead at the scene, with 2 transported to the hospital and both "declared dead" there. All six adults were also pronounced dead at the school.⁴

The Sandy Hook Interfaith prayer vigil took place Sunday, December 16, 2012, just two days after the school shooting at Sandy Hook Elementary School in Newtown, Connecticut. This shooting marked the second deadliest school shooting in U.S. history, surpassed only by the shooting at Virginia Tech University in 2007, with the ignominious distinction as the deadliest school shooting at a K-12 school.

According to the Concise Oxford English Dictionary, "vigil" is defined as "keeping awake during the time usually given to sleep, esp. to keep watch or pray." This event shared some tenets with the 9/11 interfaith service (Chapter 3), but also diverged in significant ways.

The prayer vigil took place in the Newtown High School auditorium, initiated by the Newtown Interfaith Clergy Association. Reverend Matt Crebbin, Senior Pastor of the Newtown Congregational Church provided opening remarks, emphasizing the need for the community to "come together." Reverend Crebbin's remarks are an interesting admixture of previewing the raison d'être for the event and offering a sort of theological disclaimer, in saying,

> We are not here to ignore our differences or diminish our core beliefs which define our many different faith traditions. But to offer our love, care and prayers to our families and our community. We wanted to offer our voices in the form of words from our sacred text(s) and prayers from the depths of our being, but we also wanted to gather together in silence.⁵

After approximately 36 minutes of assembling and awaiting the arrival of President Obama, the service began with Rev. Matt Crebbin's opening remarks. He informed the attendees that the participants who will be speaking on the auditorium stage will be seated in the auditorium prior to ascending the steps of the stage, as "a symbolic gesture that we ourselves are with you and among you in these coming days."⁶ Reverend Crebbin provides a preview of the range of theologies and faiths represented by the participants, reminding them of the reasons for congregating: "Let us come together. Let us pray. Let us listen. And let us seek the comfort of our various faiths."⁷ He seems to allay concerns circumscribing the Establishment Clause of the First Amendment of the Constitution by telling the attendees that the Newtown Interfaith Clergy Association asked the Selectwoman and the School Superintendent if it would be permissible for the prayer vigil to take place at the high school, which is a public entity to which the Establishment Clause would apply.

Reverend Crebbin's remarks were followed by the first pair of participants: Rabbi Shaul Praver of Newtown's Adath Israel Synagogue, and Reverend

Mel Kawakami, Senior Pastor of Newtown's United Church. Rabbi Praver chanted *El Mali Rachamim*, the Hebrew Memorial Prayer, accompanied by an English translation adapted to the Sandy Hook tragedy. Next, with an invitation by Kathleen Adams-Shepherd, Rector of the Trinity Episcopal Church, accompanied by Reverend Jim Solomon, Pastor of the New Hope Community Church, and a third individual who did not speak and was not identified in the video, or the script, she asked everyone to join her in reciting the 23rd Psalm. This prayer was followed by Muadh Bhavnagarwala, a young boy of the Al-Hedaya Islamic Center, chanting a prayer from the Qur'an in Arabic, followed by Jason Graves, also from the Center, reciting passages from the Qur'an in English. Reverend Jane Sibley of Newtown's United Methodist Church offered a prayer to the first responders. Dr. John Woodall, Baha'i Community Leader and Unity Project Founder, followed by an unidentified religious leader, and then Leo McIlrath, Ecumenical Chaplain of Lutheran Home of Southbury, Connecticut. E. Patricia Llodra, First Selectman spoke next, who then introduced Governor of Connecticut Dannel Malloy, who then introduced President Barack Obama.

After President Obama spoke, Monseigneur Bob Weiss of the St. Rose of Lima Catholic Church approached the podium and spoke, followed by another unidentified speaker, and then prayers by Monseigneur Bob Weiss. Reverend Rob Morris approached the podium and delivered the final benediction prayer, which served as the basis for a major controversy, arguably tarnishing what should have been a wholly uncontroversial event, at least with respect to the intent of offering succor to grieving people.

Reverend Morris, in his first year of service as Pastor of Christ the King Lutheran Church in Newtown, Connecticut, delivered the benediction at the Sandy Hook prayer vigil, causing an uproar with the Lutheran Church—Missouri Synod.[8] Reverend Matthew Harrison, President of the Missouri Synod, rebuked Reverend Morris, compelling him to apologize for "violating its prohibition against joint worship with other religions."[9] According to the Missouri Synod, participation in an interfaith prayer service "could be seen as an endorsement of faiths that do not regard Jesus alone as a savior or as a suggestion that differences between religions are not important," even adhering to the belief that Islam and Baha'i propagate "teachings of false religions."[10] In his lengthy letter of apology, dated January 31, 2013, Reverend Morris apologized profusely, but did in fact defend his participation in the service, adducing the following "defense," without really denying the claims advanced by the Synod, writing the following:

> Prior to the events of 12/14, I had already spent hours with my own congregation, catechizing them as to the differences between our Lutheran understanding of Scriptural teaching, the various other denominations' teachings, and the teachings of false religions such as Islam or B'Hai.[11]

Regarding his benediction specifically, Reverend Morris said that he

> was sharing 'a final blessing of the hope which is ours through faith in Jesus Christ, using the words of St. John and St. Paul.' I then read from Revelation 21, and I prayed the Trinitarian benediction from Paul's letter to the Corinthians which we say as part of our Lutheran daily offices.[12]

Reverend Morris's defense includes an abnegation of his participation as "an act of joint worship, but one of mercy and care to a community shocked and grieving an unspeakingly horrific event."[13]

In a stunning volte-face approximately two weeks after Reverend Morris's apology, Reverend Matthew Harrison himself apologized in a video statement, for his mishandling of the situation in his recriminations against Reverend Morris, conceding the "plan failed miserably."[14] Although his plan intended to defuse the situation, it was exacerbated, whereby critics of Reverend Harrison from within and outside of the Synod, "charged that he was intolerant and insensitive to the town's grieving residents."[15] Reverend Harrison conceded that the Missouri Synod denomination is actually conflicted over the rule against joint worship, where "some see it as an endorsement of other religions, while others see it as an opportunity to share their faith with the community."[16] Just as the government did not construe the use of the school for the prayer service as an endorsement of religion in violation of the Establishment Clause, the same can be applied analogously: interfaith services do not inexorably yield syncretism, and the separation of religions can certainly be maintained. The conflict was all the more magnified and injurious to the community, since one of the children who was killed at Sandy Hook was a member of Reverend Morris's congregation. This regrettable and unfortunate fallout precipitated rancor, while situating succor in an attenuated frame.

Through the prism of the models of interreligious prayer, Reverend Crebbin could be seen as the host, albeit his remarks are tinged with caveats and disclaimers. Knowing what was learned ex post facto about Reverend Morris's participation and his apology, one could conclude that some disingenuousness inhered in the service.[17] In the second model, "serial interfaith occasions," people of different faiths convene where "the rites of one tradition cross paths with the rites of another religious tradition."[18] As each religion is accorded distinction and integrity, this interfaith event affords everyone the opportunity to come together to pray, not pray together.[19] The Sandy Hook service was clearly more aligned with the former (coming together to pray), rather than the latter (praying together). Although the third model, "inter-riting"[20] can potentially engender misappropriation and inauthenticity, resulting from the more "fluid boundaries," unlike the 9/11, which achieved inter-riting without devolving into syncretism, the Sandy Hook service did not reach the level of inter-riting. In the 9/11 service, each religion positioned itself autonomously and interdependently through the conception of the *mise-en-scène* and the overarching theme within the parameters of the service in its entirety. The Sandy Hook service with its scaled back environs, possessed a more rudimentary *mise-en-scène*, but nonetheless, exuded potent dimensions of succor. Also, worth noting within the Sandy Hook service was the inclusion of local, state, and national political leaders, the most noteworthy being President Barack Obama.

Our analysis of President Obama's eulogy at the interfaith service presages the paradigm of a parental theology of political responsibility, where some of the families of the slain children and adults at Sandy Hook Elementary School spent the last decade engaged in various acts of advocacy through civic engagement and litigation in pursuit of legal justice in the courts of civil law. Tragically aware of the fact that their children and family members cannot be brought back in this life, they felt that redress was *sine qua non*, regardless of how long it would take.

In a December 15th issue of *The New York Review of Books*, responding to the tragic murder of children and adults at Sandy Hook Elementary School in Newtown, Connecticut, 2012, Gary Wills observed:

> We guarantee that crazed man after crazed man will have a flood of killing power readily supplied him. We have to make that offering, out of devotion to our Moloch, our god. The gun is our Moloch. We sacrifice children to him daily.[21]

In the face of the nation's worst school shooting and given the fact that 20 first graders were murdered at the hands of Adam Lanza, Wills' analogy of gun violence to the Old Testament, pagan god of child sacrifice is soberingly apt and reveals glaring hypocrisy for a so called "Christian," pro-life nation. On December 16, 2012, adopting the all too familiar persona of "Commander in Grief," President Obama performed the ritual of national eulogy for the victims of Sandy Hook at an interfaith prayer vigil. Though, this time it was different from Tucson, Blacksburg, Fort Hood, and Aurora, primarily since the scene was a school and a preponderance of the victims were children. Obama's words comported with the generic conventions of eulogy, providing succor for the suffering, honoring the dead, and trussing together a community torn asunder by bloodshed. Given the event was constituted as an interfaith prayer vigil, special emphasis was devoted to sacred and scriptural allusions. Obama's eulogy is more illustrative of rhetorical scholar Lawrence Rosenfield's etymological conception of *epideixis*, which translates "to shine or show forth," with the aim of illuminating new truths often interwoven with religious revelation.[22] The new truth of Obama's eulogy, based on the tragically unique nature that the victims of gun violence were school children, we contend is manifested in a parental theology of political responsibility.[23] Such a bravura paradigm of epideictic eloquence prompted Obama's biographer David Maraniss to acclaim the speech "his Gettysburg address."[24] However,

Obama's eulogy is also noteworthy in that by framing gun violence as a public health crisis and demanding responsible political action to prevent such violence in the future,[25] his address exemplifies what Jamieson and Campbell delineate as a "rhetorical hybrid" that shifts from epideictic to deliberative oratory.[26] Obama articulated a painful incongruity between the protection of our second amendment right to, what Wills calls, "private protected killing machines" and the collective, political responsibility of parents and governments to protect children and keep them safe. The failure of America to do this after Sandy Hook is what led Obama to declare the Sandy Hook shooting as the "saddest and angriest moment of his presidency."[27]

Wills' words and reference to Moloch are relevant to consider in a rhetorical evaluation of Obama's eulogy. Citing Milton's *Paradise Lost*, Wills notes Milton depicted Moloch as the first pagan god who joined Satan's war on humankind:

> First *Moloch*, horrid king, besmear'd with blood
> Of human sacrifice, and parents' tears,
> Though for the noise of Drums and Timbrels loud
> Their children's cries unheard, that pass'd through fire
> To his grim idol.[28]

Milton's poetic *ekphrasis* resonates an uncanny, contemporary, and visceral description of the shocking scene at Sandy Hook. Of the "besmear'd blood," the "pass'd through [gun] fire," and the "parents' tears" of Milton's verses, it is Obama's emphasis on the status of the parents of the slain children and the parental relationship with its *sui generis* responsibility to the love and protection of children that is the central focus of our analysis.

Craig Rood illuminates how Obama's prolonged push for gun control in his eulogy employs amplification of the memories of Sandy Hook victims and how the consubstantial, familial obligation to "our children" functions as a "warrant of the dead."[29] In an examination of how an indecorous rhetoric of pro-gun ideology responded to the Sandy Hook shooting, in part, by emphasizing the testimonial narratives of the victims as personal calamities, isolated from the welfare of the civic polity, Christopher Duerringer employs the Burkean conceptions of piety, decorum, and circumference to demonstrate how such a rhetorical ideology demeans human life and reinforces the status quo.[30] In this chapter, we explore Barack Obama's eulogy at the Sandy Hook prayer vigil as a sacred rhetoric of succor that comforts the mournful and calls for a political responsibility regarding gun violence while simultaneously mollifying the rancor at senseless, indiscriminate violence against children. Beyond that, it is our contention that Obama's discourse achieves these fitting responses through a parental theology of political responsibility grounded in a communitarian ethic. Moreover, Obama's scriptural and politically inspired advocacy for gun reform emphasizes a commitment to civic well-being and the values of love, protection, and perseverance as antidotes to gun violence. In this respect, our analysis amalgamates and extends the exceptional work of David Frank, Craig Rood, and Christopher Duerringer by illustrating how a close reading of Obama's eulogy manifests a religious rhetorical construction and interpretation of the parent-child covenant and its abiding civic obligations to act against gun violence.

David Frank's exceptional analysis of Obama's Sandy Hook eulogy illuminates how Obama employed the scriptural rhetoric of St. Paul's 2 Corinthians and the Gospel of Luke 18:16 to inspire love, protection, and perseverance for the Newtown community and the nation.[31] Frank remarks that "victims and their status can be a crucial determinant of national eulogies, shaping how an address will unfold and the influence it might have."[32] Frank explicates how Martin Luther King's 1963 eulogy for the martyred children of the Birmingham church bombing, "built on the uniquely tragic nature of the attack and the profoundly innocent character of its victims (children worshiping in church...)." King's religious eloquence goaded American society to "transform horror and grief into action and policy."[33] Obama's eulogy resembles concomitant rhetorical and religious strategies. The economy of Obama's speech progresses through the cyclical thematic topos of love. This love is covenantal and unconditional, mutually shared between God and his people. Such a covenant is analogically and biblically represented by the parent/child relationship.[34] Obama dramatizes how such a love provides comfort through inspiring acts of courage, faith, and sacrifice. Secondly, a shift from inspiration to frustration/righteous indignation at society's failure to protect children transpires. Finally, questions regarding America's priorities, promises, and the necessary protection of the most vulnerable and innocent of citizens, children, are raised by Obama. He then proclaims a promise of his own, a plan for preventive action (while not specific, the overture is made), whereby Obama invites conversion from worship of the pagan Moloch to a true faith in American democracy's responsibility to protect its own children.

After the obligatory expression of gratitude to the governor of Connecticut, Obama addresses the primary audience of his eulogy, "To all the families."[35] It should come as no surprise that the familial motif and the parental second persona would be part of Obama's rhetorical strategy in his Sandy Hook eulogy.[36] In addition to Obama's favored rhetorical maneuvers, the communal and the familial are *topoi* endemic to the epideictic genre. Celeste Condit argues for the significance of the epideictic "family" of discourse. She contends, the primary function of epideictic is to engender, uphold, and transform a community's existence.[37]

Obama's Sandy Hook eulogy stays true to the traditional task of the epideictic genre. Immediately after quoting sacred scripture, 2 Corinthians, principally for its comforting thesis, Obama clearly articulates his purpose. "We gather here in the memory of twenty children…"[38] Those children all had parents. Indicating the collective unity, solidarity, and sympathy of the nation and all parents Obama included, he uttered, "we have wept with you, pulled our children tight…Newtown you are not alone."[39] The familial construct of love and protection yoked with a message of comfort finds its telos in the final verse of the scripture passage, "we know that if the earthily tent we live in is destroyed, we have a building from God, an eternal house in heaven, not built by human hands." Frank asserts that these "pairing[s] yoke the suffering of the world to a strengthening of the soul," thereby providing eschatological hope.[40]

Rhetorically, St. Paul fashions a coalescence of the antithetical and the architectural in an effort to dispense allopathic succor for any grieving people overwhelmed by the death of children. Ephemeral human existence is metaphorically compared to the unstable, fragile, and itinerant quality of a tent. Whereas the saintly life is likened to the permanence of a sound structure, a "heavenly house" constructed by the divine creator. Such a spiritual abode promises to be one where the family, although torn asunder by an earthly world of troubles, outwardly waste, and destruction, will inhabit a familial edifice internally and eternally renewed in the familial glory of a holy and wholly unity. Moreover, St. Paul's structural metaphors of tents and buildings, earthly dwellings, and heavenly homes, delineate God's parental and covenantal relationship with his chosen people from the Old Testament. In unifying the architectural with parental covenant, St. Paul provides the people of Corinth with an intertextual typology articulated in an Old Testament letter to the Hebrews. The author of Hebrews 11:1–2, 8–9, addresses the audience in the familial language of "brothers and sisters" then, in referencing God's covenant with the patriarch Abraham, remarks that in sojourning in the promised land, Abraham dwelled in "tents with Isaac (his son) and Jacob, heirs to the same promise." The author then notes that Abraham was "looking forward to the city with foundations, whose architect and maker is God." Due to their faith in God, Abraham, and his wife Sarah, who was sterile, generated "descendants as numerous as the stars in the sky." For the faithful children of these parental paragons, the earthly, tent dwelling life is fugacious and their offspring "desire a better homeland, a heavenly one… and their God…has prepared a city for them." Obama draws on St. Paul's words for their comfort, eschatological hope, but also, as we hope to illustrate, for the analogical reasoning of covenantal love and protection between parents and children, God and faithful people, and responsible governments and their citizens.

Obama provides exemplary and inspirational anecdotes of Sandy Hook and Newtown community members' strength, resolve, sacrifice, and love. The summit of Obama's succor and familial commitment came when he mentioned that in the face of "indescribable violence" and "unconscionable evil," the Newtown community "looked out for each other, and you've cared for one another, and you've loved one another...and with time, and God's grace, that love will see you through."[41] The communitarian and ethical virtues enacted by the people of Newtown become representative anecdotes and perform an evidentiary function that lays the sacred foundation for an articulation and expression of Obama's parental theology. Such a perspective reinforces the ideals of Christian love while exhorting a secular call for political action on the issue of gun violence and thereby demonstrates the hybrid genre of epideictic and deliberative speech.[42]

The rhetorical correlation between Obama's use of 2 Corinthians and his parental theology of political responsibility is clearly established in the eighth paragraph. A close reader will recall Obama opens his eulogy with St. Paul's sacred exhortation "do not lose heart. Though outwardly we are wasting away... inwardly we are being renewed day by day." The signification of heart in this case is to mean faith, do not lose faith in God's promise of eternal life, secured by the parental covenant between God the father and his children. Yet, in paragraph eight, Obama employs heart as a metaphor for parenthood.

> The joy and anxiety of parenthood is the equivalent of having your heart outside your body all the time, walking around. With their very first cry, this most precious, vital part of ourselves—our child—is suddenly exposed to the world, to possible mishap and malice. And every parent knows there is nothing we can do to shield our children from harm. And yet, we also know that with that child's first step, and each step after that, they are separating from us; that we won't—that we can't always be there for them...[43] And we know we can't do it by ourselves... no matter how much you love these kids, you can't do it by yourself. That the job of keeping our children safe...is something we can only do together, with the help of friends and neighbors, the help of a community, and the help of a nation. And in that way, we can come to realize that we bear a responsibility for every child because we are counting on everybody to help look after ours; that we're all parents; that they're all our children.[44]

Evoking the metaphor that parents' hearts, their children, are worn "outside your body all the time" is a tacit recapitulation of St. Paul's words regarding the outwardly and ephemeral nature of our earthly life. Obama remarks, since parents cannot always be there for their children, first, we must be reassured by the sacred comfort and eschatological hope provided by Paul's words that there is an inward renewal of eternal glory. Secondly, from a secular vantage, "we bear a responsibility for every child because we're counting on everybody else to look after ours; that we're all parents, that they're all our children."[45] Moreover, this paragraph epitomizes Obama's parental theology of political and community responsibility. Since we are "so often unable to discern God's heavenly plans,"[46] Obama remarks later, and we know that we are not doing enough to protect our children from gun violence; Sandy Hook proves this, therefore change is demanded. Obama's mandate is rooted in a communitarian orientation of mutual responsibility for the safety and protection of "all our children." Beyond this,

Obama's charge is the fundamental promise of parents as well as a democratic polity, "our first task—caring for our children…if we don't get that right, we don't get anything right."[47] Cherishing and protecting "all our children" is a moral imperative, not just parentally but civically. Obama then brilliantly conflates the sacred and the secular by aligning concern for the well-being of children with our socio-political obligations. "That is how, as a society, we will be judged."[48] There is subtle semantic ambiguity in Obama's choice of the word "judged." A subtending religious connotation can be gleaned as if to argue that as a nation America will not just be assessed empirically or politically on how we responded to the scourge of murdered children at the hands of assault weapons in the court of history but, rather, if we do not act to change the continued practice of child sacrifice, clearly a vitiation of a foundational societal value, we will be judged morally in the heavenly court of the Almighty. Here the generic boundaries of forensic and epideictic discourse become less divergent.

Obama, on the question of getting right the care and protection of America's children, employs the use of anacoenosis, a subspecies of rhetorical questions whereby a rhetor asks the opinion of a certain audience with the aim of having them respond in a particular way.[49]

> And by that measure can we truly say, as a nation, that we are meeting our obligations? Can we honestly say that we're doing enough to keep our children—all of them—safe from harm? Can we claim, as a nation, that we're all together there, letting them know that they are loved, and teaching them to love in return? Can we say that we're truly doing enough to give all the children in this country the chance they deserve to live out their lives in happiness and with purpose?

A central rhetorical feature of the epideictic genre, of which eulogy is a subspecies, is its capacity to cultivate identification and reinforce communal values. Forsyth argues that anacoenosis encourages an audience to realize how much they have in common.[50] Anacoenosis essentially asks questions in an effort to elicit similar answers. Obama's rhetorical questioning is intended to underscore his parental theology of political responsibility undergirding and reinforcing, through the repetition of "Can we…," shared values of love, safety, and happiness. Clearly Obama's anacoenosis invites his audience to weigh their responses vis-à-vis the mass shooting at Sandy Hook and the continued communal exigence of gun violence. In what follows, Obama's anacoenosis may also be considered hypophora, another form of rhetorical question in which a rhetor provides an audible response to their antecedent inquiry. To Obama's previous queries, he responds, "The answer is no. We're not doing enough. And we have to change."[51]

This section of rhetorical questions permits Obama to argue more deliberately and deliberatively for political action. While it may appear Obama is deviating from the precinct of the epideictic, he is not. As Perelman and Olbrechts-Tyteca contend, epideictic reinforcement preserves an existing "disposition toward action by increasing adherence to the values it lauds."[52] Obama begins with his own empirical evidence by quantifying the number of times he has had to console a community ravaged by gun violence. "Since I've been president, this is the fourth time we have come together to comfort a grieving community torn apart by a mass shooting. The fourth time we've hugged survivors. The fourth time we've consoled the families of victims."[53] Obama's use of anaphoric *accumulatio* amplifies the severity of the social ill. Obama clearly acknowledges the pathology of gun violence and demands the tragic sacrificing of children must stop; change is imperative. He, then, uses the argumentative strategy of prolepsis, or anticipatory refutation stating, "We will be told that the causes of such violence are complex and that is true." "No single law…can eliminate evil from the world or prevent every senseless act of violence in our society." Obama again imbricates the existential and the political with the abstract and theodicy (the problem of evil in our world) and just like "being unable to discern God's plans," is no excuse for inaction, so, too, is the argument that evil cannot be purged from society. Despite these complexities and aporias, Obama offers assurances. For it is out of our love and obligation for one another, "the only one thing we can be sure of… the love we have—for our children, for our families, for each other," that we should at least try to prevent more tragedies like Sandy Hook. Obama's words here illustrate his theology of parental love and political responsibility.

Before ending his eulogy, Obama vows to bring together various constituencies from law enforcement to parents and educators to exercise our obligation to try and stop gun violence. Obama returns to the strategy of rhetorical questioning to again to expose an odious incongruity between, a nation of Moloch worshipers whose values are antithetical to parental love and civic responsibility. "Because what choice do we have? Are we really prepared to say that we're powerless in the face of such carnage, that the politics are too hard? Are we prepared to say that such violence visited upon our children year after year is somehow the price of our freedom?" The communal answer to Obama's question is there should be no choice. There is but one true response, to choose the life of children over the intransigent politics of the so called "gundamentalists," whose right to bear arms trumps the safety of our children.

Obama saves the most percussive instantiation of his parental theology of political responsibility for the end. Obama remarks that the one thing we can be sure of is the "boundless love we feel for them (our children), a love that takes us out of ourselves." Here the ephemeral and the transcendent harken back to the opening Corinthians passage and bind the audience to something larger. "We know that is what matters." Metaphysically, the eternal and theological view that Obama underscores here is what should drive the nation forward in everything we do (and the subtextual action here is like comprehensive gun reform); "as long as God sees fit to keep us on this Earth."[54]

Although we have failed to protect our children here on earth, they are now in the care of the Lord and have entered the eternal kingdom, the parental covenant reaches its telos in our children's heavenly home. After Obama, as president and civic representative of political responsibility implored the nation to, at least, try to militate against gun violence; he ended his eulogy and parental theology where he began with the words of sacred scripture. "Let the little children come to me…and do not hinder them—for to such belongs the kingdom of heaven."[55] Mindful that God calls us each by name, Obama, as if to enact the voice Jesus Christ's invitation, calls each of the deceased children by name. The ineffability of the horrific tragedy of Sandy Hook and all its irredeemable evil is vanquished, linguistically brought to light with the faithful and transcendent belief that these slain children, "all our children," now abide in the eternal dwelling of God the father. Obama is able to entwine 2 Corinthians with this passage from Matthew 19:14. The outward temporal tents are transfigured, like the earthly Jesus himself, to inward, permanent buildings that make up the kingdom of heaven. The verity of this is affirmed and constituted in the very somber and stoic speech act of naming them. And if only in that evanescent moment of articulation, Obama's panegyric epitaphs engender a rhetorical memorial inscribed in history and on the hearts of all parents, providing eternal hope in the parental covenant and goading our nation to enact political responsibility to end the scourge of gun violence that in the case of Sandy Hook has destroyed our very hearts.

One of the legal victories of the Sandy Hook victims' families was realized with the case circumscribing unlawful marketing practices in *Soto v. Bushmaster Firearms Int'l, L.L.C.*, 202 A.3d 262 (Conn 2019). The provenance of the families' successful lawsuit belies the strength of the legislation which they were up against. In 2005, Congress passed the protection of lawful Commerce in Arms Act (PLCAA), barring,

> causes of action against manufacturers, distributors, dealers, and importers of firearms or ammunition products…for harm solely caused by the criminal or unlawful misuse of firearm products by others when the product functioned as designed and intended.[56]

The exigence motivating Congressional Republicans and the lobbying efforts of the National Rifle Association (NRA) to support the federal legislation, serving to immunize the gun industry, was a spate of lawsuits against gun manufacturers in the face of tens of thousands of deaths and injuries in which guns were used. Indubitably, at the forefront in pursuing this legislation was the potential financial liability. For all intents and purposes, the statute, signed into law by George W. Bush, ostensibly shut down any possible litigation against the gun manufacturers for a third party "criminal or unlawful misuse of a [firearm]…"[57] However, in 2019, daylight emerged for the Sandy Hook families, with a legal peripeteia which could not have been foreseen, although the loophole of "predicate exception" inhered in the PLCAA, perhaps as an ineffectual or rarely used exception, allowing "suits against gun manufacturers who knowingly violate a State or federal statute applicable to the sale or marketing of firearms, and by that violation, proximately cause a gun victim's harm."[58] The plaintiffs propounded the legal case that

> Bushmaster had violated the Connecticut's unfair trade practice law (CUTPA), by advertising and marketing the XM15-E2S in an unethical, oppressive, immoral, and unscrupulous manner that promoted illegal offensive use of the rifle, and as such, could be sued under the predicate exception to the PLCAA due to the promotional tactics' causal relationship to all or some of the injuries inflicted during the Sandy Hook massacre.[59]

In February 2022, relatives of nine victims of Sandy Hook (five children and four adults) settled with Remington, the manufacturer of the Bushmaster rifle for an unprecedented seventy-three million dollars "in a mass-shooting related case against a gun manufacturer."[60] The families lawsuit claimed that Remington encouraged illegal and dangerous behavior effectuated by the marketing and advertising tactics in violation of state consumer law.[61]

Originally filed in 2014, the families ultimately appealed to the Connecticut State Supreme Court, allowing the case to proceed. The defendant appealed to the U.S. Supreme Court which denied the appeal.[62] The families adduced evidence that Remington's marketing strategy promoted the guns' "assaultive qualities, military uses, and lethality."[63] As brilliantly reported by Elizabeth Williamson, in her book-length study *Sandy Hook*, Adam Lanza led a dark and disturbingly isolated life. As told by Williamson, "he taped dark plastic bags over the windows of his downstairs bedroom, where he played violent computer games and compiled data on mass shootings dating to the 1970s."[64] The gun used by Adam Lanza, including the duct-taped magazines found at the site of the massacre, appear in the video game Call of Duty, and this photographic evidence was successfully marshalled in the lawsuit.[65] The company also trafficked in marketing and advertising, using "flashy militaristic pitches with macho slogans like 'Forces of opposition, bow down,' 'Clear the room,' and 'Consider your man card reissued.'"[66]

In the wake of a video broadcast by Alex Jones on April 22, 2017, titled "Sandy Hook Vampires Exposed,"[67] the defamation lawsuit filings against Alex Jones and Infowars began in 2018, reaching successful fruition in a series of trials in 2022, with subsequent upcoming trials having taken place in March 2023.[68] In 2017, Lenny Pozner and Veronique De La Rosa, the parents of Noah Pozner, the youngest victim of the Sandy Hook shooting, and Neil Heslin, the father of Jesse Lewis, were the first plaintiffs to hold Jones accountable in a court of law.[69]

Parents and relatives of victims, in addition to an FBI agent who survived the Sandy Hook massacre when he responded to the scene, have successfully sued

Alex Jones and Infowars as legally accountable in a series of defamation lawsuits, sending a powerful message that words matter, and when scrutinized and adjudicated through the lens of defamatory speech and infliction of emotional distress, a speaker's words are not assumed to be protected by the First Amendment. An ignominious and abhorrent media personality, Alex Jones's legal woes began in earnest in 2018 with the initial filings of lawsuits, for what Mark Bankston, the plaintiffs' lawyer in the first trial in Austin, Texas, called "the most despicable and vile campaign of defamation and slander in American history."[70]

According to First Amendment Watch at New York University, consequential false claims were propagated by Jones, a notorious conspiracy theorist, who used his website and media platform Infowars to spread falsehoods and disinformation, which rose to the legal standard of defamation. Jones referred to the "so-called massacre" as "a 'giant-hoax,' and a 'false flag.'" He falsely claimed that the parents were hired by the government as crisis actors, and that no murders occurred, including the falsity that a gun was in the car trunk, and that the whole theatrical event was designed as an attack against the Second Amendment, including the seizure of guns.[71]

The major questions posed which are pivotal in determining if Jones's speech was protected include the following: whether the plaintiffs are public figures or deemed private individuals; whether the disinformation constituted actual malice or a reckless disregard; whether expression of opinion is protected speech; and whether rhetorical hyperbole is a justifiable defense.[72] Although the defense emphatically and unequivocally used the First Amendment against the defamation charge, and the burden is heavy on the plaintiffs to prove defamation against a media entity, the lawsuits against Jones state that "the First Amendment has never protected demonstrably false, malicious statements like the defendants,"[73] an affirmation of the landmark Supreme Court decision, *New York Times v. Sullivan* (1964).

As civil suits, the plaintiffs sued Jones for monetary damages for his dissemination of "defamatory falsehoods against private persons..."[74] Jones's brand of prevarication and calumny were uniquely and consummately egregious, exacerbated by his preferred modality of communication—the internet—maximizing the defamation with the portmanteau "defamacast," as a cross between libel and slander, insofar as the defamatory statements possessed the posterity of libel as originally conceived through the written word, and the orality and ephemerality of slander as originally conceived through the spoken word, both predicated on the common-law distinction.[75]

In the first trial in Austin, Texas, July 26, 2022, Neil Heslin and Scarlett Lewis, Jesse Lewis's parents, testified as having "endured years of accusations and threats."[76] Originally asking for compensatory damages of 150 million dollars,[77] the plaintiffs' lawyer Mark Bankston, argued that the false statements that Jones created and trafficked in were nonpareil. The jury did award Jesse Lewis's parents four million dollars in compensatory damages and forty-five million dollars in punitive damages.⁷⁸ Judge Maya Guerra Gamble believed that the damage to the family was so beyond the pale, that she ordered Jones to pay the four million in compensatory and the forty-five million in punitive damages that the jury originally awarded them,⁷⁹ calling it "a rare case,"⁸⁰ notwithstanding the fact that this award surpassed the cap in Texas law.

In the second trial in Waterbury, Connecticut, fifteen plaintiffs sued on behalf of eight shooting victims and an FBI agent who responded to the scene at Sandy Hook Elementary school.⁸¹ On October 12, 2022, the plaintiffs were awarded almost one billion dollars.⁸² The two-week trial culminated in a staggering award of almost 1 billion dollars. During the trial, the plaintiffs recounted how they pleaded with Jones to stop disseminating the dangerous falsehoods, including the … "wrenching stories of harassment by conspiracy theorists who believed Mr. Jones's lies, including death and rape threats, confrontations and messages threatening to defile and dig up the victims' graves."⁸³ Christopher Mattei, the lawyer representing the families in this case makes reference to the "depravity" of Jones's falsehoods, with the plaintiffs having established "the highest degree of reprehensibility and blameworthiness."⁸⁴ A testament to the egregiousness of Alex Jones's defamatory speech are the adjustments made by Judge Guerra Gamble in the first trial in Texas and the trial in Connecticut. Superior Court Judge Barbara N. Bellis in the Connecticut trial augmented the 965 billion dollars in compensatory damages awarded by the jury with 473 million dollars in punitive damages for lawyers' fees.⁸⁵ Although two major SCOTUS cases extend First Amendment protection to the tort of infliction of emotional distress,⁸⁶ Jones was not protected from the damages "for extreme and outrageous conduct that caused severe mental or emotional harm to the plaintiff."⁸⁷

In the Texas trial, the punitive damages far exceeded the compensatory damages, whereby punitive damages in a defamation suit "are awarded as a form of punishment when the defamation has been particularly offensive, malicious, and destructive of reputation."⁸⁸ In the Connecticut trial, the damages were compensatory, divided for each plaintiff between awards for (1) defamation/slander damages, past and future, and (2) emotional distress damages, past and future,⁸⁹ with the punitive damages added by Judge Bellis in a later ruling.⁹⁰

After the Texas trial, the plaintiffs' lawyer Mark Bankston was quoted as saying, "Speech is free, but lies you have to pay for…This is a case about creating change."⁹¹ After the Connecticut trial, the plaintiffs' lawyer Chris Mattei was quoted as saying that the decision "serves to reinforce the message of this case: those who profit from lies targeting the innocent will face justice."⁹²

CHAPTER 5: PART 1

Religion and Violence

Known as "World Jew-baiter No. 1" and "the biggest bigot in the world,"[1] Julius Streicher was accused of "inciting Jewish persecution in his speeches and anti-Semitic newspaper *Der Stürmer* (The Attacker)."[2] Streicher delivered his post-Kristallnacht speech on November 10, 1938, to over 100,000 people assembled in Nuremberg at Adolf Hitler Square.[3] Streicher's speech argued for the justification of the destruction surrounding Kristallnacht. With Streicher's conviction of having committed crimes against humanity, this was the first time this crime comprised "words used as persecution."[4]

"SPEECH AFTER 'THE NIGHT OF BROKEN GLASS'"[5]

Julius Streicher

Nuremberg, Germany. November 10, 1938.

Fellow people's comrades!
 To begin, let us make this clear: You were not ordered to come here, but came of your own free will. It is a shame that it is impossible for all those curious people abroad, and all those within our county who are the secret friends of certain forces abroad, cannot stand where I am standing to see for themselves how great the will

of the people of Nuremberg and Franconia is to know the truth. You want to and shall hear the truth, and from those who have preached it for twenty years, not only in Franconia, but also to the entire world.

What happened? As the Fuhrer last Monday paused here in Nuremberg while traveling to Munich, the news came from Paris that a seventeen-year-old Jew went into the German embassy and shot Counsel vom Rath. The whole world quickly heard the news. Those who do not understand the racial question, which is the key to everything, said what all ignorant people say: Someone mentally ill, a stupid young boy who did not know what he was doing, shot someone. For those of us with understanding, however, the shots in the Paris embassy meant something different than they did to those who never want to see. We know: That Jew was the representative and agent of the Jewish people, both through blood and education.

Parisian newspapers with the courage to print the truth have said that at his first interrogation, he answered the question of why he had done the deed by saying that an irresistible drive had made him go to the German embassy and shoot a German. We know where the drive that made the Jew shoot the German comes from. We know that the Jew received his blood from all the races of the world. Negro blood, Mongolian blood, Nordic blood, Indian blood—the blood of all races flows in this bastard race. This mixed blood, forces the Jew into criminal deed. As the old German proverb has it: "He who has mixed blood in his veins follows the worst direction." That means that he is forced to do wrong. He who has pure blood has a single soul; he who has mixed blood has a divided soul. Sometimes he obeys the good blood, sometimes the bad. As a bastard, the Jew always follows the dictates of his bad blood.

Thus, this creature went to the German embassy and shot the German counsel in the service of the Jewish people because his *inferior mixed blood demanded* it of him. His divided soul needed the death of this man, and this insolent Jewish murderer declared that he was sorry that the counsel was not dead, only wounded. Those French newspapers with the courage to tell the truth report to us that this Jewish murderer stated during his interrogation that he had been a student at a rabbinical school in Frankfurt. For twenty years, I have told the citizens of Nuremberg and Franconia that, he who has gone to a rabbinical school has been educated not to the good, but to criminality. From his earliest childhood, the Jew is taught different things than we are taught. No, he is not taught "Love your neighbor as yourself" or "If someone strikes you on your right check, turn also your left cheek to him." Instead, he is taught: "You may do whatever you wish to a Gentil." He is even taught to see the execution of a Gentile as a deed that pleases Good. We have been writing that in the *Sturmer* for twenty years, we have been preaching it to the whole world for twenty years, and we have brought an understanding of the Jewish Question to millions.

Still, we know that there are individuals among us who still have pity for the Jews, individuals who are not worthy to live in this city, not worthy to belong to this people of which you are a proud part. Today we heard of a "lady" who sighed that it was heartbreaking to see all the destroyed shops. Who had pity for us when, after the war, the Jew brought down enormous misery on the German people, as the Jew brought down enormous misery on the German people, as the Jew stole our savings during the great inflation, as Germany was blockaded during the World War by Jewish orders and hundreds of thousands of women and children starved? We are used to speaking our mind and I say that those who behave like that "lady" do not belong here among us, and they can go wherever they want to with the Jews. We do not need them here!

We have done what we once said and prophesied that we would do. As I said to you twenty years ago, the time will come when Germans no longer live in barracks, but rather the Jews. Germans will the move into the fine houses. And if the Jews now move away, we will be able to give pleasure to some families with many children by allowing them to celebrate Christmas in a decent home, a home in which others previously celebrated a different holiday. The mayor will see to it that everything possible is done in the near future to relieve our present housing shortage. And the Fuhrer has assured us that, especially in Nuremberg, more will be done to alleviate the tragic inheritance others left to us. The good will is there, but you all know the state Germany was in, and what must be done to make us secure. The Fuhrer knows that the German people will bear everything proudly, including the poverty that still exists, in order to preserve our people as a whole.

It was the mixed blood and education that drove the young Jew to murder. The Jew is educated to hate all Gentiles. However, the Jew also makes distinctions. It is no accident that the boy went into the German embassy instead of the Soviet-Russian embassy, or the American, or some other one.

Why did he choose the German embassy? He wanted to strike someone belonging to the people that the Jews hate most fervently. At the end of September, the Jews in Germany were overjoyed, they were ecstatic. The Jews in the whole world were so happy that they could hardly control themselves. They hoped that the new world war that they had been dreaming and writing about for years was finally coming. They believed that they would then be able to regain their strength in German, or return to it.

We could have killed all the Jews in Germany yesterday, but we did not do it. The demonstrations in Franconia were, in general, disciplined, clear, and farsighted. They proved to the world that the days when the Jew could take out his wrath on us, whether from within or without, are finally over. They showed a world friendly to the Jews that, when necessary, the German people can do whatever has to be done. And National Socialism has proved that when it acts with determination, it is successful.

What happened yesterday and today has become history. The people demonstrated, and today the government declared that it wants the demonstrations to end. At the same time, it was announced that the Jews, who provoked the German people through their agent in Paris, will be subjected to new measures. They could have pared themselves those measures, but which now are necessary.

The Jew who fired the shot in Paris is not the only one who intended to take aim at the German people. The Jew in Paris, in the name of Jewry, wanted to strike symbolically at the heart of the German people. A short time ago, a Jew here told the police that Nuremberg Jews might attack political figures. He wanted to say that, if such a thing should happen, all Jews should not be held responsible. We believe in powers, whether human or of fate, that make revolver bullets and knives powerless. The Fuhrer and his fellow fighters escaped bullets in front of the Feldherrnhalle. And I believe that, were a Jew to attack a leading political figure in Nuremberg, nothing could stop the Franconian people from finally solving the Jewish Question in Nuremberg. I believe that if the Jews were to do what they would like to do—as did the Jew Hirsch some years ago with his hellish machine—Nuremberg's workers would say: "An eye for an eye, a tooth for a tooth!"

Let no one believe, however, that we were worried about that. We are subject to fate, we have fought for twenty years, and we move into the future with cheerful courage. We go on as people who know. We always want to come together to learn.

Do not forget that this murderer is a Jew. The Jew has the murder of Golgotha on his conscience. This people cannot be a "chosen" people. Nuremberg's teachers have decided that, in the future, they will teach children only those words that come from Christ's mouth. They refuse to teach the children any longer about a holy people of God.

In one night, the Jew butchered 75,000 Persians. As he left Egypt, he killed all the firstborn, that means the whole posterity, of Egypt. What would have happened if the Jew had succeeded in inciting the peoples into a war against us, and if we had lost that war? Under the protection of foreign bayonets, the Jew would have butchered and murdered us. Never forget what history teaches.

That Jews would have instituted a new Purim festival in Germany. In celebrations abroad, they already use a doll to represent Adolf Hitler. With howls of glee from Jews old and young, it is taken to the gallows. But the hopes of the Jews have not been fulfilled, since we are not cowards, because we are National Socialists, because we no longer have parties or classes, because workers, factory workers, help to greater this greater Germany, and because it has our full admiration. It also has my love and admiration! I could not have survived these twenty years had you not supported me, had you not been so decent from the beginning. How many of you heard me in the Hercules Hall and today have changed inwardly because you believed what I said back then: "Look at those who want to be your leaders. They are Jews!"

The Nuremberg worker is farsighted, and no coward. He goes along proudly, quietly, and strongly! The Fuhrer has often said: "If I had not had my workers, my craftsmen, I could have carried out my work." He knew that he could rely on you.

What was the meaning of that bullet in Paris? Symbolically, it was aimed at the new National Socialist Germany's heart. The Jew wanted to say: "When the time comes, this whole people will be hit by a bullet." They sent a seventeen-year-old Jew because they thought a French court would treat him gently. They hoped he would get a judge like the Jew Schwarzbart found ten or fifteen years ago. He gunned down a Ukrainian leader, and was acquitted because the Ukrainian was a leader of a people that hated Jews. We do not know what the court will rule in this case. The new Germany waits for the verdict, the new Germany that is led by Adolf Hitler and owes its life to National Socialism.

The synagogue of Nuremberg's Jews once stood where we now stand. Nuremberg citizens set the synagogue on fire [in 1347], for it was not a house of God, but rather a den of murderers. We admire those men today, and say that they lived in a great era. In centuries to come, people will say that our age is a great age, too. The name of the man who fell to the murderous bullet will also go down in history. His name will join the names of those that are holy to us. Sixteen fell at the Feldherrnhalle. Their blood sanctifies our flags. That is how we should see the death of Counsel vom Rath.

Our hope is that the Jewish people will one day receive the penalty they deserve for all the sorrow, misery, and trouble they have brought the peoples. We believe the supreme court is coming that will judge the Devil's people. Then the world will breathe more easily, and there will be peace.

And now I ask you to keep disciplined. No more demonstrations! We have made some progress, and will leave the rest to the Fuhrer. We greet him with our Sieg Heil!

***

RHETORICAL ANALYSIS

Julius Streicher is not a name possessing the same recognition as Hitler or Goebbels, the latter infamously, inextricably, and instrumentally connected with the policies and practices used to engineer the extermination of Jews, culminating in the diabolical plan called the "Final Solution." However, Streicher's name is integral to the heinous enterprise. Streicher's sphere of influence was a predominantly rhetorical sphere of influence, but one that is recognized by scholars, not only as instrumental to the efforts surrounding the genocidal events of World War II, but as one which has influenced anti-Semitic and racist rhetoric throughout the twentieth century and into the first two plus decades of the twenty-first century, with no abatement in sight.

According to Randall Bytwerk in *Landmark Speeches of National Socialism*, "national socialism was the most prolific rhetorical movement of the twentieth century," and that "everything that Nazism intended was revealed in its rhetoric."[6] The rhetoric emerged as the progenitor of the tenets of propaganda,[7] privileging pathos over logos with a fervor one usually finds in sermonic rhetoric.[8] A potent dimension of Nazi rhetoric was the use of Christian imagery, and "infusing old symbols with new meaning,"[9] and this rhetorical strategy was evident in Julius Streicher's discourse. And although Streicher was not part of the war machine in ways comparable to Nazis like Goring, Speer, Hess, and Ribbentrop, of this infamous cohort, Streicher received a sentence of death, the same sentence as Goring and Ribbintrop, for crimes against humanity.[10] Streicher's crimes against humanity were committed solely with his rhetoric.[11] The rhetorical device of antonomasia expresses Streicher's infamy with complete clarity: "World Jew-baiter No. 1" and "the biggest bigot in the world."[12]

The Nuremberg Charter, signed August 8, 1945, established the International Military Tribunal.[13] Julius Streicher was accused of "inciting Jewish persecution in his speeches and anti-Semitic newspaper *Der Stürmer* (The Attacker)."[14] With Streicher's conviction of having committed crimes against humanity, this was the first time this crime encompassed "words used as persecution."[15] This "incitement to genocide" had previously been an unprecedented prosecution, whereby "inciting mass murder [occurred] through words alone,"[16] and officially not recognized in the international community until the 1948 Genocide Convention.[17] Streicher was convicted, and found guilty under Article 6(c) of the International Military Tribunal:

> Namely, murder, extermination, enslavement, deportation, and other inhumane acts committed against any civilian population, before or during the war; or persecutions on political, racial or religious grounds in execution of or in connection with any crime within the jurisdiction of the Tribunal, whether or not in violation of the domestic law of the country where perpetrated.[18]

Applicable to all three crimes of Article 6: Crimes Against Peace (6a), War Crimes (6b), and Crimes Against Humanity (6c) is the following:

> Leaders, organizers, *instigators* and accomplices participating in the formulation or execution of a common plan or conspiracy to commit any of the foregoing crimes are responsible for all acts performed by any person in execution of such plan. [19]

The prosecution's strategy claimed that "Streicher helped to create, through his propaganda, the psychological basis necessary for carrying through a *program of persecution* which culminated in the murder of six million men, women, and children."[20] The prosecution claimed that Streicher's rhetoric served as a *"conditioning* of German citizens to being open to carrying out a mass violence campaign against a victim population, not direct calls for imminent commission of such violence."[21]

As Gordon so importantly notes, although hate speech was not mentioned in the Charter, it was a cornerstone of the prosecution of Streicher.[22] Notwithstanding the Chief Prosecutor's insistence on the "central role of 'incitement,'" that word was also absent from the Charter.[23]

Streicher refutes the causation between his rhetoric and the extermination of the Jews,[24] but confirms the link on Sept. 12, 1936. As reported in the *New York Times*, Streicher gave a speech at a meeting at the Wittelsbacha Hotel on September 12, 1936, professing that "extermination is the only real solution of the Jewish problem," and a final solution will necessarily be bloody.[25] In justifying this monstrous route, Streicher said the Jews always attained their ends through wholesale murder and have been responsible for wars and massacres. To secure the safety of the whole world they must be exterminated.[26] Despite the newspaper's longevity, with its initial issue published in May 1923,[27] and the final issue in February 1945,[28] *Der Stürmer* was not ever considered a Nazi party newspaper,[29] and its influence in facilitating the realities of the Final Solution was seemingly dubious at best.

The IMT permitted each Nazi defendant to make a final statement, and on August 31, 1946, Streicher absolved himself and the German people of any guilt, and that the killings were committed on Hitler's orders devoid of any other influences.[30] The Tribunal's judges imbued *Der Stürmer* with an influence in support of Count Four of the indictment upon which Streicher was found guilty. "Streicher's speeches and articles, week after week, month after month, had infected the German mind with the virus of anti-Semitism and incited the German people to active persecution."[31] Streicher's aspiration for the extermination of Jews was couched in the metaphor of "root and branch,"[32] and evidenced in *Der Stürmer's* articles over its two decades plus existence, A September 1938 article captured the essence and the depth of the animus directed at Jews, saying, the Jew is "a germ and a pest, not a human being, but a parasite, an enemy, an evil-doer, a disseminator of diseases who must be destroyed in the interest of mankind."[33] Clinically, was Streicher a madman? Was he insane? Prior to his trial, Streicher underwent a psychiatric/psychological examination to determine whether he was sane to stand trial.[34] Once completed, the International Military Tribunal concluded that he was sane and competent to comprehend the criminal acts which he was accused of committing.³⁵ By all accounts, Streicher possessed no redeeming qualities. He was a serial offender, charged with a multitude of offenses, including "slander, corruption, sadism, and rape."³⁶ He was also a sexual deviant and garnered satisfaction from whipping prisoners.³⁷

The verdict against Streicher was announced on September 20, 1946, and he was hanged on October 16, 1946 on the charge of "'incitement to murder and extermination' under Count Four, crimes against humanity."³⁸ Streicher's case was the first time that the crime of "incitement to murder and extermination," was treated as a "subset of crimes against humanity."³⁹ Streicher's propagandistic vehicles were construed as comparable to the crimes committed by those who were duly recognized and acknowledged to be part of the war machine. Streicher was not found to have planned, organized, or implemented the extermination plan.⁴⁰ Streicher's crime was his *mens rea*, given his knowledge and continued pronouncements in support of and with the full-throated approbation for the extermination of the Jewish populace.⁴¹ As Eastwood explains, Streicher's propaganda, as published in *Der Stürmer*, was "classified, as using 'word as persecution' under the remit of Article 6c, crimes against humanity,"⁴² under the International Military Tribunal.⁴³ The Tribunal determined that between August 1941 and September 1944, 26 articles published in *Der Stürmer* "demanded annihilation and extermination in unequivocal terms; and incited German citizens to 'active persecution' of the Jews."⁴⁴

Although Streicher admitted to having spoken of the extermination of the Jews, his defense was its figurative use and not its literal use, essentially mounting a defense of poetic/rhetorical license.⁴⁵ When Streicher was about to be hanged, he invoked the Book of Esther, shouting "Purim Festival 1946."⁴⁶

Born in Bavaria in 1885, Streicher was a formal entrant to the Nazi Party on October 8, 1922.⁴⁷ *Der Stürmer*'s preliminary issue appeared April 20, 1923, used as a venue to target his "local party enemies" and not the Jews,⁴⁸ providing denunciations of non-Jewish Germans who were "insufficiently hostile to Jews."⁴⁹ As a topos in *Der Stürmer*, anti-Semitism accounted for 60–75% of the newspaper's content.⁵⁰ To Streicher, Jews were "sub-humans, worse than Negroes," and the advertisements did not elude the anti-Semitism.⁵¹ The prototype of *Der Stürmer* began with Streicher's foray into journalism, publishing the inaugural issue of Deutsche Sozialist, June 4, 1920,⁵² and presaging his animus towards Jews. Bytwerk argues that *Der Stürmer* can lay claim as "the most infamous newspaper in history."⁵³

Showalter explains that when Streicher delivered speeches, he did so with a spectacular theatricality, notwithstanding a mediocre rhetoric which, periodically, was "of the usual kind and brought nothing new."⁵⁴ And yet, as Nina Andrews points out, one of the prosecutors, Lieutenant Colonel Griffith-Jones claimed that, Streicher's propaganda was an unimpeachable "contributory factor in Jewish persecution and deaths under the Nazi regime"[55]—the front and center evidence being Streicher's November 10, 1938, Kristallnacht speech.[56]

By the time Streicher delivered his November 10, 1938, speech, *Der Stürmer*—the centerpiece and most consequential artifact of his anti-Semitic rhetoric—had been disseminated over the course of fifteen years, with its topoi and themes pellucidly instantiated in his speech in the immediate aftermath of Kristallnacht.

Shrafstetter and Steinweis observe that the pogrom of November 1938 was not the first chapter of the Holocaust, but it was the first time that large numbers of Jews sought to escape arrest and go in search of places to hide.[57] November 9, 1938, was a watershed event, contributing to the realization of the Final Solution. On that night, and through November 10, known as Kristallnacht, and translated as "night of broken glass," Germany's synagogues were destroyed, homes of Jewish citizens in Germany were vandalized, and thousands were deported to their ineluctable destination of concentration camps.[58] Kristallnacht is also referred to as a pogrom, since as Steinweis explains, "the word 'pogrom' originated as a Russian term suggesting acts of breaking, smashing, and plundering."[59] But a pogrom only engendered a short-term solution to the Jewish problem,[60] and a more efficacious, long-range range was needed to accomplish the quintessential goal of the complete destruction of European Jewry. According to Raul Hilberg, pogroms and the tactics used November 9–10, 1938, were jettisoned for a more systematic approach which was steeped in a legal framework engineered by a "bureaucratic destruction process, which, in its step-by-step manner, finally led to the annihilation of five million victims."[61]

The proximate and pretextual rationale for the violence surrounding Kristallnacht was the assassination on November 7, 1938, of Ernst vom Rath at the German Embassy in Paris.[62] Herschel Grynszpan, a seventeen-year-old student living in Paris since 1936,[63] learned of the deportations of thousands of Polish Jews who were legally residing in Germany.[64] All of their belongings were seized, but of the 12,000 expelled,[65] only 4,000 were allowed to enter Poland, while the others were left with no habitable destination.[66] Grynszpan learned of his family's plight through a postcard he received from his sister on November 3, an account of desperation confirming the plight affecting thousands of Jews, and retribution was his determined recourse. Intending to assassinate the German Ambassador, Grynszpan instead shot vom Rath, a German counselor on November 7, 1938,[67] and he died of his wounds on November 9, 1938.[68] As Gilbert says, "from the moment that news of his death reached Hitler in Munich, an unprecedented wave of violence broke over Germany's remaining three hundred thousand Jews."[69] In the aftermath of the assassination, riots ensued with the imprimatur of Hitler, while Goebbels, the Nazi Propaganda Minister communicated with leaders "to organize demonstrations against Jews, but to make them appear as impulsive acts by ordinary German citizens."[70]

The first issue of *Der Stürmer* appeared April 1923.[71] Ironically, the paper touted itself as "a paper in the fight (or struggle) for the truth."[72] There was no erudite journalistic enterprise here. The language is characterized as banal and childish, appealing to the lowest common denominator with a "gutter sensationalism."[73] According to Showalter, "*Der Stürmer* functioned as 'a major symbol of the homicidal, genocidal anti-Semitism that continues to make the name of Nazi Germany a synonym for evil." As Showalter observes, *Der Stürmer* endeavored and succeeded in creating "an alternative psychic reality,"[74] and trafficking in the most virulent conspiracy theories. The newspaper's cartoons were created by Phillip Rupprecht, whose inaugural appearance in *Der Stürmer* December 1925,[75] and who signed the published cartoons as "Fips."[76] After November 1925, the cartoons regularly appeared with his drawn caricatures complementing the lead articles.[77] Varga does observe that, although Fips' illustrations did not comport with the legal definition of obscenity, many of Streicher's critics believed them to be obscene.[78] At the very least, they were crude, profane, disgusting and even blasphemous. The caricatures of Jews that Fipps drew were of someone who was "short, fat, ugly, unshaven, drooling, sexually perverted, bent-nosed, with pig like eyes, a visual embodiment of the message of the *Stürmer's* articles."[79]

The goal of achieving the "annihilation of European Jewry was part and parcel of the rhetoric in *Der Stürmer*."[80] With the rise of Hitler in 1933, the idea of a "final solution" was within the realm of achievability, with a contemporaneous *Der Stürmer* article stating the following: "therefore the Jewish race must be exterminated (ausgerottet) from beneath the sun."[81] By 1933, five years prior to Streicher's Kristallnacht speech, *Der Stürmer's* circulation reached almost 500,000, festooning "special notice-boards" across Germany, in addition to its presence in the schools.[82] And one month prior to the Kristallnacht speech of November 10, 1938, *Der Stürmer* included the following sentiment in the paper: "Bacteria, vermin and pests cannot be tolerated. For reason of cleanliness and hygiene we must make them harmless by *killing them off*."[83] Irrefutably, Streicher did not mitigate the invectives and vituperations against Jews.

In 1937, the Gauleiter of Danzig credits Julius Streicher and *Der Stürmer* as being indispensable to finding a solution to the Jewish question.[84] In a document dated January 23, 1935, Sami Glucksmann of Danzig filed a lawsuit predicated on claims of libel and blasphemy against four individuals, the first of whom was Julius Streicher, in his capacity as editor-in-chief of *Der Stürmer*.[85] The lawsuit accuses Streicher and his publication of trafficking in lies and false information, utilizing, as he was wont to do, perverted interpretations of sacred Jewish literature as evidence to promulgate his anti-Semitic rhetoric.[86] Glucksmann's goal, in his book *The Forgeries and falsifications in the Antisemitic Literature and My lawsuit Against Julius Streicher & Co.*, was "to expose openly the forged, or distorted Biblical and Talmudic quotations, especially before the eyes of all truth-loving

Christians. At the same time, it is his desire to present, in place of the forgeries and falsifications, the true Jewish teaching and doctrines."[87]

Streicher delivered his post-Kristallnacht speech to over 100,000 people assembled in Nuremberg at Adolf Hitler Square.[88] In his salutation to the crowd, Streicher bemoans the fact that the people of the world cannot be in Nuremberg and Franconia as first-hand witnesses of, and to relish in the deeds of the people supporting the destruction surrounding Kristallnacht. Streicher argues that the destruction was a justifiable act in avenging the killing of vom Rath, ascribing to Grynszpan—only referred to as a "seventeen-year-old Jew"—a synecdochic appellation as "the representative and agent of the Jewish people."[89] Two attributes contribute to the inferior status of the Jews, one based in nature (blood) and one in nurture (education).[90] The Jew's inferiority is attributable to his tainted blood "received...from all the races of the world," and "flows in this bastard race."[91] The tainted blood adversely affects the soul and the Jew's obeisance to the good in life is always superseded by the bad.[92] Not only did the Nazis blame the Jews for sullying the purity and tainting the blood of the white race,[93] but in addition, the Jews caused the decline, not only of Germany, but of "every great civilization," according to Hitler.[94]

However, it is Streicher's soul that has been the subject of scholarly inquiry. As scholars have studied what makes individuals and groups engage in malevolent behaviors over the centuries, Julius Streicher has been a subject of such inquiry as possessing a pathology of the soul and the mind, including its manifestations in a dysfunctional and dangerous rhetoric. Joel Dimsdale is intrigued by the greater harm engendered by disease of the soul than disease of the body: "there are more disorders of the mind than of the body, and they are of a more dangerous nature… the mind, when disordered,…can neither bear nor endure anything and is under the perpetual influence of desires."[95] Dimsdale notes the resonance of Cicero's passage in his Tusculan Disputations, in the persona of Julius Streicher.[96] As effective as his anti-semitic rantings were, Streicher was limited as far as intelligence, and his vulgarity and crudity were matched by an uncanny, preternatural ability to connect with audiences.[97]

Streicher lays the Jew's criminality at the feet of the Jewish education in rabbinical schools.[98] Streicher falsifies tenets of Judaism, as recognized and litigated by Glucksmann. Streicher claims that Jews are not instructed in the Golden Rule, which is categorically untrue, as is evidenced in Leviticus, 19:18. Streicher also claims that Jews are taught that killing Gentiles pleases God, which, too, is categorically untrue. In his "Response to antisemitic distortions of the Talmud," Dr. Maurice Mizrachi states that "the Talmud has been a favorite target of antisemites for at least a millennium," including infractions such as fabrication, truncation, and quotations taken out of their context,[99] and two examples are applicable to Streicher's claims. One claim is that "Jews don't care whether Gentiles live or die," ostensibly using the passage from the Bavli Sanhedrin 37a. However, the Yerushalmi, Sanhedrin Y 4:1 (22a) states, "whoever destroys a life is considered as if he destroyed an entire world; and whoever saves a life is considered as if he saved an entire world."[100] Another of Streicher's claims that you may do whatever you wish to a Gentile is erroneously substantiated with Sofrim 15:10 of the Talmud, where it is written, "[even] the good among the Gentiles must be killed." Dr. Mizrahi responds that the context is "in time of war."[101]

In the coalescing and summative statement of this section of the speech, Streicher claims that both "mixed blood" and education ineluctably contributed to Grynszpan's actions, given their antipathy towards all Gentiles, explicitly saying that the Jews are wholly responsible for the newly implemented draconian measures against them, with their alleged provocation against the German people.[102] Streicher then invokes the infamous "Jewish Question," the answer to which is the equally infamous "Final Solution."[103]

Streicher's publication output was not limited to the adult German audience, strategically, engaging a more expansive demographic with materials adapted for, and appealing to children.

In 1938, Julius Streicher's publishing house put out a children's book *Der Giftpilz* (The Poisonous Mushroom) by Ernst Hiemer, who, in 1934, was hired by Streicher to write articles for *Der Stürmer*.[104] *Der Stürmer* certainly was not subtle in its wish for the complete annihilation of the Jews, with a screed by Hiemer encapsulating the sentiment: "the Jewish menace will thus only be eliminated if Jewry in the whole world has ceased to exist."[105] Mary Mills, in her essay "Propaganda and Children During the Hitler Years," argues that the stories in the picture book purported "to indoctrinate young children in the most extreme anti-Semitism imaginable," as a portent/harbinger of the Final Solution, so tragically and efficaciously realized in 1942 at the Wannsee Conference.[106] As Mills further explains, "without the hate that these books sought to instill into young children, there could not have been a Final Solution."[107] One story in *The Poisonous Mushroom*, referenced in Streicher's November 10, 1938 speech is story #13—"What Christ Said About the Jews." Prior to its final passage, the story ends with a mother's admonition to her children, pictorialized in the story with all eyes a gaze upon Christ on the Crucifix: "When you see the Cross, think of the terrible murder by the Jews on Golgotha. Remember that the Jews are children of the Devil and human murderers."[108]

Streicher's indictments of Jews as murderers continue with two Biblical references: one from the *Ketuvim* and one from the Five Books of Moses. In the speech, the statement "In one night, the Jew butchered 75,000 Persians,"[109] references the Book of Esther, and the holiday of Purim, which commemorates "the deliverance of the Jews from Haman's plot to kill them,"[110] and when Streicher was executed, he uttered "Purim Feast, 1946,"¹¹¹ presumably simpatico with Haman, who was also hanged.

The Book of Esther reference is followed immediately by a reference to Exodus, 12:11 with "As he left Egypt, he killed all the firstborn, that means the whole posterity, of Egypt."¹¹² This reference in Streicher's speech to the killing of the firstborn is to the tenth plague on Passover. One of the most opprobrious motifs associated with anti-Semitism is "blood libel" which accuses Jews of killing Christian children, a false narrative that goes back to the twelfth century,¹¹³ but goes back even further to Apion's work on the second century B.C.E.¹¹⁴ This narrative survived for centuries, and used by Streicher in *Der Stürmer*, including in a special issue published May 1,1934, and titled "Ritual Murder," with the headline, "A Jewish Plan to Murder Non-Jews Unicovered."¹¹⁵ This issue included "an image of Jews filling basins with blood of Christian children, with three crosses in the background,"¹¹⁶ and which Teter claims is "one of the most notorious."¹¹⁷ As explained in the *Holocaust Encyclopedia*, Streicher's Der Stürmer made ample use of the notion of blood libel, implementing "ritual murder imagery."¹¹⁸

The nexus between "blood libel" and Passover is the allegation that Jews used the blood of Christian children ritualistically to bake the matzohs for the Passover.¹¹⁹ The calendrical proximity between Passover and Easter further amplified and exacerbated the false claim of blood libel.¹²⁰

Streicher invokes Grynszpan, first metonymically, and then speculatively, that a seventeen-year-old was sent to Paris to kill a German in the embassy so that he would benefit from the same magnanimous treatment that Scholem Schwarzbard received when he was acquitted of the murder of Symon Petliura,¹²¹ the latter living in exile in Paris, and who had served as commander of the Ukrainian Directory's army. Schwarzbard believed that Petliura was responsible for the pogroms of 1917, which killed 50,000–60,000 Jews, in addition to many more who were wounded or orphaned. and shot him in Paris on May 25, 1926.¹²² In Schwarzbard's defense, his lawyers put the pogroms on trial with Schwarzbard transformed into a "righteous avenger,"¹²³ and as a defendant bearing witness to the criminal acts (of the pogroms), perpetrated by Petliura, the narrative told by the defense exculpated and redeemed Schwarzbard, and their "rhetoric turned vengeance into a quest for humanitarian justice."¹²⁴

Schwarzbard's trial which began October 18, 1927 at Paris' Palais de Justice,¹²⁵ ended on October 26, 1927, with an acquittal after only a little more than three hours of deliberation.¹²⁶ Without denying that he had committed the crime, Schwarzbard pled not guilty, recounting the hundreds of years of antisemitism, with Petliura, a descendant of Khmelnytskyi, one of the perpetrators, whom he believed to be "a great murderer."¹²⁷

In the antepenultimate paragraph of the speech, Streicher again refers to the Jews as murderers. Streicher analogizes Kristallnacht with the Nuremberg synagogue set ablaze in the fourteenth century, adducing the rationale that the synagogue "was not a house of God, but rather a den of murderers."[128] In the penultimate paragraph, Streicher refers to the Jews as "the Devil's people,"[129] and as Bytwerk states, "Christians believed that Christ himself had said of the Jews that their father was the Devil."[130] With unadulterated irony, Streicher exhorts the assembled crowd at the speech "to keep disciplined," and discontinue any demonstration, for their work is done, and Hitler will take up the baton from this point forward.

Gerald B. Winrod, founder of the Defenders of the Christian Faith in 1925, lauded Hitler and Goebbels, and quoted *Der Stürmer*.[131] As detailed by Randall Bytwerk, the New Christian Crusade Church of Louisiana published "The Julius Streicher Memorial Edition," of what was the ritual-murder special edition originally published in 1934.[132] Bytwerk advances the argument that the burgeoning of organizations disseminating racist antisemitic material with facility and ubiquity through the internet and social media sites is as lethal as anything Streicher produced.[133]

Controversy ensues over whether Streicher's crime fit the punishment. Bytwerk notes that Streicher's notoriety and criminality inhered in a rhetoric that was perceptibly distinguishable from the criminal acts of the other International Military Tribunal defendants at Nuremberg.[134] In his groundbreaking book *Atrocity Speech Law: Foundation, Fragmentation, Fruition*, Gregory S. Gordon acknowledges, that, as an artifact, with significant longevity, *Der Stürmer*, "helped mobilize the extermination of six million Jews in the Holocaust," through the rhetoric of dehumanization and hate speech,[135] and the most efficacious way of disseminating this reprehensible rhetoric through the spoken and written modalities of communication.[136] But Gordon concedes, that "within the context of adjudicating crimes arising from inflammatory rhetoric, the jurisprudence has failed to identify categories of hate speech that could help determine how to ease the friction between the competing goals of liberal expression of ideas and meaningful protection of victims."[137] If, indeed, a "compelling empirical connection between hate speech and mass atrocity" can be established, Gordon asks, "what laws, if any, criminalize the dissemination of such rhetoric?"[138] Gordon's theory of the "Unified Liability Theory for Atrocity Speech Law"[139] would facilitate a more nuanced case within international criminal law, so as to determine whether the speech should be prosecuted or protected.[140] The flaw in the Streicher trial entailed the prosecution's "shoehorn[ing] hate speech related offenses into crimes against humanity (persecution) charges."[141]

As explained by Telford Taylor, a member of the prosecution group at the Nuremberg trial, "there was no accusation that Streicher himself had participated in any violence against Jews, so the sole (and difficult) legal issue was whether or not 'incitement' was a sufficient basis for his conviction."[142] And despite the

legal defensibility in Streicher's conviction, Taylor was dismayed by the Tribunals' lack of acknowledgement of mitigating factors, conceding that the newspaper *Der Stürmer*, "however maddening and objectionable it may be, should be touched with criminal accusations only with the greatest caution."[143] Eastwood quotes Taylor in his commenting on the Streicher conviction, that "it is hard to condone the Tribunal's unthinking and callous handling of the Streicher case."[144]
The IMT concluded that,

> Streicher's incitement to murder and extermination at the time when Jews in the east were being killed under the most horrible conditions clearly constitutes persecution on political and racial grounds in connection with War Crimes, as defined by the Charter, and constitutes a Crime Against Humanity.[145]

Some scholars note an incommensurability between the bedrock legal principle, "*nullumcrimen sine lege, nullapoena sine lege*" ("no crime without law, no punishment without law"),[146] and the prosecutorial defects against Streicher, including an incommensurability between his crimes, their lack of codification in the Charter, and the punishment meted out to him, which some view as harsher than the punishments meted out to other defendants whose crimes seemed more legally compatible with Article 6c) of the Charter. Other scholars find justification in Article 6 (c) even in the face of the adjudicatory flaws, in that "crimes against humanity" are not only morally objectionable but deserve to be punished and must be punished because of their abhorrent character if peaceful coexistence in human society is to be maintained."[147]

Alan Olson comments that Karl Jaspers' work, *The Question of German Guilt*, written in the aftermath of WWII, "probably is the most cited of all Jaspers' works being acknowledged by nearly all who venture into an investigation and analysis of the war crimes and atrocities committed by the Third Reich."[148] A less restrictive and potentially more fruitful way of understanding the Tribunal conviction and punishment of Streicher is Jaspers' paradigm of the "four concepts of guilt": criminal, political, moral and metaphysical.[149] Criminal guilt rooted in the legal arena, circumscribes the application of the law to "statutory crimes."[150] Political guilt engages the "culpability of a group or a people for crimes committed by the state to which one belongs as a citizen—even though one may not have actively supported the leaders and agents of the state responsible for these crimes."[151] Moral guilt falls on the individual and their conscience.[152] Unlike political and criminal guilt "determined by external and pragmatic considerations,"[153] moral guilt is "determined by internal and spiritual considerations,"[154] as is the last one—metaphysical guilt.[155] Metaphysical guilt, as Olson suggests, "is the kind of guilt connected with what the Nuremberg Tribunals defined as crimes against humanity."[156] As Jaspers states, "there exists a solidarity among men as human beings that makes each co-responsible for every wrong and every injustice in the world, especially for crimes committed in his presence or with his knowledge."[157] This guilt, more commonly known as "survivor's guilt" occurs when one feels "guilty in a way not adequately conceivable either legally, politically or morally."[158] In invoking the tragic cataclysms that befell the Jews, Jaspers elaborated upon the weight of this survivor's guilt:

> We did not go into the streets when our Jewish friends were led away; we did not scream until we too were destroyed. We preferred to stay alive, on the feeble, if logical ground that our death could not have helped anyone. We are guilty of being alive. We know before God, which deeply humiliates us.[159]

In order to purify one's soul, Jaspers tells the reader "that God is, is enough. When all things fade away, God is—that is the only fixed point."[160]

The rancorous and hatred filled religious rhetoric in Streicher's writings, including his Kristallnacht speech, November 10, 1938, demands a response of succor, possessing redemptive qualities. For reasons already adduced, the criminal response was not wholly satisfactory in a multitude of ways. In terms of political guilt, one must seriously reflect on the citizenry's responsibility. Arguably, a teleological approach provides the most satisfactory response, in that, some dubious means (legally/criminally), might justify greater, more important ends. The devolution in Streicher necessitates a "purification out of the depth of consciousness of guilt."[161] In a sense, the procedural and legal constraints of the international criminal law as realized in the Nuremberg Trial, are surpassed by the "consciousness of guilt" and atonement in moral and metaphysical guilt.

In the last two passages of his Kristallnacht speech, November 10, 1938, Streicher wishes to inflict a "penalty" imposed on Jews, whom he refers to as the "Devil's people." Exhorting the German people to remain disciplined, he tells them that they should not participate in any more demonstrations, since progress has already been made, and the rest should be left to Hitler.

The profane legacy of Julius Streicher and *Der Stürmer* has been dangerously reincarnated with the *Daily Stormer*, the website launched on July 24, 2013, by Andrew Anglin.[162] The site, which is an homage to Streicher's newspaper, traffics in hate speech, antisemitism and racism, and in July 2016, the *Daily Stormer* ranked as "the most popular English-language website of the radical right."[163] On the heels of Trump's victory November 2016, subsequent to Hillary Clinton's concession speech, Anglin said, "Our Glorious Leader has ascended to Go Emperor."[164] Anglin did not exhibit any modesty in taking credit for the website's influence, saying, "Make no mistake about it: we did this. If it were not for us, it wouldn't have been possible."[165] Luke O'Brien characterizes Anglin as "the alt-right's most accomplished propagandist."[166] Although Anglin maintains an ambiguous stance regarding the *Daily Stormer's* ironic stance, the messages seem starkly unambiguous and bereft of the irony trope, where he states, "I do want to gas kikes."[167]

Seventy-seven years ago, Jaspers' portentous statement should be taken to heart:

> And yet, we are oppressed by one nightmarish idea: if a dictatorship in Hitler's style should ever rise in America, all hope would be lost for ages. We in Germany could be freed from the outside. Once a dictatorship has been established, no liberation from within is possible. Should the Anglo-Saxon world be dictatorially conquered from within, as we were, there would no longer be an outside, nor a liberation.[168]

In stunning comments reminiscent of Hitler, Trump claimed that immigrants coming to the borders of the United States were "poisoning the blood of our country."[169] Believe him when he says what he says. The electorate should not be lulled into a Cassandra-like Syndrome of disbelief or complacency. Believe Trump when he says, "No, no, no—other than Day 1," when asked by Fox News host Sean Hannity at a townhall in Davenport, Iowa, "you're not going to be a dictator are you?"[170]

CHAPTER 5: PART 2

Religion and Violence

On November 9, 2018, Josef Schuster, president of Germany's Central Council of Jews, along with President Frank-Walter Steinmeier, German Chancellor Angela Merkel, and other speakers, honored the victims of Kristallnacht and commemorated its eightieth anniversary. Schuster served as the religious representative of victimized people. Through the use of archetypal metaphor of fire among other rhetorical devices, Schuster's words of remembrance sought to provide succor for the painful, tragic, and violent history of Kristallnacht. But equally as important, Schuster raised concerns about the recent resurgence of anti-Semitism, anti-immigration, and violence experienced in contemporary Europe and America.

"SPEECH BY DR. JOSEF SCHUSTER, PRESIDENT OF THE CENTRAL COUNCIL OF JEWS IN GERMANY, AT THE CEREMONY MARKING THE 80TH ANNIVERSARY OF REICHSPOGROMNACHT"[1]

Josef Schuster

Berlin, Germany. November 9, 2018.

Ladies and gentlemen,

It was the middle of the night when the manhole cover flew through the synagogue window. Glass shattered. The next morning, the leader of the congregation was shaken. "It is terrifying to see what force anger and hatred can create," she said.

The manhole cover which hit the synagogue in Gelsenkirchen was not thrown in 1938.

It was 2014.

It is wrong to draw parallels.

Yet when we remember the state-led rioting against Jews in November 1938 80 years ago, we are doing so not just in awareness of the worst crime against humanity in history and focusing on the lessons that we have drawn from it. We are also doing so in the knowledge that injustice is happening to this day.

Things are still happening which bring back horrendous memories.

Such incidents particularly traumatise one group of people, namely the survivors of the Shoah and their descendants who are deeply horrified when they hear such news.

Today, on this day of remembrance, we bow down before the survivors, whether they are here with us today or elsewhere.

And we bow our heads in grief and perpetual remembrance of the six million murdered Jewish women, men and children and all victims of National Socialist crimes.

Even though one day we will have no-one left who themselves witnessed this delirium of destruction, we will never let the flame of remembrance go out.

Ladies and gentlemen,

the targeted, state-led violence against Jews, Jewish businesses and synagogues in November 1938, can be viewed as a staging post on the road to implement the radical National Socialist ideology, indeed to consummate this ideology in horrific fashion.

The night now known as Reichspogromnacht did not come from nowhere. The process to exclude Jews from German and, from 12 March 1938, also from Austrian society had long since been given a legal basis. Upon taking power in 1933, the National Socialist government began laying the legal foundation for excluding Jews from society. In 1935, this process of exclusion reached an initial perverse culmination in the Nuremberg race laws.

And in 1938 alone, countless other steps followed. Jewish citizens, for example, had to register their assets. In May, so-called "Degenerate Art" was seized including that of Jewish artists by dint of their being Jewish. In the euphemistically named June Action, countless Jews were arrested due to minor offences and deported to concentration camps. In July, all Jewish doctors lost their license. And soon afterwards, Jews were forced to use Sara or Israel as middle names – the first visible marking of Jews before the yellow star was introduced in 1941.

You can see just how difficult life became for the Jews in the exhibition "1938 Projekt – Posts from the past." We are presenting parts of this exhibition created by the Leo Baeck Institute today. They are compelling accounts which say so much more than mere numbers.

Late in the evening of 9 November 1938, the violence erupted: SA and SS officers attacked synagogues and Jewish businesses. They attacked thousands of unsuspecting Jews in their homes. All in all, some 1,400 synagogues, half of the synagogues at the time, were damaged or destroyed.

Synagogues here in Berlin, also this one in Rykestrasse, were set alight on the night of 9 to 10 November. The fire was put out pretty quickly but only to protect neighbouring houses.

Some 30,000 Jews were deported to concentration camps. Approximately 1,300 Jewish citizens were murdered or driven to suicide.

The brutal violence opened the eyes of many Jewish citizens. The blind destructive range, the violence which literally exploded – previously they would not have thought the civilised German nation capable of such behaviour. Emigration figures shot up as a result, although new regulations made it extremely difficult to leave.

We now know from reliable sources that Reichspogromnacht was state-controlled. And even back then, most citizens realised that it had not been a spontaneous outpouring of rage, as Goebbels presented it, but that the SA and SS had been acting on orders.

There is one point I would like to make: even if on these days in November it was essentially only the SA and SS who were actively involved, we are still talking about thousands of Germans. The two organisations were so large that the pogrom could easily be launched simultaneously all across the German Reich and in Austria.

Many citizens clearly reacted by distancing themselves from what had happened, even with disgust. This is what most reports tell us. Yet, their reaction gave the Nazis valuable information: hardly anyone protested. There was no opposition to the SA and the SS. There were only isolated cases of harassed Jews receiving assistance. Hitler's reign of terror and anti-Semitic propaganda had borne fruit. After 9 November 1938, the leadership could be sure that our citizens would not get in the way even if greater violence was used against Jews.

They were to be proven right.

There were only very few people who showed human decency and courage. Wilhelm Krützfeld was one of them. In the early hours of 10 November, the Berlin police officer stood with other officers from his beat blocking the path of the SA in front of the New Synagogue in Oranienburger Strasse. He prevented the exterior of the building being set alight and ensured that the fire which had been started inside was put out.

This example of the police officer Wilhelm Krützfeld leaves a deep impression to this day. Many will wonder if they would have had the same courage.

We can of course also ask ourselves this question today. After all, today too, we are dealing with arsonists.

With mental arsonists but also with real ones.

I want to use some statistics to make my point.

In 2016, there were almost 1000 attacks on refugee housing, more than 60 of these were cases of arson. More than 60 cases of arson. That is an average of five arson attacks a month on buildings providing housing for people who have sought refuge here.

In 2017, there were only 16 cases of arson. I tell you this quite deliberately. Sometimes it seems to me that I can hear a sigh of relief that the number of attacks on refugees and refugee housing has dropped significantly.

Yes, they have dropped. But that is no reason for complacency!

The very fact that some 300 refugees were injured in attacks in 2017 alone, that housing for asylum-seekers is a regular target for attacks – this is scandalous!

And it is also a scandal that more and more mosques are being daubed with slogans of hatred or subjected to even more serious attacks.

And it is a scandal the same thing happens to synagogues about every two weeks in Germany although they are protected by the police.

And you will all remember the Jewish restaurant-owner in Chemnitz who was recently and repeatedly attacked by neo-Nazis. Shortly after, in October, neo-Nazis targeted a Persian restaurant in Chemnitz seriously injuring the Iranian owner.

It is a disgrace for our country that such things are happening in Germany in 2018!

It is behind these people who attack refugees, Muslims or Jews, that we find the mental arsonists. My impression is that they are growing in number in Germany.

They are fueling the fear of refugees. With their choice of words and disproportionate level of attention paid to individual incidents, they are inciting the people. They are inciting hatred against asylum-seekers and particularly against Muslims.

A party sitting on the far right in the Bundestag have perfected their skills in incitement. They are mental arsonists.

There is nothing they respect. They instrumentalise the courageous White Rose resistance movement for their own ends. They deride the victims and survivors of the Shoah by relativising National Socialist crimes. They are misrepresenting history and want to destroy our culture of remembrance.

It would have been unbearable for the Jewish community, today, 80 years after Pogromnacht, to have representatives of this party in our midst. That is why this was the only parliamentary group of the German Bundestag which we did not invite.

These forces must not be allowed to gain yet more ground. On the contrary. They must be pushed back so far that they are consigned to oblivion.

After all, to use the words of Karl Jaspers, there must be no freedom to destroy freedom.

It is up to us!

Each of us bears responsibility for ensuring that respect and tolerance define Germany's profile.

What we need now are courageous and convinced democrats. We need people who show civil courage. People who speak out.

Civil courage starts in everyday situations. Each and every one of us can ask ourselves: do I speak out when people tell jokes about gays in the pub? Or if people speak disrespectfully about women? Or if people talk about the alleged influence of Jews from the American east coast?

Or am I afraid of being seen as a spoilsport or a stick-in-the-mud. Do I just try and fit in? Do I remain silent or do I chuckle along so as not to stand out from the crowd? Do I pretend not to hear if a colored man is insulted in the train?

If we do not stand up for the values anchored in our Basic Law, for human dignity, when it comes to the small stuff, we cannot expect it to work on the big stuff.

As Richard von Weizsäcker put it in his famous speech marking the 40th anniversary of the end of the war, the Weimar Republic did not fail because there were too many Nazis too early, but because for too long there were too few democrats.

This is an accurate analysis and highlights precisely the difference between then and now.

Today there are enough democrats. There is no risk attached to standing up for basic rights. We need to remember, we are serving as a role model in the way we behave.

No child is born a racist.

No child is born an anti-Semite.

And yet the word "Jew" is used as an insult in school playgrounds.

That is why above all teachers need to be courageous and convinced democrats. Whether in sport, chemistry or religious education lessons - anti-Semitism and racism are never acceptable. The context is immaterial. There can be no understanding for anti-Semitism and racism. There has to be a clear red line here.

The cultural scholars Aleida and Jan Assmann, who have just been awarded the Peace Prize of the German Book Trade, found wonderful words in their acceptance speech:

"There have to be undisputed convictions and a basic consensus such as the Constitution, the division of powers, the independence of the judiciary and human rights. Not every dissenting voice warrants respect."

These convictions, this basis consensus do exist in Germany. Yet they are being called into question by the far right in a manner we have not seen for some time. That is why we need to defend this consensus.

In recent years, we have taken democracy and the rule of law for granted. Perhaps too much for granted.

Yet now we sense that democracy is not a matter of course. We have to do something for it. We have to be courageous. And we need to make both the coming generations and people from other cultures and political systems into convinced democrats.

And that is actually a wonderful task!

And if I think of the demonstrations we have seen in recent months whether under the hashtag "We are more", "Welcome United", "Indivisible" or "Heart not hassle", then I sense that something is happening.

The citizens of Germany are taking to their feet. There is a sense of a new awakening.

Today, on this day so ambivalent for Germany, we are remembering above all Reichspogromnacht. But we do not want to forget the year 1989. On 9 November 1989, the Wall fell and Germany attained its unity in freedom. The country began its journey to shared democracy peacefully and without violence.

Today, the citizens are again taking to the streets together to campaign for human rights, against racism and anti-Semitism, in their hundreds and thousands. Hundreds and thousands of courageous and convinced democrats. They are not letting Germany simply drift to the right. They are fighting for the basic consensus. They make me confident about the future.

It is the dawn of a new era where Germany makes respect into one of its core values.

Ladies and gentlemen,

in the year 1938, a 12-year-old Jewish boy from Vienna uttered the following words:

"Mum, if we are really so awful and no other country wants to take us in, it is better to call it a day and turn on the gas-tap."

Never again must we find ourselves in a situation where a human being, worse still, a child, experiences such desperation because of his background.

Thank you very much!

* * *

RHETORICAL ANALYSIS

In a ceremony on November 9, 2018, Josef Schuster, president of Germany's Central Council of Jews, along with President Frank-Walter Steinmeier, German Chancellor Angela Merkel, and other speakers, honored the victims of Kristallnacht and commemorated its eightieth anniversary. The ceremony culminated with a multimedia presentation featuring eight personal stories and experiences of German and Austrian Jews from the 1938 Project.[2]

Remembrance commemorations and memorials are patently epideictic occasions. Schuster served as the religious representative of a victimized people. His words of remembrance sought to provide succor for the painful, tragic, and violent history of Kristallnacht. But equally as important, Schuster raised concerns about the recent resurgence of anti-Semitism, anti-immigration, and violence experienced in Europe and America. Schuster opened his speech with a narrative episode involving a manhole covering flying through the window of a synagogue and glass shattering. Such a destructive image appeared to his audience to be an allusion to Kristallnacht. Then, with suspenseful, anachronistic peripety, Schuster noted "the manhole cover…was not thrown in 1938. It was 2014."[3] From that moment forward, Schuster made the case for his rhetorical use of historical analogs. In drawing contemporaneous parallels to the rise of anti-Semitism, white supremacy, toxic nationalism, and xenophobia endorsed by alt-right, anti-immigrant, and populist political parties like the Alternative für Deutschland (AfD),[4] Schuster offered a prophetic warning akin to what Karl Marx penned in chapter one of *The Eighteenth Brumaire of Louis Bonaparte*, when history repeats itself a first time it is tragic.[5] As Schuster observed, history has in fact repeated itself with an increased malice towards Jews, Muslims, and immigrants; it is tragic, it is traumatic, it is violent, and demonstrates a painful reminder of what a rancorous rhetoric of religious intolerance and indifference can ultimately unleash.

Schuster impressed upon the audience the curative need for the virtue of "civil courage" and called for "committed democrats" to "speak out" today in contrast to the indifference of the German people of 1938 who stood by as the glass of shop windows shattered and synagogues and sacred scriptures smoldered. Keenly attuned to the rhetorical relationship between *kairos* and *topos*, Schuster delivered his address from the Rykestrasse synagogue, the very house of worship which was burned on the same night in 1938 where 91 people were killed, 7,500 businesses were pillaged, and Torah scrolls were desecrated. Beyond this, and most egregious, the painful lesson of Kristallnacht that Schuster shared was that such silence and dearth of protest signaled to the Nazis and the National Socialist government that far worse crimes against humanity could be and were meted out on the Jewish people.

Described as a "rousing speech,"[6] Schuster's commemorative address inventively intertwined statistics, testimony, stories, rhetorical questions, historical allusions, and adeptly employed the archetypal metaphors of fire and arson. Schuster's address accomplished two interrelated rhetorical goals in accordance with the sacred succor/rancor armature that we have adopted as our critical approach to analyzing speeches addressing the *topoi* of religion and tragic violence. First, with the spirit of "never again," in his epideictic remembrance of Reichspogromnacht, Schuster employed the strategy of historical analogy to call for action against the alarming contemporaneous exigence facing Germany and many other Western nations experiencing an increase in far-right, hyper nationalistic ideologies, and populist political movements.[7] Yet, Schuster is not the first to imply a historical analogue regarding Kristallnacht. Eberhard Bethge recounts an anecdote about the German theologian, Dietrich Bonhoeffer, who shortly after surveying the events of Kristallnacht in Berlin is known to have annotated the biblical entry of Psalm 74:8 with the date of Kristallnacht. Psalm 74:8 references when the Babylonians destroyed the Temple and deracinated and deported the ancient Israelites. According to Bethge, Bonhoeffer was deeply moved and is said to have felt the burden of solidarity with the despairing on the night of the 1938 pogrom, thereby establishing a historical, and, as David Clark has argued, a theological, linkage between Psalm 74:8 and Kristallnacht.[8]

In the epideictic genre, auditors can expect to hear the application and amplification of more stylistic filagree and figural flourishes. Schuster does not disappoint. The second main trope Schuster employs to reinforce the link between past and present is the metaphor of fire. Early in the speech, after depicting the destructive violence of Kristallnacht, and in particular the burning of synagogues, shops, and scrolls, Schuster acknowledged that such "injustice is happening to [sic] this day…in Germany in 2018."[9] Schuster then presented statistical data that of the 1000 attacks on refugee housing in 2016, sixty of these cases involved arson.[10] Prior to his presentation of statistics, Schuster used the Promethean metaphor of "mental arsonists" several times to claim that the current violent attacks on refugees, Muslims, and Jews are motivated by an odious propaganda. "Today… we are dealing with…mental arsonists but also real ones."[11]

Schuster further solidifies the temporal link between the past and present with the literal analogy of real arsonists of 1938 and 2018. But what are we to make of the figurative analogy to "mental arsonists?" Schuster's aureate metaphor of "mental arsonists" is eminently suited to his occasion and kindles a percussive vivacity of its own, illuminating and crisscrossing not only semantic fields but also temporal dimensions. The metaphor of mental arsonists may not necessarily make an argument, but rhetorically it vivifies his statistics by elucidating how ignitable ideology and propaganda can be, and how hate speech can spread like wildfire and consume the mind. Similarly, on the rhetorical functions of the archetypal metaphor of fire, Michael Osborn wrote, "Because of its spontaneous generation and rapid reproduction, fire can represent also the birth of an idea and how it proliferates in the mind. Furthermore, just as a torch spreads flame from one place to another, and idea can leap from one mind to another."[12]

Kristallnacht was the tragic telos of not only empirical arson, but ideological. Arson is a criminal activity motivated by a deep seeded anger and typically involves some kind of accelerant, (metaphorically, words) to ignite a conflagration. Schuster awakened in the hearts and minds of his German audience a truth, when he stated, "No child is born a racist. No child is born an anti-Semite."[13] Consequently, the inculcated tragic and violent motives of "mental arson" are doused with ideological accelerant that feeds, inflames, and incites hatred, racism, intolerance, and indifference. To this point, as Schuster had laid out earlier in his speech, the pogrom of 1938 "did not come from nowhere."[14] Long before the yellow star was implemented, the anti-Semitic policies of the Nazis were part of a programmatic propaganda campaign and manifested in the material practices of legal exclusion, asset registration, and false arrests.[15] This point is unscored by Kenneth Burke in his prescient 1939 article "The Rhetoric of Hitler's Battle." Burke's psycho-textual analysis of Hitler's projection devices, scapegoating tactics, and "bastardized religious patterns," among other "medicinal appeals" to what ailed Germany, were not exactly hiding in *Mein Kampf*. Burke examined the vocabulary of Hitler's subtending motives and explicated how they would be carried out to their tragic telos.[16]

Diabolic discourse like this reaches its odious apex in violence, but perhaps most tragic is when, through a heinous hegemony, oppressed beings are themselves persuaded by and believe the mental arson to the point of being complicit in their own fatality. This traumatic reality is instantiated at the close of Schuster's address when he shared the shocking testimony of a twelve-year-old Jewish boy from Vienna, who in the 1938 uttered, "Mum, if we are really so awful and no other country wants to take us in, it is better to call it a day and turn on the gas-tap."[17] Yet, Schuster's commemorative oration called the German people to a "new awakening" despite the mental arsonists' desire to destroy the culture of remembrance. He remarked "we will never let the flame of remembrance go out"[18] lest the world succumb to historical amnesia and necessitate Elie Wiesel's metaphor of "memory transfusion."[19]

Osborn's critical insights on the metaphor of fire are aglow in Schuster's remarks as he carried the inferno symbolism further, "they [mental arsonists] are fueling the fear of refugees." With their choice of words…they are inciting hatred…and want to destroy our culture of remembrance. Since fire as, Osborn argues, is the most active and transformative of nature's elements it maintains a protean and polysemous status.[20] Fire can be viewed as a pharmakon, both as infernal force of incineration and destruction as well as a purifying succor of eternal, covenantal remembrance.[21] The rhetorical manner in which Schuster transvalues the metaphorical material and spiritual fire functions much like Kenneth Burke explicates, "Language develops by metaphorical extension, in borrowing words from the realm of the corporeal, visible, tangible and applying them by analogy to the realm of the incorporeal, invisible, intangible; and finally, poets regain the original relation, in reverse, by a 'metaphorical extension' back from the intangible into a tangible equivalent (the first 'carrying-over' from the material to the spiritual being compensated by a second 'carrying-over' from the spiritual back into the material)"[22]

Moreover, the rhetorical alchemy of Schuster's metaphorical fire transmutes the rancorous heat of hatred and violence manifested at Kristallnacht and in Shoah crematoriums to a sacred succor of infinite memorial. A metaphorical metamorphosis like this performs what Paul Ricoeur refers to as "redescriptions." Ricoeur argues, "metaphor is a rhetorical process by which discourse unleashes the power that certain fictions have to redescribe reality." By linking fiction and redescription in this way, we restore the full depth of meaning to Aristotle's discovery in the *Poetics* that the *poiesis* of language arises out of the connection between mythos (*muthos*) and *mimesis*.[23] The metaphoric figures of fire and arson interlarded with references to the historicity of Bonhoeffer's Psalm, the persecution of ancient Jews in Babylon, Kristallnacht itself, and Schuster's own connective chronicling of contemporary hate crimes indeed demonstrate Ricoeur's observation of metaphor's rhetorical power of melding the mythic and the mimetic. Under the dynamic trope of metaphor, Schuster's speech reveals not merely a mechanistic repetition/representation of, or allusion to, historical events but an inventive faculty for unifying mythos and mimesis, poetry and rhetoric, history and the *hic et nunc*, engendering a radically new palimpsest predicated on hoary and tragic motives.

The strength of Schuster's analogical claims is that both his literal and temporal (historical to contemporary comparisons of violence, 1938–2018) as well as his figural, metaphorical comparisons ("mental arsonists") are united and work in rhetorical harmony with each other. His transhistorical analogy provides persuasive evidence in the form of statistics and makes an argument for the resemblance of cases of violent, destructive arson perpetrated against Jewish people in 1938 and 2018. The brilliance of Schuster's fire trope is his eloquence draws on the pharmakon-like quality and hermeneutic variance of fire, transvaluating meanings from hate to the healing needed to heed the lessons of history, from a rancorous rhetorical poison to a palliative panegyric on the eightieth anniversary of Kristallnacht, and from violent destruction and incineration to the eternal flame of remembrance, enlightenment, and covenantal promise. Overall, Schuster's speech attempts to perform the religious and rhetorical act of what Kant has called "regeneration," the healing and hopeful capacity for human change after experiencing radical immorality and tragic violence.

CHAPTER 6: PART 1

Borders/Immigration and Violence

In Fort Wayne, Indiana, on June 14, 2018, Attorney General Jeffery Sessions, spokesperson for the Trump Administration, propagated a divisive immigration policy. The audience was the Fort Wayne Rotary Club, the Fort Wayne Business Forum, the Allan County Bar Association, and local, state, and federal law enforcement officers. One of the main topoi of Sessions's speech included articulating the criteria for asylum.

> "ATTORNEY GENERAL SESSIONS ADDRESSES
> RECENT CRITICISMS OF ZERO TOLERANCE
> BY CHURCH LEADERS"[1]
>
> Jefferson Sessions
>
> Fort Wayne, Indiana. June 14, 2018

Thank you, Tom for that kind introduction; thank you for your eight years of service to the Department of Justice, and congratulations on your appointment as United States Attorney.

Thank you to the Fort Wayne Rotary Club, the Fort Wayne Business Forum, the Allan County Bar Association—and most of all thank you to law enforcement officers from the federal, state, and local levels.

Thank you all for being here.

It is good to be back in the Hoosier state. On my previous trip, I enjoyed being with your dedicated and professional Attorney General Curtis Hill as we explored the 10 Point Coalition neighborhood.

This is an exciting and important time. We have an historic opportunity to—finally—fix an immigration system that has been broken for decades.

The American people have been begging and pleading with our elected officials for an immigration system that is lawful and that serves our national interest—one that we can be proud of. There is nothing mean-spirited about that. They are right, decent and just to ask for this.

But for more than a decade now, the elites and Washington insiders have prioritized the interests of certain corporate interests and activist groups over what is best for the American people.

Beginning in 2009, the previous Administration released most aliens apprehended at the border who requested asylum into the United States with a document asking them to show up for a hearing at some later date. Word spread quickly that by asserting a fear of returning to one's home country, one could remain in the United States.

The results are just what one would expect. The number of illegal entrants has surged. Asylum claims skyrocketed, and the percentage of meritorious asylum claims—those actually granted—declined.

That's because the vast majority of the claims are not valid. For the last five years, only 20 percent of claims have been found to be meritorious after a hearing before an Immigration Judge. In addition, some fifteen percent are found invalid by during the initial screening by the U.S. Citizenship and Immigration Service.

In addition, in 2009, the Department of Homeland Security reviewed more than 5,000 initial asylum screenings. By 2016, only seven years later, that number had increased to 94,000. The number of these aliens placed in immigration court proceedings went from fewer than 4,000 to more than 73,000 by 2016—nearly a 19-fold increase.

This cannot continue.

Compounding this problem, the previous administration wouldn't prosecute illegal aliens who entered the country with children. It was de facto open borders.

The results were unsurprising. More and more illegal aliens started showing up at the border with children. To illustrate, in 2013, there were fewer than 15,000 family units apprehended crossing our border illegally between ports of entry. Five years later, it was more than 75,000—a five-fold increase in five years. It didn't even have to be their child—it could be anyone. You can imagine the horrible abuses that resulted.

The open borders, pro-amnesty crowd encouraged that—and they have the gall to attack those of us who want to end this lawlessness and the dangers these children face.

And then there was the time that President Obama used his pen and phone to do something he said he couldn't legally do. In July 2012—a few months before he was up for re-election—President Obama announced that he would give legal status to 800,000 illegal aliens—along with work authorization and other benefits, like Social Security. Congress had rejected this proposal on multiple occasions—but President Obama did it anyway.

Again, the result was not a surprise: the number of unaccompanied alien children arriving at our border nearly doubled in one year. The next year, it doubled again.

That could hardly be a coincidence. The President had sent the wrong message. Criminal networks spread the lie that kids could get amnesty. As a result, tens of thousands of vulnerable children made the dangerous journey North—with terrible humanitarian consequences.

And then, in 2014, the Obama Administration doubled down and attempted to expand its unlawful amnesty to any illegal alien here since 2010.

Towards the end of the last administration, prosecutions for illegal entry and reentry both declined, and sanctuary policies were encouraged, eroding relationships with state and local law enforcement officers that had taken decades to build.

Sanctuary policies are when cities or states refuse to cooperate with federal immigration enforcement. If they've got somebody in custody who is wanted for deportation—they release them back into the community. At their root, they are a rejection of all immigration law. If you won't deport somebody who came here illegally and then committed another crime—then who will you deport?

Meanwhile in Congress, efforts to end illegal immigration have been blocked at every turn. Any law enforcement policies are attacked by open borders radicals and well-paid lobbyists.

Every time something is proposed that would end illegal immigration, it gets blocked. If it works, it gets blocked. If it doesn't work—if it won't end illegal immigration—then the elites and the Washington insiders are all for it.

Eric Holder—my predecessor as Attorney General of the United States—supports sanctuary laws. Here is his legal defense of sanctuary policies: "states have the power over the health and safety of their residents and the allocation of state resources." That's it. It's almost a non sequitur. The question is whether cities and states have the right under the Constitution to actively undermine the supreme law of the land—a question that has been settled repeatedly in the negative since 1819.

Our elites—who seem to think that they are also our betters—don't like our immigration system; they know they don't have the votes to change it—and so they have willingly embraced illegality. It is outrageous.

But the Trump administration is working to restore legality to the system and undo the damage that was done in the Obama years.

Unfortunately, there has been a lot of misinformation out there on what we at the Department of Justice are doing. The reports have been so wrong that some people might even call it "fake news."

So let me clear a few things up.

Yes, we are pursuing a "zero tolerance" prosecution policy at the border.

Under the laws of this country, illegal entry is a misdemeanor. Re-entry after having been deported is a felony.

Under the law, we are supposed to prosecute these crimes. Accordingly, I have ordered our prosecutors to pursue 100 percent of the illegal entries on the Southwest border that DHS refers to us.

If you cross the Southwest border unlawfully, then the Department of Homeland Security will arrest you and the Department of Justice will prosecute you. That is what the law calls for—and that is what we are going to do. Having children does not give you immunity from arrest and prosecution. It certainly doesn't give immunity to American citizens.

However, we are not sending children to jail with their parents. The law requires that children who cannot be with their parents be placed in custody of the Department of Health and Human Services within 72 hours.

We currently spend more than $1 billion a year in taxpayer dollars taking care of unaccompanied illegal alien minors. Most are in HHS custody. They are provided food, education in their native language, health and dental care, and transported to their destination city—all at taxpayer expense.

It should be noted the perils to which these parents subject their children. Hundreds of aliens die every year trying to make it to the border to illegally enter this country. In many cases, children are trafficked, abused, or recruited by criminal gangs. No one should subject their child to this treacherous journey—and yet the open borders lobby encourages it every day.

But the Trump administration is ending the Obama-era incentives to bring children here illegally. Last September, the Trump administration ended DACA. We agree with President Obama: he didn't have the legal authority to give any legal status to illegal aliens without Congress. That's why this unlawful policy is over.

And now that DACA is over, the criminals can't spread the lie that kids can get amnesty.

Our policies are discouraging people from making children endure that treacherous journey. Everything the open borders lobby is doing is encouraging that and endangering these children. It's that simple.

There's only one way to stop this and that is for people to stop smuggling children. Stop crossing the border illegally with your children. Apply to enter lawfully. Wait your turn.

We have also returned the asylum process to what Congress intended it to be.

If you don't meet the requirements for asylum in this country, then you do not receive asylum here. That should not be a controversial idea.

Let me take an aside to discuss concerns raised by our church friends about separating families. Many of the criticisms raised in recent days are not fair or logical and some are contrary to law.

First- illegal entry into the United States is a crime—as it should be. Persons who violate the law of our nation are subject to prosecution. I would cite you to the Apostle Paul and his clear and wise command in Romans 13, to obey the laws of the government because God has ordained them for the purpose of order.

Orderly and lawful processes are good in themselves and protect the weak and lawful.

Our policies that can result in short term separation of families is not unusual or unjustified. American citizens that are jailed do not take their children to jail with them. And non-citizens who cross our borders unlawfully—between our ports of entry—with children are not an exception.

They are the ones who broke the law, they are the ones who endangered their own children on their trek. The United States on the other hand, goes to extraordinary lengths to protect them while the parents go through a short detention period.

Please note, Church friends, that if the adults go to one of our many ports of entry to claim asylum, they are not prosecuted and the family stays intact pending the legal process.

The problem is that it became well known that adults with children were not being prosecuted for unlawful entry and the numbers surged from 15,000 in 2013 to 75,000 four years later. That policy was a declaration of open borders for family units.

Importantly, children are far more at risk attempting entry in remote areas.

I have given the idea of immigration much thought and have considered the arguments of our Church leaders. I do not believe scripture or church history or reason condemns a secular nation state for having reasonable immigration laws. If we have them, then they should be enforced. A mere desire to benefit from entry to the nation does not justify illegal entry. And, there are of course adverse consequences to illegal actions.

Once again, let me state that this nation has perhaps the most generous laws in the world.

My request to these religious leaders who have criticized the carrying out of our laws to also speak up strongly to urge anyone who would come here to apply lawfully, to wait their turn, and not violate the law.

Under the INA, asylum is available for those who leave their home country because of persecution or fear on account of race, religion, nationality, membership in a particular social group, or political opinion. Asylum was never meant to solve all problems—even all serious problems—that people face every day all over the world.

You may have heard that I have "restricted" asylum eligibility or "denied" asylum eligibility to certain people. But that's not exactly right.

I have not made new law—I have simply restated and implemented what Congress has passed: asylum is generally not for those who have suffered a private act of violence. It is for members of groups who are persecuted by the state or whom the state will not protect from persecution. Members of those groups cannot go somewhere else in their home country. Most victims of private crimes can.

Think about it. There are victims of crime all over the world—1.2 million violent crimes are committed every year in this country alone. Are all 1.2 million of these victims automatically entitled to asylum in Canada, the United Kingdom, or anywhere else they choose?

We have to make a choice: do we continue to allow the word to spread that you can come here illegally and there will be no consequences—or do we finally send the message that we enforce our laws? In the Trump administration, we enforce the law.

There is no right or entitlement—legal or moral—to come to this country. Immigration is a privilege that the American people have chosen to grant in certain cases. And let me note how generous the American people are: we allow in 1.1 million legal immigrants on a path to citizenship every year. Another 700,000 come here explicitly for jobs. Another half a million come here to attend our universities and colleges.

But we've got a choice here. We either have open borders or we have laws. It's one or the other.

Some people in the media have chosen to attack us for enforcing the law. That doesn't surprise me. But I'm not ashamed of the United States of America. I am not going to apologize for carrying out our laws. That is my duty.

President Trump ran for office promising to end the illegality and to fix our system. We are carefully and lawfully stopping the abuses in our system.

It is not a bad thing, but a good thing that President Trump is keeping his word. We intend to follow the mandate that he has received from the people. I embrace it.

President Trump made a generous offer to the Democrats in Congress. He offered to give DACA recipients true legal status if we can build a wall, close the loopholes, and switch from chain migration and the visa lottery to a merit-based system. The Democrats' refusal of this offer is baffling. He simply asked that they agree to a permanent solution to the problem. Why wouldn't you want to end the illegality?

Our goal is not radical. What is radical is the open borders policies that have been pushed on us time and again by the elites and the Washington insiders.

Our goal is that immigrants should apply, wait their turn, and that people stop making that dangerous trek across the desert rather than coming here unlawfully. If they meet the standards, then they can be admitted—and those standards should advance the national interest.

If we succeed in this—if we finally get a system we can be proud of—then we will start a virtuous cycle of lawfulness, safety, and prosperity.

The American people have been patient. We have been waiting for 30 years. They want us to seize this opportunity that we have right now. It's time that we finally deliver a lawful system of immigration that benefits them.

* * *

RHETORICAL ANALYSIS

When Jeff Sessions, the first Attorney General in the Trump Administration, spoke to an assembled group of civic and business leaders in Fort Wayne, Indiana on June 14, 2018, he did not do so in a vacuum. His message reflected a controversial policy promulgated by the Trump Administration, for which Sessions became its mouthpiece.[2]

On May 7, 2018, Jeff Sessions, then Attorney General of the United States, delivered a speech in San Diego, California, which the Department of Justice's *Justice News* titled "Remarks Discussing the Immigration Enforcement Actions of the Trump Administration."[3] In this speech, Sessions attempted to articulate a more effective and expedient policy for the immigration problem – which many see as one of the most pressing problems that the United States has grappled with and continues to do so. The problem is most critically and urgently manifest on the borders of California and Arizona and on the Southwest border of Texas. Sessions laid out five conditional statements, the initial one serving as the overarching one, and the four subsequent statements serving as the criteria of unlawful border crossing. Sessions states, "I have put in place a 'zero tolerance policy' for illegal entry on the Southwest border."[4] Then he articulates the overarching legal infraction and consequence as a conditional statement, followed by the four conditionally stated criteria statements:

> If you smuggle illegal aliens across the border, then we will prosecute you. If you are smuggling a child, then we will prosecute you and that child will be separated from

you as required by law. If you make false statements to an immigration officer or file a fraudulent asylum claim, that is a felony. If you help others to do so, that's a felony too. You're going to jail.[5]

Through extensive media reports, the American public witnessed the most conspicuously cruel and inhumane tenet of the Zero Tolerance policy. Zero tolerance has been used in the law metaphorically and euphemistically, but Sessions used it and applied it literally.[6] Notwithstanding the government's desires to mitigate access, the audio and video documentation, including testimony from eyewitness accounts, was stunning and horrifying. Children and infants were taken from their parents' arms, in some cases, literally ripping them from each other's embrace.[7] Efren Olivares, the racial and economic justice director for the Texas Civil Rights project, distilled the essence of the tragically ill-conceived policy in saying, "the big problem is that the children are being taken away before there is any determination about not only the parents' criminal liability but also their potential immigration relief."[8] Once the parents are deemed "unlawful immigrants," they are taken into federal criminal custody, at which point their children are considered unaccompanied alien minors and taken away.[9]

On June 9, the month after Sessions' zero tolerance policy pronouncement in San Diego, the United Methodist Church's (UMC) Rio Texas Conference advanced a resolution exhorting the Department of Justice to "immediately discontinue separating children from their families due to the 'zero tolerance' policy."[10] The United Methodist Council of Bishops urged the government to dispense with the family separations.[11] The United Methodist Women supported the epistolary "Women of Faith Cry Out to Keep Families Together," sent to Kristjen Nielsen, then Secretary of Homeland Security. The clarity in the women's impassioned admonition to Nielsen cannot be misconstrued:

> We *know* the harm we are doing to children with this policy, which makes this deliberated separating of children from their parents for the intent of punishing the family particularly vile. This must stop now.[12]

The United Board of Church and Society urged people to contact Congressional leaders, write op-ed essays and connect with "local immigrant advocacy and support networks."[13] High profile members of faith communities vehemently rebuked the policy as well. An ardent supporter of Trump, Rev. Franklin Graham, the late Rev. Billy Graham's son, denounced the administration's zero tolerance policy as "disgraceful" due to families being "ripped apart."[14] Cardinal Daniel DiNardo, the archbishop in Galveston/Houston said, "Our government has the discretion in our laws to ensure that young children are not separated from their parents and exposed to irreparable harm and trauma."[15]

As if the controversy surrounding the policy had not already reached a fever pitch, smacking of xenophobia, physical and emotional cruelty, Sessions' speech of June 14, 2018, "Recent Criticisms of Zero Tolerance by Church Leaders,"[16] was his egregious and ineffectual attempt to refute the criticisms and salvage the moral legitimacy of the policy as well as his own ethos as a man of faith and as a member of the UMC.

The response to Sessions' May 18 policy announcement invited vociferous colloquies which escalated after Sessions' June 14, 2018 speech in Fort Wayne, Indiana, to an audience comprised of the Fort Wayne Rotary Club, the Fort Wayne Business Forum, the Allan County Bar Association, and local, state and federal law enforcement officers. The impetus necessitating the delivery of this speech was the blowback from the religious communities, most pointedly the UMC.

In his June 14, 2018 speech in Fort Wayne, Indiana, Sessions stipulates the criteria for asylum: "persecution or fear on account of race, religion, nationality, membership in a particular social group, or political opinion."[17] He continues by parsing a false dilemma between people who "have suffered a private act of violence" and "members of groups who are persecuted by the state or whom the state will not protect from persecution."[18] Sessions erroneously sees the former as singular non-generalizable acts of violence as opposed to generalizable persecution victimizing recognizable, arguably capriciously limited demographic cohorts.[19] Clearly, this argument is a stark contravention of the Board of Immigration Appeals' (BIA's) 2014 precedent in Matter of A-R-C-G.

As integral to the cruelty contemporaneous with the Zero Tolerance policy in late spring 2018 engineered by Trump advisor Stephen Miller and Attorney General Jeff Sessions, the latter issued the decision Matter of A-B as an overruling of BIA.[20] In Matter of A-R-C-G, the BIA concluded that "married women in Guatemala, who are unable to leave their relationship" can be construed as "a particular social group," and "as a basis for asylum in the United States."[21] Menke observes that the BIA's 2014 decision affirmed "the validity of a particular social group of domestic violence victims."[22]

A significant part of the UMC's outrage was the use of the Bible—a touchstone for moral teachings—which, in this context, was perverted to justify the policy—a policy distinguished by its inhumanity and incontrovertible cruelty. In a letter dated July 18, 2018 sent to Rev. Boykin and Rev. Wines, approximately 640 clergy and laity of the UMC issued a complaint against Jeff Sessions, a member of the UMC in Mobile, Alabama as well as an active churchgoer in Arlington, Virginia.[23] In the complaint, the complainants claim that Sessions' zero tolerance policy "led to harm against thousands of vulnerable humans," urging him to "step back from his harmful actions and work to repair the damage he is currently causing to immigrants, particularly children and families."[24]

Based on Paragraph 2702.3 of the 2016 United Methodist Book of Discipline, they officially charged Sessions in his capacity as Attorney General and member of the UMN in Mobile, Alabama and Alexandria, Virginia with four stunningly serious chargeable offenses: "child abuse, immorality, racial discrimination and dissemination of doctrines contrary to the standards of doctrine of the UMC."[25] Subsumed as an evidentiary example within the last charge is Sessions' "misuse of Romans 13," which the charge states "is in stark contrast to Disciplinary commitments to supporting freedom of conscience and resistance to unjust laws."[26] Ironically, in trying to conciliate an audience comprised of people of faith in his June 14, 2018 speech, he annihilated any potential goodwill through his interpolation and mischaracterization of Romans 13. What statement in Sessions' speech could have precipitated such a hue and a cry by the faith community?

> Let me take an aside to discuss concerns raised by our church friend about separating families. Many of the criticisms raised in recent days are not fair or logical and some are contrary to law. First—illegal entry into the United States is a crime—as it should be. Persons who violate the law of our nation are subject to prosecution. I would cite you to the Apostle Paul and his clear and wise command in Romans 13, to obey the law of the government because God has ordained them for the purpose of order. Orderly and lawful processes are good in themselves and protect the weak and lawful.[27]

That one line referencing Romans 13 sparked vociferous outrage, perceived by many as a misplaced strategy to appeal to an audience, comprised in part, of those who identify as individuals of faith. Factually, the contextual reference to Romans 13 is steeped in the ignominious annals of American history. As recounted by historian John Fea, this verse was used by Southerners in the nineteenth century to defend slavery and the Fugitive Slave Act.[28] Fea also said that, few references are made to Romans 13 post Civil war since "the passage's message about submitting to authority is regarded as un-American,"[29] and Sessions' intent, in the manipulation of Scripture, was a justification of his political agenda.[30]

Critics argue that the passage cited by Sessions is utilized as a fallacious appeal to authority in which Sessions disregards the summative jussive statement in Romans 13:9, "Thou shalt love thy neighbor as thyself."[31] Gabriel Salguero reinforces the critique of Sessions' misuse of Romans 13 by stating that to fully understand Romans 13, Romans 12 (specifically Romans 12:9) must be incorporated into the hermeneutic: "*Let* love be without dissimulation. Abhor that which is evil; cleave to that which is good."[32]

The emotional appeals in Sessions's June 14, 2018 speech are revelatory of the ostensibly opaque act of violence embedded in the rhetoric, the pathos, and the consequences of the real-life tragedy, and which are best understood through Aristotle's *Rhetoric* and *Poetics*.

Sessions is unequivocally exhibiting hubris which translates as insolence.[33] As an excursus of the term in Aristotle's *Poetics*, Eugene Garver states that hubris is "wanton violence, arising from the pride of strength, passion, etc."[34] Garver adds that, for Aristotle, hubris can be understood as a crime, even be committed "by words as well as deeds,"[35] The insolence is distinguished by the individual feeling "superior to others when ill-treating them."[36] Sessions clearly sees himself as superior, instantiating Aristotle's characterization of insolence:

> A man expects to be specially respected by his inferiors in birth, in capacity, in goodness, and generally in anything in which he is much their superior: as where money is concerned a wealthy man looks for respect from a poor man; where speaking is concerned, the man with a turn for oratory looks for respect from one who cannot speak; the ruler demands the respect of the ruled, and the man who thinks he ought to be a ruler demands the respect of the man whom he thinks he ought to be ruling.[37]

And this last clause is the crux of Sessions's hubristic emotional appeal. In exemplifying this point, Aristotle invokes two lines from Homer's *The Iliad*: "Great is the wrath of kings, whose father is Zeus almighty,"[38] and "Yea, but his rancor abideth long afterward also."[39] Sessions feebly attempts to hide the rancor with succor, but to no avail, as evidenced by the ubiquitous denunciations leveled against him. In the opening words of his extraordinary first-hand account of the border crisis, Jacob Soboroff observes that he was "an unlikely eyewitness to one of the most shameful chapters in modern American history."[40] Although Sessions never really felt the emotion of shame, the UMC did feel shame, "in regard to bad things, whether present, past, or future, which seem likely to involve us in discredit."[41] Sessions did try to attenuate the perceived shame originating with the UMC and other constituencies present at the June 18, 2018 speech, however, one could not say with any degree of confidence that he felt shame surrounding his support for the Zero Tolerance policy. The UMC initially felt shame but reverted to shamelessness in the July 30, 2018 pronouncement. As stated by Rev. Dr. Debora Bishop, the district superintendent of UMC in Mobile, Alabama said,

> A political action is not personal conduct when the political officer is carrying out official policy. In this matter, Attorney General Jeff Sessions was carrying out the official policy of the President and/or the United States Department of Justice. It was not an individual act.[42]

The outrage was short-lived as evidenced by the UMC's change of heart, resulting in all four of the charges leveled against Sessions being dropped.[43] Although the July 18 complaint by the undersigned stated that they "have an ethical obligation to speak boldly when one of our members is engaged in causing significant harm in matters contrary to the Discipline on the global stage,"[44] the

Church ultimately determined on July 30, 2018, that an incompatibility between the tenets of Sessions's faith as a private citizen and his conduct as a political official is wholly acceptable, and in no way vitiates his good standing in the UMC. Needing to reconcile one's private values with professional duties and responsibilities on behalf of Sessions, the UMC set aside the interconnectedness, opting instead for a seemingly flawed mutual exclusivity, morally contrary to the kairotic moment.

As fortuitous as this peripeteia was for Sessions, this reversal of fortune for him personally from negative to positive, fundamentally contradicts the premise in the July 18, 2018 complaint:

> While other individuals and areas of the federal government are implicated in each of these examples, Mr. Sessions—as a long-term United Methodist in a tremendously public position—is particularly accountable to us, his church. He is ours, and we are his.[45]

In altering their conclusion about Sessions, the UMC contributed to the "misery and bad fortune" of the separated families.[46] Within a Judeo-Christian framework, the complaint is a uniquely significant passage. This last line is reminiscent of the Song of Solomon (*Shir Hashirim*) 6:3: "*Ani L'Dodi, V'Dodi Li*": I am my Beloved's and my Beloved is mine.[47] This espousal between Sessions and the UMC is undoubtedly more metaphorical than the more literally driven betrothal in the Song of Solomon, but the complete extrication and tearing asunder of the two in the Church's July 30, 2018 decision could not leave one more nonplussed.

Bemoaning the previous administration's lack of or indifference to the virtue of foresight, and with the current administration's critique, benefitted partially by 20/20 hindsight since major challenges still prevail with unaccompanied minors crossing into the United States at the Southern border,[48] Alejandro Mayorkas, the newly sworn in Secretary of Homeland Security in the Biden administration, excoriated the Trump administration for having "dismantled our nation's immigration system in its entirety."[49] Secretary Mayorkas accuses them of engendering a moribund department shamelessly distinguished by facilities which were not "available or equipped to administer the humanitarian laws" which had been passed in Congressional legislation.[50] But with the multitude of committed breaches, Mayorkas declares that "the most powerful and heartbreaking example of the cruelty that preceded this administration…is the intentional separation of children from their parents."[51] En route to righting this egregious and grievous wrong, Mayorkas has been named as chairman of the Family Reunification Task Force.[52] This moral outrage has been transformed into a "moral imperative for the Biden administration."[53] The Biden administration is making a concerted effort to mitigate a significant amount of the damage with respect to family separation.[54] Whether all of the families can be made whole with as minimal irreparable damage as possible has yet to be determined, but irrefutably, the Biden administration's efforts thus far are well-intentioned.

But the legal, political, and ethical imbroglios circumscribing the immigration issue are far from resolved. Notwithstanding several months of bipartisan efforts in the Senate to pass a border security bill, Mike Johnson, the House Speaker, refused to bring it to the House for a vote, and even Senate Republicans who initially supported the bill defected, abandoning a bill that provided more to the Republicans than to the Democrats.[55] And on the heels of that legislative debacle, in a second attempt, the House of Representatives voted to impeach Alejandro Mayorkas, the Secretary of Homeland Security, by the slimmest margin, 214–213. Unprecedentedly, Mayorkas is "the first sitting Cabinet secretary in United States history to be impeached."[56] The long-range consequences are staggering, insofar as the bar for impeachment charges has sunk, where the criteria no longer appeared to be high crimes and misdemeanors.[57] What is the motive? Cravenly and cynically, it was engineered to create a campaign talking point for Trump: Keep it broken so that he can say it is broken, and that only he can fix it.[58]

CHAPTER 6: PART 2

Borders/Immigration and Violence

Pope Francis's apostolic sojourn to Mexico ended with Catholic Mass at the border in Ciudad Juárez. The Mass, celebrated on February 17, 2016, was synchronously broadcast across the Rio Grande to an audience in El Paso, Texas. At the border, Francis delivered a homily and reasoned the central cause of the immigration problem to be a selfish indifference, a comfortable desensitization to the suffering of the immigrant other. Francis's homily achieved its purpose by applying a hermeneutic reading of the prophetic narrative of Jonah augmented with affect theory.

"HOMILY OF HIS HOLINESS POPE FRANCIS AT CIUDAD JUÁREZ FAIR GROUNDS"[1]

Pope Francis

Ciudad Juárez, Mexico. February 17, 2016

In the second century St. Irenaeus wrote that the glory of God is the life of man. It is an expression which continues to echo in the heart of the Church. The glory of the Father is the life of his sons and daughters. There is no greater glory for a father than to see his children blossom, no greater satisfaction than to see his children grow up, developing and flourishing. The first reading that we have just heard points to this. The great city of Nineveh was self-destructing as a result of oppression and dishonour, violence, and injustice. The grand capital's days were numbered because the violence within it could not continue. Then the Lord appeared and stirred Jonah's heart: the Father called and sent forth his messenger. Jonah was summoned to receive a mission. "Go", he was told, because in "40 days Nineveh shall be overthrown" (Jon 3:4). Go and help them to understand that by the way they treat each other, ordering and organizing themselves, they are only creating death and destruction, suffering and oppression. Make them see this is no way to live, neither for the king nor his subjects, nor for farm fields nor for the cattle. Go and tell them that they have become used to this degrading way of life and have lost their sensitivity to pain. Go and tell them that injustice has infected their way of seeing the world. "Therefore, go Jonah!" God sent him to testify to what was happening, he sent him to wake up a people intoxicated with themselves.

In this text, we find ourselves before the mystery of divine mercy. Mercy, which always rejects wickedness, takes the human person in great earnest. Mercy always appeals to the goodness of each person, even though it be dormant and numbed. Far from bringing destruction, as we so often desire or want to bring about ourselves, mercy seeks to transform each situation from within. Herein lies the mystery of divine mercy. It seeks and invites us to conversion, it invites us to repentance; it invites us to see the damage being done at every level. Mercy always pierces evil in order to transform it. It is the mystery of God our Father: he sends his Son who pierced into what was evil, he took on sin in order to transform evil. This is his mercy.

The king listened to Jonah, the inhabitants of the city responded and penance was decreed. God's mercy has entered the heart, revealing and showing wherein our certainty and hope lie: there is always the possibility of change, we still have time to transform what is destroying us as a people, what is demeaning our humanity. Mercy encourages us to look to the present, and to trust what is healthy and good beating in every heart. God's mercy is our shield and our strength.

Jonah helped them to see, helped them to become aware. Following this, his call found men and women able to repent, and able to weep. To weep over injustice, to cry over corruption, to cry over oppression. These are tears that lead to transformation, that soften the heart; they are the tears that purify our gaze and enable us to see the cycle of sin into which very often we have sunk. They are tears that can sensitize our gaze and our attitude hardened and especially dormant in the face of another's suffering. They are the tears that can break us, capable of opening us to conversion. This is what happened to Peter after having denied Jesus; he cried and those tears opened his heart.

This word echoes forcefully today among us; this word is the voice crying out in the wilderness, inviting us to conversion. In this Year of Mercy, with you here, I beg for God's mercy; with you I wish to plead for the gift of tears, the gift of conversion.

Here in Ciudad Juárez, as in other border areas, there are thousands of immigrants from Central America and other countries, not forgetting the many Mexicans who also seek to pass over "to the other side". Each step, a journey laden with grave injustices: the enslaved, the imprisoned, and extorted; so many of these brothers and sisters of ours are the consequence of a trade in human trafficking, the trafficking of persons.

We cannot deny the humanitarian crisis which in recent years has meant migration for thousands of people, whether by train or highway or on foot, crossing hundreds of kilometers through mountains, deserts, and inhospitable zones. The human tragedy that is forced migration is a global phenomenon today. This crisis which can be measured in numbers and statistics, we want instead to measure with names, stories, families. They are the brothers and sisters of those expelled by poverty and violence, by drug trafficking and criminal organizations. Being faced with so many legal vacuums, they get caught up in a web that ensnares and always destroys the poorest. Not only do they suffer poverty but they must also endure all these forms of violence. Injustice is radicalized in the young; they are "cannon fodder", persecuted and threatened when they try to flee the spiral of violence and the hell of drugs. And what can we say about the many women whose lives have been unjustly robbed?

Let us together ask our God for the gift of conversion, the gift of tears, let us ask him to give us open hearts like the Ninevites, open to his call heard in the suffering faces of countless men and women. No more death! No more exploitation! There is always time to change, always a way out and always an opportunity, there is always the time to implore the mercy of God.

Just as in Jonas' time, so too today may we commit ourselves to conversion; may we be signs lighting the way and announcing salvation. I know of the work of countless civil organizations working to support the rights of migrants. I know too of the committed work of so many men and women religious, priests, and lay people in accompanying migrants and in defending life. They are on the front lines, often risking their own lives. By their very lives they are prophets of mercy; they are the beating heart and the accompanying feet of the Church that opens her arms and sustains.

This time for conversion, this time for salvation, is the time for mercy. And so, let us say together in response to the suffering on so many faces: In your compassion and mercy, Lord, have pity on us… cleanse us from our sins and create in us a pure heart, a new spirit (cf. Ps 51[50]:3, 4, 12).

And now I also want to greet from here all our beloved brothers and sisters who are joining us simultaneously from the other side of the frontier, especially those who are gathered in the Stadium of the University of El Paso, known as The Sun Bowl, under the guidance of your Bishop, Monsignor Mark Seitz. Thanks to technology, we can pray, sing, and celebrate together that merciful love which God gives us, and which no frontier can prevent us from sharing. Thank you, brothers and sisters of El Paso, for making us feel one single family and one same Christian community.

***

RHETORICAL ANALYSIS

Since his election in 2013, Pope Francis has made what he calls "forced migration" a hallmark issue of his pontificate. Hailing from Latin America and being the son of immigrants, Pope Francis has been a resolute advocate for migrants, refugees, victims of human trafficking, and all those fleeing manifold forms of violence. According to the United Nations' Global Trends Report, as of 2016, there are over sixty-five million refugee people displaced across the world.[2]

Displacement is perilous and often involves violence and tragic death. The increasing number of drownings of thousands of migrants attempting to cross the Mediterranean is one of the many tragic consequences of migration. Such human suffering and death have intensified to a full-blown humanitarian crisis, exacerbated by what Francis condemns as the "globalization of indifference."[3]

The salience of the invisibility and tragic loss of so many migrant and refugee people for Francis was made limpid in two initial gestures. First, in late May of 2013, Francis gave the plenary address to the Pontifical Council for the Pastoral Care of Migrants and Itinerant People in which he appealed to the international community to develop new approaches to policies that will protect the dignity and improve the life of marginalized people.[4] Second, the holy father wasted little time putting into action his grand pastoral commission to "go out" beyond the secure borders of Roman basilicas and journeyed to Lampedusa for his first apostolic visit. Lampedusa, "the island of tears" as Francis called it, is a small island located in the Mediterranean Sea between Sicily and Libya; it serves as a way station for the exodus of refugees from African countries as well as Syria who often brave the perilous crossing in small, crowded fishing vessels and unsafe rubber dinghies. To date, crossing the Mediterranean, "a vast cemetery" to use Francis's words, is the deadliest migrant route in the world. According to the website infomigrants.net, in the last six years, 19,000 migrants have been reported missing or dead since October 2013.[5]

Upon hearing about thousands of migrants, mostly women and children, who drowned and washed ashore in "boats which were vehicles of hope and became vehicles of death," Francis, confessed it pierced like a "thorn in my heart."[6] On July 8, 2013, at Lampedusa before and audience of 15,000, the lugubrious pontiff offered a penitential Mass, called for solidarity, and urged the faithful to aid persecuted migrants and comfort the families of the deceased. Shortly after that, Francis would take a similar message to the US-Mexican border and later the Greek Island of Lesbos where he would return to Rome with three refugee families, a total of 12 people.[7] It is Francis's Homily at the US-Mexican border in Ciudad Juarez, just south of El Paso that we feature as a relevant instance of the sacred succor/rancor rhetorical dynamic.

In February of 2016, amid a contentious Republican primary, Donald Trump accused the Pope of being a "very political person," Mexico's "political pawn," and continued to stoke the flames of xenophobia by fomenting fears about the dangers of an open border.[8] Trump vowed that if he was elected president, he would force Mexico to finance the building of a border wall.[9] In the now famous in-flight press conference following the apostolic journey to Mexico, Francis responded to a Reuters' journalist who asked him about Trump's comments. Francis replied, "a person who thinks only of building walls, wherever it may be, and not of building bridges, is not Christian. This is not the Gospel."[10] The Trump administration's hyper-nationalistic, anti-immigrant, calls for mass deportations, and initiation of the "family separation policy," officially adopted and applied to the US-Mexican border from April to June 2018,[11] perpetrates precisely the kind of violence against immigrants that Pope Francis finds anathema to Gospel principles.

Pope Francis's six-day trip to Mexico culminated with a Mass at the border in Ciudad Juárez and was simultaneously broadcasted across the Rio Grande to El Paso, Texas. As a rhetor, Francis never misses the symbolic power of the *mise-en-scène*. Adorned in a violet vestment (a symbol of penance), and in solidarity with thousands of immigrants seeking a better life only to find violence in what has become a full-scale humanitarian crisis, Francis placed flowers at the base of a massive cross erected on a makeshift platform for the ceremony. The cross for Catholics is an icon of suffering as well as salvation, a rhetorical reminder that the Christian narrative embodies both succor and rancor. Francis gazed across the Rio Grande, made the sign of the cross, waved to the throngs of people gathered there, and prayed silently. For Francis, the central pathology of the immigration crisis is a selfish indifference, a comfortable desensitization to the suffering of the immigrant other.

The immigration crisis as destructive violence is featured as a principal theme in Francis's homily. His religious rhetoric exemplifies a sacred succor evident in an elegant imbrication of scriptural exegesis with a fitting response to the exigence of indifference to forced migration. In what follows, we provide a brief analysis of these discursive dynamics at work in Francis's homily.

Francis begins with the Old Testament story from the book of the beleaguered prophet Jonah. Before he softened, Jonah was an example par excellence of indifference to human suffering. Declining to bring God's mercy to Nineveh, Jonah absconds to Tarshish. As Francis would later write of what he called "the Jonah syndrome," a disorder so analogous to Francis's US-Mexican border context, "He [Jonah] had erected a fence around his soul with the barbed wire of his certainties divided the world into good and bad, and closing the door to God's action. Today, so many people act like Jonah…they complain and disdain; and feeling their identities threatened they get involved in battles…in order to feel more secure…in their Tarshishes of self-righteousness."[12] In employing the scriptural narrative of Jonah, Francis aims to draw a parallel between Jonah's initial isolated and prideful superiority and Francis's US audience.

After Jonah's "whale" of a conversion, God dispatched him to the great walled city of Nineveh that was "self-destructing as a result of oppression, dishonour, violence, and injustice."[13] The violence plaguing Nineveh was no way to live and if it continued, Nineveh would be overthrown, such was the message Jonah brought to the king. Employing the pharmakos hermeneutic, Francis rhetorically depicts violence and the evil of indifference in the form of the pharmakon: first, as anesthesia; then, as disease; and, finally, as poison. Paraphrasing God's instructions to Jonah, Francis, anaphorically exhorts, "Go and tell them that they have become used to this degrading way of life and have lost their sensitivity to pain. Go and tell them that injustice has infected their way of seeing the world. [God] sent him [Jonah] to wake up a people intoxicated with themselves."[14] When a people become inebriated with hubris and infected with the "virus of isolated conscience,"[15] a rhetor can strike them with a sobering dose of *kataplexis*.[16] Aristotle's rhetorical concept of *kataplexis* signifies the strong emotional arousal of excessive shame and distress associated with disgrace.

More recently, affect theorist, Silvan S. Tompkins defines shame as "an innate *affect auxiliary* response and a specific inhibitor of continuing interest and enjoyment."[17] In evoking shame, Tompkins further explicates, we are hindered by acting on positive affect. Indifference breeds a positively felt detachment; there is a joy that one appreciates in self-atomization and isolation from the suffering "Other" which promulgates what Sedgwick refers to as a social (for Francis, spiritual) death.[18] As we will witness, Francis's main criticism of indifference is its capacity to foment social and spiritual death which ironically lives in the uninhibited enjoyment of a privileged socio-political homophily.[19] Such an affective state is antithetical to Catholic social teaching and the scriptural vocation of Jonah that Francis highlighted in his homily. Humility and sometimes humiliation can be powerful antibodies to such selfishness and excessive individualism.

How does the emotional appeal to shame function as a pharmakon in Pope Francis's rhetoric? First, Francis is aware that more than an inert, detached pity for the suffering of immigrants is needed. His audience must be shamed out of their apathy, a word meaning "insensible to feeling" or "without suffering." What Francis's rhetoric provides is a conversion therapy affording an afflicted audience divine mercy. However, such redemptive salve is granted only after an acknowledgement of one's sins. Francis's religious and rhetorical prescriptions involve a two-step process. First, he dispenses an analeptic stimulant to awaken the numbness of indifference. Fear, racism, indifference to the suffering of others are all psychological walls that divide and occlude mercy and conversion. Francis observed that "mercy always appeals to the goodness of each person, even though it be dormant and numbed."[20]

The pontiff stood at the US-Mexican border, his words induced unity and solidarity for the often tragic, transitional context of the immigration crisis and the nameless faces who writhe from its pain. In an ironic inversion of Wordsworth's "borderer," Francis promoted not the romantic revolutionary ideology of individual liberty, but an empathetic embrace of the suffering and otherness of the human person. His words open a dialogic space and serve as a visual, empirical, and existential bridge inviting audiences on both sides to, like Jonah commanded, "look to the present" across the border, through the walls, and to visually bear witness to the damage being done at every level. Francis avowed:

> Here in Ciudad Juárez, as in other border areas, there are thousands of immigrants from Central America and other countries, not forgetting the many Mexicans who also seek to pass over "to the other side." Each step, a journey laden with grave injustices: the enslaved, the imprisoned and extorted; so many of these brothers and sisters of ours are the consequence of a trade in human trafficking, the trafficking of persons.[21]

The shameful denial of the humanitarian crisis of forced migration is laid bare by Francis' descriptions of the violence endured. The poorest lives are destroyed. They are banished by poverty and violence, drug tracking, and criminal organizations. Trying to escape the hellish spiral of violence and drugs, they find that they are ensnared in a web; their lives unjustly robbed.[22]

Next, to expunge his audiences' selfish and indifferent myopia, Francis deploys a homeopathic gift in the form of healing and cleansing tears, induced by emoting shame. The festering shame and disgrace must be purged, flushed out with tears. Cathartic tears become the purgative succor for the violence of indifference. These tears of conversion function homeopathically converting the shameful to the salubrious. Weeping serves a cathartic and intercessory function. St. Augustine observes that tears are the surest sign that an audience is being moved to action.[23] As a repudiation of the "Doctrine of Stoical Apathy," John Lesley wrote, "weeping…is a means of purifying our own soul…to enter heaven we must passé through the Purgatory of Weeping."[24] In his most recent encyclical *Fratelli Tutti*, Francis mentions St. Paul's epistolary exhortation to the Romans to "weep with those who weep."²⁵ The Holy Father affirmed, "When our hearts do this, they are capable of identifying with others without worrying about where they were born or come from. In the process, we come to experience others as our own flesh."²⁶ The percussive beauty and conversionary action inherent in weeping Francis calls us to experience are what Cardinal Luis Antonio G. Tagle calls the "Gospel of tears."²⁷

Francis informs his audience that the king of Nineveh adhered to Jonah's conversionary prescriptions and God's mercy entered the hearts of the inhabitants, producing peace and penance. Furthermore, attendant Jonah's prophetic rhetoric, Francis's words invite the conversion therapy of divine mercy. Change of heart for the Ninevites took the form of awareness, repentance, and weeping. Thus, unlike Jonah's own conversion, Francis calls his audience to conversion by a different kind of "wail." Cathartic tears become the purgative succor/rancor for the violence of indifference. Francis's sermonic repetition explained,

> To weep over injustice, to cry over corruption, to cry over oppression. These are the tears that lead to transformation, that soften the heart; they are tears that purify your gaze and enable us to see the cycle of sin into which very often we have sunk. They are tears that can sensitize our gaze and our attitude hardened and especially dormant in the face of another's suffering. They are the tears that can break us, capable of opening us to conversion. This is what happened to Peter after having denied Jesus; he cried, and those tears opened his heart.²⁸

Francis analogizes weeping as the conversionary process by which one is cleansed from the illness of injustice and the sin of indifference. Likewise, Elizabeth S. Belfiore contends that conceptions of catharsis linked to moral purification have been identified with homeopathic as well as allopathic theories.²⁹ Moreover the *Catechism of the Catholic Church* teaches conversion is accompanied by a "salutary pain and sadness."³⁰ Purification as a means of obtaining forgiveness with one's neighbor is reconciled through the "tears of repentance."³¹ Conversion in Francis's instance is a radical reorientation that shakes a people awake from their noxious apathy and tears become the antidote to indifference. Injustice infects our way of seeing the world and as Francis teaches elsewhere, tears are "the glasses needed to see Jesus."³²

Francis brings the comparative argument home when he states, just as in Jonah's time, so, too, today may we commit ourselves to conversion. Francis' homilies that address violence and tragic loss in our world function both as sacred succor and rancor. As a religious rhetor, Francis's adept exegesis of scripture is masterly made ever so relevant to his contemporaneous exigences and audiences. Francis's words are a salubrious bridge of consolation and repentance, not a wall of fear or state-sponsored separation.

Afterword

The work of rhetorical criticism, as this volume most presciently exemplifies, equips us to reckon with the rancor of fascist religious rhetoric and violence currently escalating across the world. As Oldenburg and Hacker Daniels's analyses in this volume demonstrate, sacred rhetoric (succor) functions to relieve and mediate the paradoxical, and even dissonant, entanglements of religion and violence in both contemporary U.S. and historical global conflicts. Rancor is the rhetoric that characterizes the object of a community's source of suffering, often materialized through violence. Globally, Christian Nationalism has emerged as a political ideology, defined through discursive succor/rancor, that fuses and privileges a particular form of Christianity in a country's public and civic realms.[1] Global affairs scholar Niya Saiya explains that Christian Nationalism is "at once both descriptive and prescriptive: Christian nationalists believe that their countries are defined by Christianity and that their governments and citizens should take steps to keep it that way. In the case of the [U.S.] Capitol insurrection, the rioters were literally trying to take back their country for God."[2] According to Oldenburg and Hacker Daniels, succor is an inventional resource which mediates cognitive, political, and spiritual deliberation through the suffering of community tragedy and violence. Thus, Christian Nationalist rhetoric constitutes bodies imagined from succor and rancor to achieve its aims. As Christian Nationalist politics gain influence, we must recognize the ways in which the succor of religious rhetoric produces a rancorous reality for marginalized subjects and its material consequences for the world. To do so, I suggest we further examine the advancement of trans necropolitics in the state of Florida, under the fascistic governance of Ron DeSantis.

At this moment in the United States, we are experiencing a deadly, systematic backlash to the neoliberal inclusion and biopolitical regulation of transgender and gender-nonconforming life as it flourishes within the public sphere of a contemporary colonial apparatus. 2023 marks the fourth consecutive year of escalating anti-trans legislation with 549 anti-trans bills proposed this year alone at both the state and national levels.[3] 69 of these bills have been signed into law across GOP-controlled state legislatures and supermajorities.[4] Undeniably, the mass mobilization of anti-trans rhetoric across the public sphere in recent years has facilitated much of the political and discursive maneuvering behind the backlash. Perhaps one of the most notable rhetorical moves vilifying transgender people, but also implicating queer people more broadly, is the (re-)emergence of "groomer" and indoctrination rhetoric related to trans panic in public bathrooms.[5] For example, Florida's H.B. 1521, the "Safety in Private Spaces Act," encompasses this panic by explicitly criminalizing people (namely transgender and gender non-conforming people) who do not use the facilities corresponding to their sex assigned at birth in publicly-leased buildings to "maintain public safety, decency, decorum, and privacy."[6]

Within anti-trans and queer discourses, groomer rhetoric sustains Christian Nationalist fervor for gender traditionalism and conformity through the discursive succor of protecting the Christian family and securing its reproduction as salvation against gender and sexual deviance. In this case, the Christian Nationalist emphasis on reproductive and gender/sexual conformity is reified in the bill's definition of sex as "the classification of a person as either female or male based on the organization of the body of such person for a specific reproductive role, as indicated by the person's sex chromosomes, naturally occurring sex hormones, and internal and external genitalia present at birth." H.B. 1521 is only part of the bioessentialist, necropolitical schema for criminalizing, erasing, and eliminating transgender life in the state. The state has also passed S.B. 1438, titled "Protection of Children," which threatens businesses with revocation of their licenses if children are found to attend "adult live performances," (i.e., drag performance, at their establishments).[7] Of major bodily and material consequence, S.B. 254, "Treatments for Sex Reassignment," fully restricts transgender children's access to gender-affirming healthcare through a wholesale ban, with the possible recourse of removing children from their family homes into state custody if suspected of being subjected to any treatment.[8] Additionally, under S.B. 254, transgender adults' access to gender-affirming care is significantly restricted through a new informed consent process that delimits physicians as the only healthcare professionals allowed to provide treatment, while also expanding civil liability for gender-affirming healthcare providers.[9] Anti-trans rancor is ultimately enacted through the violence of forced detransition and elimination from public spaces.

The violence enacted from rhetorical rancor must be attended to through the material reality in which it is grounded. In Jack Selzer and Sharon Crowley's seminal volume on material rhetoric and bodies, *Rhetorical Bodies*, Selzer explains that material rhetoric is a "meditation on the material aspects and groundings of language as rhetorical action as it is traditionally conceived, and on the rhetorical nature of material realities, whether they are literate realities or not."[10] Material rhetoric prompts rhetorical critics to "take very seriously the materials conditions that sustain the production, circulation, and consumption of rhetorical power."[11] The themes and analyses of the present volume's case studies enable us to understand the development and imbrication of Christian Nationalism into contemporary social and political discourses around race, gender, religion, mass public violence, and borders/immigration. In the context of the present volume, succor/rancor are inventional sources of rhetorical power for achieving deliverance from the material conditions that create the need for succor/rancor itself.

From a materialist perspective, rhetorical power facilitates the circulation of material and discursive conditions that ultimately constitute reality. By analyzing the arrangement and fashioning of discourses, this volume's themes can be understood as the material conditions fomenting the rhetorical power of global Christian Nationalist politics. Of U.S. rhetoric, rhetorical critic Michael Lechuga describes it as "a specific public-facing communication practice that organizes people and materials (especially land) to serve the needs of a settlement."[12] Further, Lechuga frames U.S. rhetoric through assemblage theory to understand how bodies and materials are mobilized and arranged across territories through logics of settler desire which is particularly motivated to create the conditions that allow the ongoing reproduction of settler logic. In fact, the (re-)emergence of groomer rhetoric, as evidenced in Chapter 2's Harvey Milk case study, highlights the reproduction of settler logics and suggests that we analyze the material conditions that prompt the (re-)circulation of oppressive discourses. This conception of U.S. rhetoric positions Lechuga to make an important observation: "what one feels as an effect (or affect) from assemblages is the sense that territories are being reshaped and recoded to be more conducive to the reproduction of the assemblage."[13] As Saiya demonstrates, Christian Nationalism exists globally in various formations, cultural or "creedal," through an assemblage of various sociopolitical conditions.[14] However, Christian Nationalism, as a U.S. rhetoric, engages the felt conditions of a colonial reality, grounded in Christianity, through succor and rancor, in service of reproducing the material conditions that enable coloniality. Thus, the exercise of rhetorical power is conducted through deceptive and misleading religious rhetoric clothed in succor, but really espousing a rancor that assembles a reality based in the oppression and subjugation of nonnormative subjects.

By centering anti-trans discourses, anti-trans legislation in Florida arguably engenders the most eliminating and deadliest formation of trans necropolitical backlash in the U.S. *thus far*. Although anti-trans rhetoric is a significant feature of the contemporary fascist state apparatus, it is not the only exercise of Christian Nationalism's succorous and rancorous rhetorical power. Following his reelection, Governor DeSantis pronounced that Florida is "Where Woke Goes to Die."[15] This pronouncement encompasses an assemblage of Christian Nationalist politics that centers oppositional rancor to marginalized empowerment and liberation cohered as "woke ideology." The necropolitical severity of this pronouncement cannot be underestimated. As the Florida state legislature corporally legislated its anti-woke hostility onto transgender bodies, embodiments of "wokeness" were targeted and eliminated through state-wide book banning rituals, rejecting marginalized history curriculum, dismantling administrative diversity and equity structures in higher education, and prohibiting the free expression of nonnormative gender and sexual identity across grades K-12.[16]

The enactment of bodily elimination is an especially material practice. Recently, Florida passed S.B. 1718, "Immigration," which effectively prohibits the existence of undocumented immigrants in the state by mandating citizenship E-verification through employers (the bill implicates any employer with 25 or more employees must comply), prohibiting local governments from issuing government identification cards and invalidating any pre-existing out-of-state identification held by immigrants, in addition to requiring hospitals to collect and report data on patients' citizenship status.[17] The consistent pattern in bodily domination and deployment of settler of logics of elimination undergirding Christian Nationalist politics and rhetoric should signal to rhetorical critics the importance of materialist rhetorical analyses when engaging with instances of rhetorical power. Bodily domination and elimination are constitutive of hierarchies of colonial difference, and the discursive pronouncement of anti-wokeness highlights the rhetorical power of this difference through the material conditions needed to sustain it.

While rhetorical critics do not have the ability to predict the future, with material rhetoric, we do have the capacity to critically engage with texts/bodies/materials to trace the mobility of discursive formations and understand the conditions behind the real production of life and death. For rhetorical critics interested in advancing an anti-colonial future that challenges and disrupts the reproduction of coloniality within rhetorical studies, Lechuga prompts us to "imagine a future where a study of rhetoric combats antiblack and anti-indigenous ideologies by aligning with activists to cocreate a political future outside and beyond the settler imaginary." A praxis-driven method, as Lechuga advocates for, privileges the voices and actions of vulnerable communities and working with activists to develop an on-the-ground-theory for meeting the violence and power where it happens. This praxis-driven method recenters the relational importance of criticism as a critical act, and contributes to a much-needed material, anti-colonial project within academic scholarship. Within theology studies, scholar Joseph Drexler-Dreis advances an orientation of decolonial love that:

> (1) exposes the idolatry of Western modernity and creates space for an alternative; (2) It situates the human person in relationship to a transcendent and irreducible, even if unnameable, reality; (3) And, it commits to catalyzing and authenticating historical movement—that is, hastening the end of the modern world-system. In these three moments, decolonial love is a posture by which to face up to reality.[18]

Similar to succor/rancor, the love/violence dichotomy showcases the inconsistencies between the divine and the discursive. For Drexler-Dreis, decolonial love is a site of salvation, or revelation to the idolatry and coloniality of the modern world system, and productively embracing the tension that arises between love and violence. Decolonial love as epistemic and as praxis moves us to relational action and movement based in the real material incongruities between the divine and Western modernity. Both of these perspectives highlight that undoing or the end of the World is a relational struggle, as well as a site of contestation, but most importantly, it remains grounded in an anti-colonial and liberatory ontology.

The heightened legislative hostility and escalating violence towards minority subjects in the U.S. is increasingly, and uneasily, forcing subjects farther from the margins towards necropolitical elimination. It is important that we recognize as critics that lives are materially already in precarity, not just by the acceleration of necropolitical legislation, but by the very being of the fascistic, colonial apparatus that regulates life and death. We cannot ignore the imminent danger a politically and socially rancorous climate presents to marginalized subjects. As we see in Chapter 2's case study on Tony Kushner's admonishment of the U.S. Christian Right following the lynching of Matthew Shephard, the response to the violence fomented by this climate of rancor only amounted to spectacular outcry then indifference. Indifference to the deadliness of our current era will only escalate to fatal danger because the colonial order in its most necropolitical form cannot afford to contain bodies that destabilize the order it seeks to instill.

Without the intervention of revolutionary praxis like decolonial love, we risk becoming complicit in stabilizing and normalizing the violence of Christian Nationalist succor/rancor as it goes uncontested to reproduce the colonial reality that will only continue to be reassembled over the bodies it disposes. With an orientation towards decolonial love, we can remain affirmed and supported in our commitment to unbounding bodies and the world from the succor/rancor that have contained its excesses. When we imagine an anti-colonial future, an afterward, we hope to redeem dignity where it has been systematically denied, to illuminate a passion for healing and relational redemption. Precarity and uncertainty, though evoke rancorous and uneasy feelings, are our greatest source of knowledge to dismantle and abolish the basis of our bounded and assembled oppression. This is our moment to turn.

Notes

Foreword

1 Martin. J. Medhurst, "The Contemporary Study of Public Address: Renewal, Recovery, and Reconfiguration," *Rhetoric & Public Affairs*, 4, no. 3 (2001): 505.

Introduction

1 Kenneth Burke, *The Philosophy of Literary Form: Studies in Symbolic Action* (Berkeley: University of California Press, 1973), 61.
2 René Girard, *Oedipus Unbound: Selected Writings on Rivalry and Desire* (Palo Alto: Stanford University Press, 2004), 13. For more on Girard, rhetoric and religion, see: Paul Lynch, *Persuasions of God: Inventing the Rhetoric of René Girard*, (State College: Penn State University Press, 2024).
3 Kenneth Burke, *The Rhetoric of Religion* (Berkeley: University of California Press, 1970), v.
4 Andrew L. Whitehead and Samuel L. Perry, *Taking America Back for God* (Oxford: Oxford University Press, 2020), 228.
5 Carl Schmitt, *Political Theology*, translated by George Schwab (Cambridge: MIT Press, 1988), 22.
6 Benedict Anderson, *Imagined Communities: Reflections on the Origin and Spread of Nationalism* (New York: Verso, 1983), 19–20.
7 Matthew Loh, "Adam Kinzinger warns that some Christians now 'equate Donald Trump with the person of Jesus Christ,' calls out pastors who support Trumpism" *Business Insider*,

August 17, 2022, https://www.businessinsider.com/adam-kinzinger-warns-of-christians-equate-trump-with-jesus-christ-2022-8.

8 Belinda Luscombe, "Theologian Russell Moore Has a Message for Christians Who Still Worship Donald Trump," *Time*, January 21, 2021, https://time.com/5932014/donald-trump-christian-supporters/.
9 David Knowles, "GOP Rep. Kinzinger publishes 'unhinged' voicemail threats left by Trump supporters," *Yahoo News*, July 5, 2022, https://news.yahoo.com/gop-rep-kinzinger-publishes-unhinged-voicemail-threats-left-by-trump-supporters-173631901.html?guccounter=1.
10 Knowles, "GOP Rep. Kinzinger publishes 'unhinged' voicemail threats."
11 Knowles, "GOP Rep. Kinzinger publishes 'unhinged' voicemail threats."
12 Hent de Vries, *Religion and Violence: Philosophical Perspectives from Kant to Derrida* (Baltimore: The Johns Hopkins University Press, 2002), 1.
13 René Girard, *Violence and the Sacred* translated by Patrick Gregory (Baltimore: The Johns Hopkins University Press, 1977), 8, 31.
14 Daniel Panneton, https://www.theatlantic.com/ideas/archive/2022/08/radical-traditionalist-catholic-christian-rosary-weapon/671122/
15 Bishop Daniel Flores, quoted in Panneton, https://www.theatlantic.com/ideas/archive/2022/08/radical-traditionalist-catholic-christian-rosary-weapon/671122/
16 Panneton, "How Extremist Culture Gun Culture Is Trying to Co-op the Rosary," *The Atlantic*, August 14, 2022.
17 Chole Folmar, "Boebert: Jesus Didn't have enough AR-15 to 'Keep his Government from Killing Him,'" *The Hill*, June 19, 2022. https://thehill.com/homenews/house/3528049-boebert-jesus-didnt-have-enough-ar-15s-to-keep-his-government-from-killing-him/
18 Folmar, "Boebert: Jesus Didn't have enough AR-15s."
19 See Joe Dallas, *Christians in a Cancel Culture: Speaking with Truth and Grace in a Hostile World* (Eugene: Harvest House Publishers, 2021); Steven E. Strang, *God and Cancel Culture: Stand Strong Before It's Too Late* (Lake Mary: Frontline, 2021).
20 Katherine Fung, "Marjorie Taylor Greene Keeps Comparing COVID to Holocaust Amid Backlash, Likens Vaccine Passports to 'Gold Star,'" *Newsweek*, May 25, 2021, https://www.newsweek.com/marjorie-taylor-greene-keeps-comparing-covid-holocaust-amid-backlash-likens-vaccine-passports-1594538.
21 Fung, "Marjorie Taylor Greene Keeps Comparing COVID to Holocaust."
22 Idan Zonshine, "Marjorie Taylor Greene compares mask mandate to Holocaust-era 'gold star,'" *The Jerusalem Post*, May 23, 2021, https://www.jpost.com/diaspora/antisemitism/marjorie-taylor-greene-compares-mask-mandate-to-holocaust-era-gold-star-668816.
23 Fung, "Marjorie Taylor Greene Keeps Comparing COVID to Holocaust."
24 Wolfgang Palaver, "Mimetic Theories of Religion and Violence," in *The Oxford Handbook of Religion and Violence*, ed. Mark Juergensmeyer, Margo Kitts, and Michael Jerryerson (Oxford: Oxford University Press, 2013), 536.
25 Alan L. Berger, ed., *Trialogue and Terror: Judaism, Christianity, and Islam after 9/11* (Eugene, OR: Cascade Books, 2021), 2.
26 Berger, *Trialogue and Terror*, 2.
27 Jessie Kratz, "The National Archives' larger-than-life statues," *National Archives: Pieces of History*, May 22, 2018, https://prologue.blogs.archives.gov/2018/05/22/the-national-archives-larger-than-life-statues/.
28 Kratz, "The National Archives' larger-than-life statues."

29 Mark I. Wallace and Theophus H. Smith, *Curing Violence* (Sonoma: California Polebridge Press, 1994), xvii.
30 Palaver, "Mimetic Theories of Religion and Violence," 541.
31 Palaver, "Mimetic Theories of Religion and Violence," 543.
32 Stephen Howard Browne, *Angelina Grimke: Rhetoric, Identity, and the Radical Imagination* (East Lansing: Michigan State University Press, 1999), 150–151.
33 Browne, *Angelina Grimke*, 37, 40, 141, 151.
34 Erin J. Rand, "Thinking Violence and Rhetoric," *Rhetoric & Public Affairs*, 12, no. 3 (2009): 461–477.
35 Jeremy Engels, "Introduction to the Forum on the Violence of Rhetoric," *Quarterly Journal of Speech*, 99, no. 2 (2013): 180–181.
36 Nathan Stormer, "On the Origins of Violence and Language," *Quarterly Journal of Speech*, 99, no. 2 (2013): 182–190.
37 Nathan Crick, *Rhetoric and Power: The Drama of Classical Greece* (Columbia: University of South Carolina Press, 2015), 5.
38 Jennifer Rose Mercieca, "The Culture of Honor: How Slave Holders Responded to the Abolition is Mail Crisis of 1835," *Rhetoric & Public Affairs*, 10, no. 1 (2007): 51–76.
39 See Nathan Crick, *Rhetoric and Power*, Chapter 1.
40 Merceica, "The Culture of Honor" 71.
41 Merceica, "The Culture of Honor" 71.
42 Milton Rokeach, *Beliefs, Attitudes, and Values: A Theory of Organization and Change* (San Francisco, Jossey-Bass, 1972), 6–12.
43 Christopher Lewis, "The Argument for Interfaith Prayer and Worship," in *Interfaith Worship and Prayer: We Must Pray Together*, eds. Christopher Lewis and Dan Cohn-Sherbok (United Kingdom: Jessica Kingsley Publishers, 2019), 22.
44 Lewis, "The Argument for Interfaith Prayer and Worship," 22.
45 Lewis, "The Argument for Interfaith Prayer and Worship," 23.
46 Heraclitus of Ephesus Quotes," *Ancient Scholars*, 19 November 2019, https://ancient-scholars.blogspot.com/2019/11/heraclitus-of-ephesus-quotes.html.
47 Burke, *Philosophy of Literary Form*, 23.

Chapter 1: Part 1 Race, Gender, and Violence

1 C-SPAN, "President Biden Remarks on 1921 Tulsa Race Massacre," C-SPAN video, June 1, 2021, https://www.c-span.org/video/?512210-1/president-biden-recalls-horror-1921-tulsa-race-massacre. Public Domain.
2 Citi, "Citi: new Black Wall Streets: 30," YouTube video, 0:30, February 22, 2022, https://www.youtube.com/watch?v=FP-TK9hIn4U. See also Victor Luckerson "How Greenwood Grew a Thriving Black Economy," *New York Times*, May 26, 2023, https://www.nytimes.com/2023/05/26/headway/how-greenwood-grew-a-thriving-black-economy.html?smid=em-share; and Matthew Thompson, "The Elusive Quest for Black Progress," *New York Times*, May 26, 2023, https://www.nytimes.com/2023/05/26/headway/black-americans-racial-progress.html?smid=em-share.
3 Guha Krishnamurth and Peter Salib, "Constitutionanlity and the Model of Civil Damages," *Tulsa Law Review*, 57, no. 1 (2022): 303.

4 Lynne Marie Kohm, Katrina Sumner, and Peyton Farley, "Empowering Black Wealth in the Shadow of the Tulsa Race Massacre," *Tulsa Law Review*, 57, no. 1 (2022): 244.
5 Thomas. E. Nelson and Darlley Josellis, "Cultural Attributions for Racial Inequality," *Politics, Groups and Identities* (2022): 1.
6 Nelson and Josellis, "Cultural Attributions for Racial Inequality," 1.
7 For an excellent piece about President Harding's visit to Lincoln University, see James D. Robenalt, "The Republican president who called for racial justice in America after Tulsa massacre," *Washington Post*, June 20, 2021, https://www.washingtonpost.com/history/2020/06/21/warren-harding-tulsa-race-massacre-trump/.
8 "HARDING EXHORTS NEGROES TO STUDY," *New York Times*, June 7, 1921, https://nyti.ms/3zJkIem.
9 Oklahoma Commission to Study the Tulsa Race Riot of 1921, *Tulsa Race Riot: A Report by the Oklahoma Commission to Study the Tulsa Race Riot of 1921* (Oklahoma City: Oklahoma Commission to Study the Tulsa Race Riot of 1921, 2001), 220.
10 Scott Ellsworth, *The Ground Breaking: An American City and its Search for Justice* (New York: Dutton, 2021), 101–102.
11 "Oklahoma City Bombing," *Federal Bureau of Investigation*, https://www.fbi.gov/history/famous-cases/oklahoma-city-bombing#Additional-Information.
12 Christopher S. Wren, "McVeigh Is Executed for Oklahoma City Bombing," *New York Times*, June 11, 2011, https://www.nytimes.com/2001/06/11/national/mcveigh-is-executed-for-oklahoma-city-bombing.html?smid=em-share.
13 Ellsworth, *The Ground Breaking*, 103.
14 Ellsworth, *The Ground Breaking*, 103.
15 Michael Wines, "Bill Clinton Leads Tribute on 20th Anniversary of Oklahoma City Bombing," *New York Times*, April 19, 2015, https://www.nytimes.com/2015/04/20/us/oklahoma-city-bombing-20th-anniversary-bill-clinton.html; Neil MacFarquhar, "Oklahoma City Marks 25 Years Since America's Deadliest Homegrown Attack," *New York Times*, April 19, 2020, https://www.nytimes.com/2020/04/19/us/Timothy-McVeigh-Oklahoma-City-Bombing-Coronavirus.html.
16 Sam Howe Verhovek, "75 Years Later, Tulsa Confronts Its Race Riot," *New York Times*, May 31, 1996, https://www.nytimes.com/1996/05/31/us/75-years-later-tulsa-confronts-its-race-riot.html.
17 Verhovek, "75 Years Later."
18 Verhovek, "75 Years Later."
19 Verhovek, "75 Years Later."
20 Oklahoma Commission to Study the Tulsa Race Riot of 1921, *Tulsa Race Riot*, 24.
21 Oklahoma Commission to Study the Tulsa Race Riot of 1921, *Tulsa Race Riot*, 32.
22 Richard Lanham, *A Handlist of Rhetorical Terms*, 2nd ed. (Berkeley: University of California Press, 2012), 164.
23 Aristotle, and Eugene Garver, trans. and ed., *Poetics and Rhetoric* (New York: Barnes and Noble Classics, 2005), 120
24 Richard Johannesen, ed., *Contemporary American Speeches: A Sourcebook of Speech Forms and Principles* (Dubuque, IA: Kendall/Hunt Publishing Company, 2000), 245–246.
25 Johannesen, *Contemporary American Speeches*, 246.
26 Johannesen, *Contemporary American Speeches*, 246.
27 Johannesen, *Contemporary American Speeches*, 245.
28 Kathleen Hall Jamieson and Karlyn Kohrs Campbell, "Rhetorical Hybrids: Fusions of Generic Elements," *Quarterly Journal of Speech*, 68, no. 2 (1982): 147.

29 Jamieson and Campbell, "Rhetorical Hybrids," 146.
30 Jamieson and Campbell, "Rhetorical Hybrids," 150.
31 Jamieson and Campbell, "Rhetorical Hybrids," 152.
32 Jamieson and Campbell, "Rhetorical Hybrids," 152.
33 Celeste Michelle Condit. "The functions of epideictic: the Boston massacre Orations as Exemplar." *Communication Quarterly*, 33, no. 4 (Fall 1985): 284.
34 Condit, "The functions of epideictic," 288.
35 Condit, "The functions of epideictic," 288.
36 Condit, "The functions of epideictic," 288.
37 Condit, "The functions of epideictic," 288.
38 Condit, "The functions of epideictic," 288.
39 Condit, "The functions of epideictic," 290.
40 Condit, "The functions of epideictic," 285.
41 Condit, "The functions of epideictic," 285.
42 Condit, "The functions of epideictic," 286.
43 Condit, "The functions of epideictic," 286.
44 Lanham, *A Handlist of Rhetorical Terms*, 165.
45 Condit, "The functions of epideictic," 287.
46 Condit, "The functions of epideictic," 297.
47 Aristotle and Garver, *Poetics and Rhetoric*, 165.
48 Jamieson and Campbell, "Rhetorical Hybrids," 146.
49 C-SPAN, "President Biden Remarks on 921 Tulsa Race Massacre."
50 Hughes Van Ellis, brother of Viola Ford Fletcher, died in October 2023. See Christine Hauser, "Hughes Van Ellis, Tulsa Massacre Survivor, Dies at 102," *New York Times*, October 10, 2023, https://www.nytimes.com/2023/10/10/us/hughes-van-ellis-dead-tulsa-race-massacre.html.
51 Scott Ellsworth, *Death in a Promised Land*, with a foreword by John Hope Franklin (Baton Rouge: Louisiana State University Press, 1992), 8.
52 Ellsworth, *Death in a Promised Land*, 9; Oklahoma Commission to Study the Tulsa Race Riot of 1921, *Tulsa Race Riot*, 38.
53 Ellsworth, *Death in a Promised Land*, 9–10.
54 Ellsworth, *Death in a Promised Land*, 10–11.
55 Ellsworth, *Death in a Promised Land*, 11.
56 Ellsworth, *Death in a Promised Land*, 14.
57 Ellsworth, *Death in a Promised Land*, 15; Daniel Victor, "At 107, 106, and 100, Remaining Tulsa Massacre Survivors Plead for Justice," *New York Times*, May 20, 2021, https://www.nytimes.com/2021/05/20/us/tulsa-massacre-survivors.html.
58 Oklahoma Commission to Study the Tulsa Race Riot of 1921, *Tulsa Race Riot*, 39.
59 Oklahoma Commission to Study the Tulsa Race Riot of 1921, *Tulsa Race Riot*, 39.
60 Oklahoma Commission to Study the Tulsa Race Riot of 1921, *Tulsa Race Riot*, 47.
61 Ellsworth, *Death in a Promised Land*, 102–103.
62 Oklahoma Commission to Study the Tulsa Race Riot of 1921, *Tulsa Race Riot*, 47.
63 Ellsworth, *Death in a Promised Land*, 45.
64 Oklahoma Commission to Study the Tulsa Race Riot of 1921, *Tulsa Race Riot*, 56.
65 Ellsworth, *Death in a Promised Land*, 46.
66 Oklahoma Commission to Study the Tulsa Race Riot of 1921, *Tulsa Race Riot*, 57; There are some disputes accounts that private planes were used to bomb the Black neighborhood. Planes

were used, according to Ellsworth while the violence ensued, as well as after the riot, "to observe any unusual activity," see Ellsworth, *Death in a Promised Land*, 63.
67 Oklahoma Commission to Study the Tulsa Race Riot of 1921, *Tulsa Race Riot*, 58.
68 Oklahoma Commission to Study the Tulsa Race Riot of 1921, *Tulsa Race Riot*, 58.
69 Oklahoma Commission to Study the Tulsa Race Riot of 1921, *Tulsa Race Riot*, 58.
70 Oklahoma Commission to Study the Tulsa Race Riot of 1921, *Tulsa Race Riot*, 58.
71 Oklahoma Commission to Study the Tulsa Race Riot of 1921, *Tulsa Race Riot*, 58–59.
72 Ellsworth, *Death in a Promised Land*, 49.
73 Karlos K. Hill, *The 1921 Tulsa Race Massacre*, with a foreword by Kevin Matthews (Norman: University of Oklahoma Press, 2021), 262.
74 Hill, *The 1921 Tulsa Race Massacre*, 263.
75 Oklahoma Commission to Study the Tulsa Race Riot of 1921, *Tulsa Race Riot*, 63; Ellsworth, *Death in a Promised Land*, 52.
76 Ellsworth, *Death in a Promised Land*, 52.
77 Oklahoma Commission to Study the Tulsa Race Riot of 1921, *Tulsa Race Riot*, 64.
78 Oklahoma Commission to Study the Tulsa Race Riot of 1921, *Tulsa Race Riot*, 64.
79 Oklahoma Commission to Study the Tulsa Race Riot of 1921, *Tulsa Race Riot*, 66.
80 Ellsworth, *Death in a Promised Land*, 57.
81 Ellsworth, *Death in a Promised Land*, 61.
82 Oklahoma Commission to Study the Tulsa Race Riot of 1921, *Tulsa Race Riot*, 86.
83 Oklahoma Commission to Study the Tulsa Race Riot of 1921, *Tulsa Race Riot*, 88; 600 interned, Death, 63; 1000 businesses and homes destroyed. (Death, 66)
84 Oklahoma Commission to Study the Tulsa Race Riot of 1921, *Tulsa Race Riot*, 89.
85 Hill, *The 1921 Tulsa Race Massacre*, 270.
86 "Tikkun Olam: Repairing the World," *My Jewish Learning*, https://www.myjewishlearning.com/article/tikkun-olam-repairing-the-world/.
87 Alfred Brophy, *Reconstructing the Dreamland: The Tulsa Race Riot of 1921: Race, Reparations and Reconciliation* (Oxford: Oxford University Press, 2003), 105.
88 Brophy, *Reconstructing the Dreamland*, 105–106.
89 Brophy, *Reconstructing the Dreamland*, 106.
90 Brophy, *Reconstructing the Dreamland*, 106.
91 Brophy, *Reconstructing the Dreamland*, 106–107.
92 Brophy, *Reconstructing the Dreamland*, 117.
93 Caleb Gayle, "100 Years After the Tulsa Massacre, What does Justice Look Like?" *New York Times*, May 25, 2021, https://www.nytimes.com/2021/05/25/magazine/tulsa-race-massacre-1921-greenwood.html.
94 Brophy, *Reconstructing the Dreamland*, 117.
95 Amir Vera, Omar Jimenez, Ashley Killough, and Leonel Mendez, "Tulsa race massacre reparations lawsuit survives motion to deny and will move forward, judge rules," *CNN*, May 2, 2022, https://www.cnn.com/2022/05/02/us/tulsa-race-massacre-hearing-trial/index.html.
96 Scott Ellsworth, *The Ground Breaking: An American City and its Search for Justice* (New York: Dutton, 2021), 249.
97 Ellsworth, *The Ground Breaking*, 249.
98 Ellsworth, *The Ground Breaking*, 251–252; Brakkton Booker, "Oklahoma Lawsuit Seeks Reparations In Connection To 1921 Tulsa Massacre," *NPR*, September 3, 2020, https://www.npr.org/sections/live-updates-protests-for-racial-justice/2020/09/03/909151983/oklahoma-lawsuit-seeks-reparations-in-connection-to-1921-tulsa-massacre/.

99 Ellsworth, *The Ground Breaking*, 253.
100 Ellsworth, *The Ground Breaking*, 236.
101 Ellsworth, *The Ground Breaking*, 263, 265.
102 Ellsworth, *The Ground Breaking*, 268.
103 Campbell Robertson, "Search for Victims of the Tulsa Race Massacre," *New York Times*, June 9, 2021, https://www.nytimes.com/2021/06/09/us/tulsa-burial-race-massacre.html; Victor Luckerson, *Built from the Fire* (New York: Penguin Random House, 2023); Lauren McCarthy, "Tulsa Reaches 'Breakthrough' in Search for Massacre Victims," *New York Times*, April 15, 2023, https://www.nytimes.com/2023/04/15/us/tulsa-race-massacre-murders-dna.html?smid=em-share.
104 Robertson, "Search for Victims."
105 Oklahoma Commission to Study the Tulsa Race Riot of 1921, *Tulsa Race Riot*, 11–12.
106 Eliott McLaughlin, "As Tulsa digs for victims of the 1921 race massacre, victims say the road to justice is a long one," *CNN*, May 31, 2021, https://www.cnn.com/2021/05/31/us/black-wall-street-massacre-victims-burial/index.html.
107 McLaughlin, "As Tulsa digs for victims of the 1921 race massacre."
108 Brophy, *Reconstructing the Dreamland*, 112.
109 Lynne M. Kohm, Katrina Sumner, and Peyton Farley, "Empowering Black Wealth in the Shadow of the Tulsa Race Massacre," *Tulsa Law Review*, 57, no. 1 (2022): 244.
110 Kohm, Sumner, and Farley, "Empowering Black Wealth," 264.
111 Kohm, Sumner, and Farley, "Empowering Black Wealth," 264.
112 Lebeil Estrin, ed., "Judaism: Facts and Fundamentals," *The Aleph Institute*, 2017, 10, http://alephne.org/media/pdf/724/1Rwg7244564.pdf.
113 Estrin, "Judaism," 100; Kohm, Sumner and Farley construe this dictum as "replacing and identifying with the loss of another." In "Empowering Black Wealth in the Shadow of the Tulsa Race Massacre," 265.
114 Carmen Forman, "Stitt, Tulsa Race Massacre Commission at odds over law limiting lessons on race, gender," *Oklahoman*, May 11, 2011, https://www.oklahoman.com/story/news/2021/05/11/oklahoma-gov-stitt-faces-criticism-over-critical-race-theory-law/5044899001/.
115 Forman, "Stitt, Tulsa Race Massacre Commission at odds."
116 Michael Levenson, "Tulsa Race Massacre Commission Ousts Oklahoma Governor," *New York Times*, May 14, 2021, https://www.nytimes.com/2021/05/14/us/Oklahoma-critical-race-theory-Tulsa-massacre.html.
117 Levenson, "Tulsa Race Massacre Commission Ousts Oklahoma Governor."
118 C-SPAN, "President Biden Remarks on 921 Tulsa Race Massacre."
119 See Robert Turner, "The 1921 Tulsa Race Massacre," Karen Gantt, "Black Wall Street: Wealth and Lessons for Today," Warigia M. Bowman, "Connections Between Black Wall Street and Oklahoma's All-Black Towns," and Lynne Marie Kohm, Katrina Sumner, and Peyton Farley, "Empowering Black Wealth in the Shadow of the Tulsa Race Massacre," in *Tulsa Law Review*, 57, no. 1 (2022).
120 Aristotle and Garver, *Poetics and Rhetoric*, 501.
121 C-SPAN, "President Biden Remarks on 921 Tulsa Race Massacre."
122 Alexander Pope, and Henry Morley, ed. *An Essay on Man* (Urbana, Illinois: Project Gutenburg, 2007), https://www.gutenberg.org/files/2428/2428-h/2428-h.htm.

123 Theodore Parker, *Ten Sermons of Religion* (Boston: Crosby, Nichols, and Company, 1853), 84–85; Mychal Denzel Smith, "The Truth About 'The Arc of The Moral Universe,'" *Huffington Post*, January 18, 2018, https://www.huffpost.com/entry/opinion-smith-obama-king_n_5a5903e0e4b04f3c55a252a4.

124 "I'll overcome someday," Hymnary.org, https://hymnary.org/text/this_world_is_one_great_battlefield.

125 *Continuing Injustice: The Centennial of the Tulsa-Greenwood Race Massacre, Subcommittee on the Constitution, Civil Rights, and Civil Liberties*, 117th Cong. (2021) (state of Lessie Evelyn Benningfield ("Mother") Randle, Tulsa Race Massacre Survivor).

126 Tamara R. Piety, "Introduction—The Remains of the Day: Tulsa 1921:2021," *Tulsa Law Review*, 57, no. 1 (2022): 13.

Chapter 1: Part 2 Race, Gender, and Violence

1 Marius Robinson, "Woman's Rights Convention," *Salem (OH) Anti-Slavery Bugle*, June 21, 1851: 4. Public Domain.

2 F. D. Gage., "Sojourner Truth," *New York Independent*, April 23, 1863: 1. Public Domain.

3 "She...shows what a great intellect slavery has crushed." Lucy Stone, "Sojourner Truth," *The Woman's Journal* 5 (August 1876): 252, quoted in Suzanne Pullon Fitch and Roseann M. Mandziuk, *Sojourner Truth as Orator: Wit, Story, and Song* (Westport: Greenwood Press, 1997), 19.

4 Kenneth Burke, *Permanence and Change An Anatomy of Purpose*, 3rd ed. Berkeley, CA. (University of California Press, 1984), 133. Exorcism by misnomer, Burke says, occurs when one "casts out devils by misnaming them." He explains, "It is not the naming in itself that does the work, but the conversion implicit in such naming."

5 See Suzanne Fitch and Roseann M. Mandziuk, *Sojourner Truth As Orator: Wit, Story, and Song* (Westport: Greenwood Press, 1997). A copy of a promotional poster is appended in the opening pages; the image is courtesy of the Sojourner Truth State archives of Michigan.

6 See: Sojourner Truth and Olive Gilbert, *Narrative of Sojourner Truth: A northern Slave, Emancipated from Bodily Servitude by the State of New York, in 1828: with a Portrait* (Boston, MA: Printed for the author, 1850); Sojourner Truth, Olive Gilbert, and Frances W. Titus, *Narrative of Sojourner Truth; a Bondswoman of Olden Time, Emancipated by the New York Legislature in the Early Part of the Present Century; with a History of Her Labors and Correspondence, Drawn from her "Book of Life"* (Boston, MA: Published for the Author, 1875); Corinne Brown Galvin, "Sojourner Truth, the Libyan Sibyl," *New York Folklore Quarterly* (Spring 1950): 5–21; Arthur Huff Fauset, *Sojourner Truth: God's Faithful Pilgrim* (New York: Russell & Russell, 1971); Carleton Mabee and Susan Mabee Newhouse, "Sojourner Truth, Bold Prophet: Why Did She Never Learn to Read?" *New York History* 69 (1988): 55–77; Also see: Suzanne Fitch and Roseann M. Mandziuk, *Sojourner Truth As Orator: Wit, Story, and Song* (Westport: Greenwood Press, 1997), 60–72, 77–83; Carleton Mabee and Susan Mabee Newhouse, *Sojourner Truth: Slave, Prophet, Legend* (New York: New York University Press, 1993).

7 Fitch and Mandziuk, *Sojourner Truth As Orator*, 3–6; Roseann M. Mandziuk and Suzanne Pullon Fitch, "The Rhetorical Constructions of Sojourner Truth," *Southern Journal of Communication*, 66, no. 2 (2001): 120–138; Roseann M. Mandziuk, "Commemorating Sojourner Truth: Negotiating the Politics of Race and Gender in Spaces of Public Memory," *Western Journal of Communication*, 67, no. 3 (2003): 271–291; Also see Karlyn Kohrs Campbell

"Agency: Promiscuous and Protean," *Communication and Critical/Cultural Studies*, 2, no. 1 (2005): 8–9; Roseann M. Mandziuk, "'Grotesque and Ludicrous, but Yet Inspiring': Depictions of Sojourner Truth and Rhetorics of Domination," *Quarterly Journal of Speech*, 100, no. 4 (2014): 468–469.

8 Fitch and Mandziuk, *Sojourner Truth As Orator*, 3–6; Mandziuk and Suzanne Pullon Fitch, "The Rhetorical Constructions of Sojourner Truth," 120–138; Mandziuk, "Commemorating Sojourner Truth," 271–291; Also see Campbell "Agency: Promiscuous and Protean," 8–9; Mandziuk, "'Grotesque and Ludicrous, but Yet Inspiring,'" 468–469.

9 By rhetorical hauntology, we invoke and apply Derrida's term to illustrate the discursive power of Truth's words to strategically militate against essentializing her. Also see Karlyn Campbell, "Agency: Promiscuous and Protean," *Communication and Critical/Cultural Studies*, 2, no. 1 (2005): 1–19.

10 See Michael Phillips-Anderson, "Sojourner Truth. 'Address at the Woman's Rights Convention in Akron, Ohio,' (29, May 1851)" *Voices of Democracy* 7, (2012): 21–46, http://voicesofdemocracy.umd.edu/wp-content/uploads/2013/08/truth-essay-pdf1.pdf; Phillips-Anderson's interpretative essay examines both Marius Robinson's as well as Frances Gage's versions of Truth's 1851 Akron, Ohio address at the Women's Rights Convention.

11 See Carlton Mabee, *Sojourner Truth: Slave, Prophet, Legend* (New York: New York University Press, 1995); Fitch and Mandziuk, *Sojourner Truth As Orator*, 56–83; Jacqueline Bacon, "God and a Woman: Women Abolitionists, Biblical Authority, and Social Activism" *Journal of Communication and Religion*, 22, no. 1 (1999): 1–39; Isabelle Kinnard Richman, *Sojourner Truth: Prophet of Social Justice* (New York: Routledge, 2016); Jami L. Carlacio, "'Aren't I a Woman (ists)?': The Spiritual Epistemology of Sojourner Truth," *Journal of Communication and Religion*, 39, no. 1 (2016): 5–25; Helane Androne and Leland G. Spencer, "The Sacredness of Black Life: Ritual Structure, Intersectionality, and the Image of God" *Journal of Communication and Religion*, 43, no. 3 (2020): 18–28.

12 Wilson Jeremiah Moses, *Black Messiahs and Uncle Toms: Social and Literary Manipulations of a Religious Myth* (University Park: The Pennsylvania State University Press, 1982), 49–66; James Jasinski, "Constituting Antebellum African American Identity: Resistance, Violence, and Masculinity in Henry Highland Garnet's (1843) 'Address to the Slaves,'" *Quarterly Journal of Speech*, vol. 93. No. 1 (2007), 29–45.

13 Kenneth Burke, *A Grammar of Motives* (Berkeley: University of California Press, 1969), 39.

14 Nathan Crick, *Rhetoric and Power: The Drama of Classical Greece*, Columbia: University of South Carolina Press, 2015, 49.

15 Crick, *Rhetoric and Power*, 49.

16 Harry M. Orlinsky, *The So-Called "Suffering Servant" in Isaiah 53* (Cincinnati: The Hebrew Union Press, 1964), 3.

17 Father Matthew Carr, "Reflection on the Suffering Servant," Catholic Exchange, March 22, 2001, https://catholicexchange.com/the-suffering-servant/.

18 Theophus H. Smith, *Conjuring Culture: Biblical Formations of Black American* (Oxford: Oxford University Press, 1995), 233.

19 Quoted in Richard P. McCormick, "William Whipper: Moral Reformer," *Pennsylvania History* 43 (1976): 23–46.

20 Smith, *Conjuring Culture*, 230–233. For more on redemptive suffering see, Simone Weil, *Gravity and Grace*, trans. by Arthur Wills (Lincoln: University of Nebraska Press, 1997), 72–73.

21 Wilson Jeremiah Moses, *Black Messiahs and Uncle Toms*, 5, 54–57.

22 James Jansinski, "Constituting Antebellum African American Identity," 33. Relatedly, the double edge sword of such a religious tradition constitutes suffering in terms of "offering up" and "to bear one's cross" and can function as a hegemonic discourse that invalidates violent and traumatic experiences.
23 Theophus Smith, *Curing Violence*, 235–236.
24 The Suffering Servant and the Glory of the Servant, Isaiah 53:5, 53: 10, New International Version Bible, https://www.biblegateway.com/passage/?search=Isaiah%2052%3A13-53%3A12&version=NIV
25 Fr. Matthew Carr, "Reflection on the Suffering Servant." Scholars, both Jewish and Christian have recently explored its prehistoricity. See *The Suffering Servant Isaiah 53 in Jewish and Christian Sources* edited by Bernd Janowski and Peter Stuhlmacher, trans. by Daniel P. Bailey (Cambridge: William B. Erdmans Publishing Company, 2004).
26 C.D. Smalley, M. L. Gilbert, and E. Robinson, "Women's Rights Convention," *Salem (OH) Anti-Slavery Bugle*, March 29, 1851.
27 Quoted in Bernice Lowe, "Michigan Days of Sojourner Truth," *New York Folklore Quarterly* 12 (Summer 1956): 127–135.
28 "Sojourner Truth," *Daily Inter Ocean* [Chicago] 1 Jan. 1881: 4.
29 The Suffering Servant and the Glory of the Servant, Isaiah, 53:5.
30 Dwight L. Dumond, *Antislavery: The Crusade for Freedom in America* (New York: Norton Library, 1961), 50.
31 Dumond, *Antislavery*, 50.
32 Gage, "Sojourner Truth." New York Independent. April 23, 1863: 1.
33 Marius Robinson, "Woman's Rights Convention." Salem (OH) Anti-Slavery Bugle. June 21, 1851: 4.
34 Helane Androne and Leland G. Spencer, "The Sacredness of Black Life: Ritual Structure, Intersectionality, and the Image of God," *Journal of Communication and Religion*, 43, no. 3 (2020): 23.
35 Simone Weil, *Gravity and Grace*, trans. Arthur Wills (Lincoln: University of Nebraska Press, 1997), 143.
36 Gage, "Sojourner Truth," 1.
37 Smith *Conjuring Culture*, 188, 192.
38 Sojourner Truth and Olive Gilbert, *Narrative of Sojourner Truth: A northern Slave, Emancipated from Bodily Servitude by the State of New York, in 1828: with a Portrait* (Boston, MA: Printed for the author, 1850), 82–83.
39 Truth and Gilbert, *Narrative of Sojourner Truth*, 37.
40 Most scholars are quick to point out the inaccuracy in the number of children Truth had. She had five children, not thirteen. Francis Gage is responsible for this erroneous embellishment in her 1863 reporting of Truth's 1851 Akron Address. The error was later corrected by Truth's friend Francis W. Titus with an addendum to the "Book of Life" section in Truth's *Narrative*. For more on this see, Roseann M. Mandziuk and Suzanne Pullon Fitch, "The Rhetorical Construction of Sojourner Truth" *Southern Journal of Communication*, 66, no. 2 (2001), 126.
41 Campbell "Agency: Promiscuous and Protean," 10; Michael Phillips-Anderson, "Sojourner Truth. 'Address at the Woman's Rights Convention in Akron, Ohio,' (29, May 1851)" *Voices of Democracy*, 7, (2012): 32.
42 F. D. Gage., "Sojourner Truth," New York Independent, April 23, 1863: 1.

43 Fitch and Mandziuk, *Sojourner Truth as Orator*, 77. For other oratorical instances where Truth employs examples of biblical women, particularly Ester and Mary of Magdala, see Fitch and Mandziuk *Sojourner Truth as Orator*, 78–80.
44 Phillips-Anderson, "Sojourner Truth," 33.
45 Robinson, "Woman's Rights Convention," 4.
46 Helane Androne and Leland G. Spencer, "The Sacredness of Black Life: Ritual Structure, Intersectionality, and the Image of God" *Journal of Communication and Religion*, 43, no. 3 (2020), 23.
47 Androne and Specer, "The Sacredness of Black Life," 23.
48 James Arnt Aune, "Lincoln and the American Sublime" *Communication Reports* 1, no. 1 (1988): 15–18.
49 Jason A. Springs *Healthy Conflict in Contemporary American Society: From Enemy to Adversary* (Cambridge: Cambridge University Press, 2018), 186–187.
50 These sentiments are mostly strongly articulated in Sojourner Truth's "Abolition Slavery Address," Proceedings of the New York City Anti-Slavery Society, September 4, 1853.
51 Quoted in Fitch and Manduziuk, *Sojourner Truth as Orator*, 139.
52 David A. Frank, "The Act of Forgiveness in Barack Obama's Eulogy for the Honorable Clementa Pinckney, Charleston, South Carolina, June 26, 2015," in *Rhetoric, Race, Religion, and The Charleston Shootings: Was Blind but Now I See*, ed. Sean Patrick O'Rourke and Melody Lehn (Lanham: Lexington Books, 2020), 118.

Chapter 2: Part 1 LGBTQ and Violence

1 Liz Tracey, "Proposition 6 (The Briggs Initiative): Annotated," *JSTOR Daily*, October 28, 2022, https://daily.jstor.org/proposition-6-the-briggs-initiative-annotated/.
2 Caitlin O'Loughlin-Rosa wrote a brief, but interesting essay, "Briggs, Milk and the Battle For Teacher Privacy: Rethinking Debate Performance Through Thematic Transcription," making the argument that the conventional criteria used to evaluate the success of debates in a debate performance should be supplanted with the assessment metrics of "floor control and idea resonance." In pursuing this thesis, O'Loughlin-Rosa uses the September 6, 1978 debate transcript in Emery's volume, applying a simplified version of the seminal essay on Conversational Analysis, "A Simplest Systematics for the organization of Turn-Taking For Conversation," in addition to thematic transcription, adapted from Edelsky's "Who's Got the Floor." O'Loughlin-Rosa's analysis uses lines 17–71 of the dialogue for the Conversation Analysis, and lines 26–56 for the thematic description. O'Loughlin-Rosa concludes from the sections analyzed, that Briggs actually won the debate, although our analysis does not support that conclusion.
3 Emery, *The Harvey Milk Interviews*, 246.
4 Emery, *The Harvey Milk Interviews*, 246; This analysis draws text from the taped excerpts of the Milk-Briggs debate. See Jon Brooks, "The Times of Harvey Milk," *KQED*, March 23, 2014, https://www.kqed.org/arts/128579/california-films-the-times-of-harvey-milk.
5 Steven Clayman and John Heritage, *The News Interview: Journalists and Public Figures on the Air* (Cambridge: Cambridge University Press, 2002), 1.
6 Harvey Milk, Jason Edward Black, and Charles E. Morris, eds., *An Archive of Hope: Harvey Milk's Speeches and Writings* (Berkeley: University of California Press, 2013), 227–229. By kind permission of University of Callifornia Press.

7   "Remarks by President Biden and Vice President Harris at Signing of H.R. 8404, the Respect for Marriage Act," The White House, December 13, 2022, https://www.whitehouse.gov/briefing-room/speeches-remarks/2022/12/13/remarks-by-president-biden-and-vice-president-harris-at-signing-of-h-r-8404-the-respect-for-marriage-act/.
8   *Dobbs v. Jackson Women's Health Organization*, 597 U.S. ___ (2022).
9   "Remarks by President Biden and Vice President Harris at Signing of H.R. 8404."
10 H.B. 1557, Leg. Sess. 124(R) (Fl. 2022), https://legiscan.com/FL/bill/H1557/2022.
11 Edward Swidriski, "Florida's "Don't Say Gay" Law Raises Serious Legal Questions," American Bar Association, November 22, 2022, https://www.americanbar.org/groups/labor_law/publications/labor_employment_law_news/fall-2022/florida-do-not-say-gay-law/.
12 Swidriski, "Florida's "Don't Say Gay" Law Raises Serious Legal Questions."
13 Swidriski, "Florida's "Don't Say Gay" Law Raises Serious Legal Questions."
14 Anthony Izaguirre, and Adriana Gomez Licon, "'Don't Say Gay' law brings worry, confusion to Florida schools," *PBS*, August 15, 2022, https://www.pbs.org/newshour/education/dont-say-gay-law-brings-worry-confusion-to-florida-schools.
15 Anthony Izaguirre, "DeSantis to expand 'Don't Say Gay' law to high school classes," *PBS*, March 22, 2023, https://www.pbs.org/newshour/politics/desantis-to-expand-dont-say-gay-law-to-high-school-classes.
16 Kathryn Varn and Douglas Soule, "Florida LGBTQ advocates: Expanding so-called 'Don't Say Gay' law says 'quiet part out loud,'" *Tallahassee Democrat*, March 24, 2023, https://www.tallahassee.com/story/news/politics/2023/03/24/florida-dont-say-gay-law-expansion-lgbtq-advocates-terrified-desantis/70039050007/; Sareen Habeshian, "DeSantis administration moves to expand 'Don't Say Gay' law in Florida," *Axios*, March 22, 2023, https://www.axios.com/2023/03/22/florida-desantis-dont-say-gay-expansion; Izaguirre, "DeSantis to expand 'Don't Say Gay' law to high school classes."
17 Varn and Soule, "Florida LGBTQ advocates."
18 Liz Tracey, "Proposition 6 (The Briggs Initiative): Annotated," *JSTOR Daily*, October 28, 2022, https://daily.jstor.org/proposition-6-the-briggs-initiative-annotated/.
19 Trudy Ring, "The Briggs Initiative: Remembering a Crucial Moment in Gay History," *Advocate*, August 31, 2018, https://www.advocate.com/politics/2018/8/31/briggs-initiative-remembering-crucial-moment-gay-history/.
20 Lillian Faderman, *Harvey Milk: His Lives and Death* (New Haven: Yale University Press, 2018), 184.
21 Vince Emery, *The Harvey Milk Interviews: In His Own Words*, 2nd ed. (San Francisco, CA: Vince Emery Productions, 2017), 20.
22 Emery, *The Harvey Milk Interviews*, 180; Annabelle Williams, "Sally Miller Gearhart, Lesbian Separatist and Activist, Dies at 90," *New York Times*, July 26, 2021, nytimes.com/2021/07/26/us/sally-miller-gearhart-dead.html.
23 Williams, "Sally Miller Gearhart."
24 Sally Miller Gearhart, "The Womanization of Rhetoric," *Women's Studies International Quarterly*, 2, no. 2 (1979): 195.
25 Gearhart, "The Womanization of Rhetoric," 195.
26 Gearhart, "The Womanization of Rhetoric," 196.
27 Gearhart, "The Womanization of Rhetoric," 196.
28 Gearhart, "The Womanization of Rhetoric," 200.
29 Wayne Booth, *The Rhetoric of Rhetoric: The Quest for Effective Communication* (Malden, MA: Blackwell Publishing, 2004), 10–11.

30 Cheryl Glenn and Andrea A. Lunsford, "Foresights from a foremother: Sally Miller Gearhart," *Introspection*, no. 2 (2019): 1–11, https://sites.google.com/murraystate.edu/intraspection/home/all-issues/issue-2-2019/foresights-from-a-foremother.
31 Emery, *The Harvey Milk Interviews*, 19.
32 Faderman, *Harvey Milk*, 181.
33 Faderman, *Harvey Milk*, 182.
34 Jon Brooks, "The Times of Harvey Milk," *KQED*, March 23, 2014, https://www.kqed.org/arts/128579/california-films-the-times-of-harvey-milk.
35 Bay Area Television Archive, "Harvey Milk Meets John Briggs," DIVA San Francisco State University, accessed, May 22, 2023, https://diva.sfsu.edu/collections/sfbatv/bundles/190667.
36 Bay Area Television Archive, "Harvey Milk Meets John Briggs;" Faderman, *Harvey Milk*, 182.
37 Bay Area Television Archive, "Harvey Milk Meets John Briggs;" Faderman, *Harvey Milk*, 182.
38 Faderman, *Harvey Milk*, 182.
39 Faderman, *Harvey Milk*, 182.
40 Williams, "Sally Miller Gearhart."
41 New York Times Editorial Board, "Texas is Silencing the Will of Millions of Voters," *New York Times*, June 3, 2023, https://www.nytimes.com/2023/06/03/opinion/texas-preemption-bill.html.
42 Molly Spragyregen, "Florida teachers forced to explain they're not teaching kids to be gay," *LGBTQ Nation*, June 1, 2023, https://www.lgbtqnation.com/2023/06/florida-teachers-forced-to-explain-theyre-not-teaching-kids-to-be-gay/.
43 Randy Shilts, *The Mayor of Castro Street* (New York: St. Martin's Press, 1982), 155.
44 Shilts, *The Mayor of Castro Street*, 155.
45 Tracey, "Proposition 6 (The Briggs Initiative): Annotated."
46 Tracey, "Proposition 6 (The Briggs Initiative): Annotated."
47 Ramy K. Khalil, "Harvey Milk and California Proposition 6: How the Gay Liberation Movement Won Two Early Victories," M.A. thesis (Western Washington University, 2012), 74, https://cedar.wwu.edu/wwuet/208.
48 Faderman, *Harvey Milk*, 143.
49 Khalil, "Harvey Milk and California Proposition 6," 74.
50 Shilts, *The Mayor of Castro Street*, 157.
51 Shilts, *The Mayor of Castro Street*, 157.
52 Tracey, "Proposition 6 (The Briggs Initiative): Annotated."
53 "Voter Information Guide for 1978, General Election," UC Law SF Scholarship repository, accessed May 27, 2023, https://repository.uclawsf.edu/ca_ballot_props/844.
54 Emery, *The Harvey Milk Interviews*, 29.
55 Emery, *The Harvey Milk Interviews*, 30.
56 Emery, *The Harvey Milk Interviews*, 9.
57 Emery, *The Harvey Milk Interviews*, 230.
58 Emery, *The Harvey Milk Interviews*, 240.
59 Emery, *The Harvey Milk Interviews*, 24–25.
60 Emery, *The Harvey Milk Interviews*, 25.
61 Emery, *The Harvey Milk Interviews*, 26–28.
62 Emery, *The Harvey Milk Interviews*, 29.
63 Emery, *The Harvey Milk Interviews*, 29.
64 Emery, *The Harvey Milk Interviews*, 14–16.

65 Milk, Black, and Morris, *An Archive of Hope*, 39.
66 Milk, Black, and Morris, *An Archive of Hope*, 39; Faderman, *Harvey Milk*, 3, 30.
67 "Harvey Milk Forever Stamp Dedicated at White House Today," *USPS*, May 22, 2014, https://about.usps.com/news/national-releases/2014/pr14_033.htm.
68 Deepa Shivaram, "The U.S. Navy has christened a ship named after slain gay rights leader Harvey Milk," *NPR*, November 7, 2021, https://www.npr.org/2021/11/07/1053330774/navy-ship-harvey-milk.
69 Brett Krutzch, *Dying to be Normal* (New York: Oxford University Press, 2019), 15.
70 Krutzch, *Dying to be Normal*, 15.
71 William K. Gilders, "Harvey Milk's (sexual and sacred) body," *Body and Religion*, 5, no. 1 (2022): 8.
72 Gilders, "Harvey Milk's (sexual and sacred) body," 9.
73 Gilders, "Harvey Milk's (sexual and sacred) body," 9.
74 Krutzch, *Dying to be Normal*, 15.
75 Gregg Drinkwater, "Creating an embodied queer Judaism: Liturgy, ritual and sexuality at San Francisco's Congregation Sha'ar Zahav, 1977–1987," *Journal of Modern Jewish Studies*, 18, no. 2 (2019): 177.
76 Drinkwater, "Creating an embodied queer Judaism," 179.
77 Shilts, *The Mayor of Castro Street*, 372.
78 Shilts, *The Mayor of Castro Street*, 374–375.
79 Faderman, *Harvey Milk*, 220.
80 Faderman, *Harvey Milk*, 221.
81 Faderman, *Harvey Milk*, 221.
82 Faderman, *Harvey Milk*, 222.
83 Faderman, *Harvey Milk*, 196.
84 Shilts, *The Mayor of Castro Street*, 292.
85 Faderman, *Harvey Milk*, 5.
86 Krutzch, *Dying to be Normal*, 42.
87 Faderman, *Harvey Milk*, 4–5.
88 Krutzch, *Dying to be Normal*, 40.
89 Krutzch, *Dying to be Normal*, 40.
90 Krutzch, *Dying to be Normal*, 40.
91 Krutzch, *Dying to be Normal*, 42–43.
92 Krutzch, *Dying to be Normal*, 44; *Milk*, directed by Gus Van Sant, 2008 (San Francisco, CA: Focus Features).
93 Faderman, *Harvey Milk*, 5.
94 Faderman, *Harvey Milk*, 5
95 Krutzch, *Dying to be Normal*, 44.
96 Krutzch, *Dying to be Normal*, 45.
97 Paul Ricœur, *The Rule of Metaphor*, trans. Robert Czerny, with Kathleen McLaughlin and John Costello, S.J. (Toronto: University of Toronto Press, 1993), 3.
98 Aristotle and Eugene Garver, eds., *Poetics and Rhetoric* (New York: Barnes & Noble Classics, 2006), 61.
99 Aristotle and Garver, *Poetics and Rhetoric*, 63.
100 Ricœur, *The Rule of Metaphor*, 13.
101 Aristotle and Garver, *Poetics and Rhetoric*, 27, 37–38.

102 Aristotle and Garver, *Poetics and Rhetoric*, 17.
103 Ricœur, *The Rule of Metaphor*, 12.
104 Arlene Stein, "Whose Memories? Whose Victimhood? Contests for the Holocaust Frame in Recent Social Movement Discourse," *Sociological Perspectives*, 41, no. 3 (1998): 535.
105 Stein, "Whose Memories?," 520.
106 Stein, "Whose Memories?," 520.
107 Stein, "Whose Memories?," 522.
108 Stein, "Whose Memories?," 523.
109 Shilts, *The Mayor of Castro Street*, 11.
110 Shilts, *The Mayor of Castro Street*, 364.
111 "Paragraph 175 and the Nazi Campaign Against Homosexuality," *Holocaust Encyclopedia*, May 4, 2021, https://encyclopedia.ushmm.org/content/en/article/paragraph-175-and-the-nazi-campaign-against-homosexuality.
112 "Gay Men Under The Nazi Regime – Photographs," Holocaust Encyclopedia, accessed, May 26, 2023, https://encyclopedia.ushmm.org/content/en/gallery/gay-men-under-the-nazi-regime-photographs?parent=en%2F45421; Stein, "Whose Memories?," 527.
113 "Gay Men Under The Nazi Regime – Photographs."
114 Stein, "Whose Memories?," 527.
115 Faderman, *Harvey Milk*, 4.
116 Faderman, *Harvey Milk*, 179.
117 Faderman, *Harvey Milk*, 179.
118 Faderman, *Harvey Milk*, 179.
119 Faderman, *Harvey Milk*, 179.
120 Erik N. Jensen, "The Pink Triangle and Political Consciousness: Gays, Lesbians, and the Memory of Nazi Persecution," *Journal of the History of Sexuality*, 11, no. 1/2 (2002): 325.
121 Jensen, "The Pink Triangle and Political Consciousness," 325.
122 Jensen, "The Pink Triangle and Political Consciousness," 325.
123 Shilts, *The Mayor of Castro Street*, 365.
124 Shilts, *The Mayor of Castro Street*, 368.
125 Krutzch, *Dying to be Normal*, 44.
126 Milk, Black, and Morris, *An Archive of Hope*, 140.
127 Faderman, *Harvey Milk*, 170.
128 Faderman, *Harvey Milk*, 17.
129 Faderman, *Harvey Milk*, 17.
130 Stein, "Whose Memories?," 533.
131 Stein, "Whose Memories?," 533.
132 Stein, "Whose Memories?," 534.
133 Stein, "Whose Memories?," 534.
134 Stein, "Whose Memories?," 534.
135 Stein, "Whose Memories?," 535.
136 Stein, "Whose Memories?," 535.
137 Caitlin O'Loughlin-Rosa wrote a brief, but interesting essay, "Briggs, Milk and the Battle For Teacher Privacy: Rethinking Debate Performance Through Thematic Transcription," making the argument that the conventional criteria used to evaluate the success of debates in a debate performance should be supplanted with the assessment metrics of "floor control and idea resonance." In pursuing this thesis, O'Loughlin-Rosa uses the September 6, 1978 debate transcript

in Emery's volume, applying a simplified version of the seminal essay on Conversational Analysis, "A Simplest Systematics for the organization of Turn-Taking For Conversation," in addition to thematic transcription, adapted from Edelsky's "Who's Got the Floor." O'Loughlin-Rosa's analysis uses lines 17–71 of the dialogue for the Conversation Analysis, and lines 26–56 for the thematic description. O'Loughlin-Rosa concludes from the sections analyzed, that Briggs actually won the debate, although our analysis does not support that conclusion.

138 Emery, *The Harvey Milk Interviews*, 246.
139 Emery, *The Harvey Milk Interviews*, 246.
140 Emery, *The Harvey Milk Interviews*, 246; This analysis draws text from the taped excerpts of the Milk-Briggs debate. See Jon Brooks, "The Times of Harvey Milk," *KQED*, March 23, 2014, https://www.kqed.org/arts/128579/california-films-the-times-of-harvey-milk.
141 Steven Clayman and John Heritage, *The News Interview: Journalists and Public Figures on the Air* (Cambridge: Cambridge University Press, 2002), 1.
142 Clayman and Heritage, *The News Interview*, 7.
143 Clayman and Heritage, *The News Interview*, 1–2; The following timeline delineates classified debates and interviews from Emery's *The Harvey Milk Interviews*, 19–20:

September 6, 1978-Debate, New San Remo Restaurant in San Francisco.

September 15-Debate, Northgate High School Auditorium in Walnut Creek.

September 26-Milk is interviewed by Juana Samayoa live on KBHK TV's program *News Talk*.

October 11-Debate, Mission High School in San Francisco, KQED, between Milk/Gearhart and Briggs/Batema. Questions from KQED reporters Randy Shilts and Rollin Post.

November 1-Debate at Pacifica High School in Garden Grove (Briggs's district).November 2-Debate in Los Angeles live on KABC-TV and/or KABC radio.November 3-Debate at Temple Sinai in Oakland.November 5-Debate on KJAZ radio in San Francisco.

144 Emery, *The Harvey Milk Interviews*, 246.
145 Clayman and Heritage, *The News Interview*, 12.
146 Clayman and Heritage, *The News Interview*, 299.
147 Clayman and Heritage, *The News Interview*, 334.
148 Clayman and Heritage, *The News Interview*, 299.
149 Clayman and Heritage, *The News Interview*, 335.
150 Clayman and Heritage, *The News Interview*, 335.
151 Clayman and Heritage, *The News Interview*, 300.
152 Paul Drew and John Heritage, "Introduction," in *Conversational Analysis*, vol. 1 (London: SAGE Publications 2006), xxii; For an excellent discussion for the background of the CA methodology for examining news interviews, see Heritage and Clayman, *Talk in Action*, 7–19.
153 Drew and Heritage, "Introduction," xxii.
154 Drew and Heritage, "Introduction," xxiv.
155 Clayman and Heritage, *The News Interview*,18.
156 Gerda Lauerbach, "Argumentation in Political Talk Show Interviews," *Journal of Pragmatics*, 39, no. 8 (2007): 1388.
157 Lauerbach, "Argumentation in Political Talk Show Interviews," 1388.
158 Lauerbach, "Argumentation in Political Talk Show Interviews," 1390.
159 Lauerbach, "Argumentation in Political Talk Show Interviews," 1391; Also, see Stephen Toulmin, *The Uses of Argument* (Cambridge University Press, 2003), 87–134.

160 Bay Area Television Archive, "Harvey Milk Meets John Briggs," DIVA San Francisco State University, accessed, May 22, 2023, https://diva.sfsu.edu/collections/sfbatv/bundles/190667.
161 Lauerbach, "Argumentation in Political Talk Show Interviews," 1390.
162 Clayman and Heritage, *The News Interview*, 300.
163 Clayman and Heritage, *The News Interview*, 313–314.
164 David Greatbatch, "On the Management of Disagreement Between News Interviewees," in *Talk at Work*, edited by Paul Drew and John Heritage (Cambridge: Cambridge University Press, 1992), 283.
165 Milk, Black, and Morris, *An Archive of Hope*, 280.
166 Milk, Black, and Morris, *An Archive of Hope*, 7.
167 Faderman, *Harvey Milk*, 3.
168 Faderman, *Harvey Milk*, 4.
169 Aristotle and Garver, *Poetics and Rhetoric*, 173.
170 Aristotle and Garver, *Poetics and Rhetoric*, 173.
171 Aristotle and Garver, *Poetics and Rhetoric*, 173.

Chapter 2: Part 2 LGBTQ and Violence

1 Tony Kushner, "Matthew's Passion," The Nation, November 11, 1998, https://web.archive.org/web/20030730084624/http://www.class.uidaho.edu/diversity/tkon.htm. From The Nation. © 1998 The Nation Company. All rights reserved. Used under license.
2 Kenneth Burke, *A Rhetoric of Motives* (Berkeley: University of California Press, 1969), 260–267. Also see Gregory Desilet, *Cult of the Kill: Traditional Metaphysics of Rhetoric, Truth, and Violence in a Postmodern World* (Bloomington: Xlibris, 2006), 20, 25, 26, 39, 111, 112, 123, 167; For references to Christianity, see 113, 162, 173, 174.
3 James Brooke's article in *The New York Times* was one of the first to describe the killing of Matthew Shepard as a "crucifixion." James Brooke, "Gay Man Dies from Attack, Fanning Outrage and Debate," *New York Times* 13, October, 1998. https://www.nytimes.com/1998/10/13/us/gay-man-dies-from-attack-fanning-outrage-and-debate.html. Tom Kenworthy's *Washington Post* coverage of Shepard's funeral used the phrase "light of the world" taken from Shepard's eulogy, and the scriptural passage John 8:12 where Jesus Christ state's "I am the light of the world." See Tom Kenworthy, "Hundreds Gather to Remember Slain Man as 'Light of the World'" *Washington Post* 17, October, 1998.https://www.washingtonpost.com/archive/politics/1998/10/17/hundreds-gather-to-remember-slain-man-as-light-to-the-world/a45ca bbb-3a31-43eb-8256-1414ee27e7b9/; Joseph Trevino, "Religious Leaders Decry Wyoming Man's Slaying," *Los Angeles Times* (Los Angeles, CA), October 15, 1998; Rembert Truluck, "Matthew Died for You and Me," *Whosoever*, November/December 1998: AG. Tony Kushner's November 11, 1998 trenchant opt ed in *The Nation* is titled "Matthew's Passion," a clear mimesis of "Christ's Passion;" Jude Sheerin's BBC report, "Matthew Shepard: The Murder that Changed America," denoted Matthew Shepard's ashes being interred at the National Cathedral in Washington DC in October of 2018 as "secular sainthood" and the "consecration" of a "perfect icon." https://www.bbc.com/news/world-us-canada-45968606; Also *The Advocate*, November 10, 1998 employs the paronomasia "The Good Shepard," joining Mathew Shepard with the this well-known sobriquet for Jesus Christ, who in John 10:11–18 "lays down his life for his sheep;" Melanie Thernstrom, "The Crucifixion of Mathew Shepard," *Vanity Fair*,

March 1998: 209.; Mark Miller, "The Final Days of a Gay Martyr," *Newsweek*, December 21, 1998: 30.; Guy Trebay, "Beyond the Fence: Conjuring the Lives of Martyr Mathew Shepard," *Village Voice*, November 3, 1998.Scott W. Hoffman, "Last Night I Prayed to Matthew: Matthew Shepard, Homosexuality, and Popular Martyrdom in Contemporary America," *Religion and American Culture: A Journal of Interpretation*, 21, no. 1 (2011); For a more recent academic exploration of the Christ figure/martyr archetype, see chapter 2 "The 'Crucifixion' of 'Anyone's Gay Son': Matthew Shepard," Brett Krutzsch, *Dying to be Normal: Gay Martyrs and the Transformation of American Sexual Politics* (Oxford: Oxford University Press), 2019, 47–83.

4   Beth Loffreda, *Losing Matt Shepard: Life and Politics in the Aftermath of Anti-Gay Murder* (New York: Columbia University Press, 2000), 18. Also see Michael Cobb, *God Hates Fags: Rhetorics of Religious Violence* (New York: New York University Press, 2006), 2–3.
5   Beth Loffreda, *Losing Matt Shepard*, 92. Also see Cobb, *God Hates Fags*, 2.
6   Loffreda, *Losing Matt Shepard*, x.
7   See Loffreda, *Losing Matt Shepard*; Brian L.Ott and Eric Aoki "The Politics of Negotiating Public Tragedy: Media Framing of the Matthew Shepard Murder" *Rhetoric & Public Affairs* 5.3 (2002): 483–505; Cobb, *God Hates Fags*; Thomas R. Dunn, "Remembering Matthew Shepard: Violence, Identity, and Queer Counterpublic Memories," *Rhetoric & Public Affairs*, 13, no. 4 (2010); Scott W. Hoffman, "Last Night I Prayed to Matthew: Matthew Shepard, Homosexuality, and Popular Martyrdom in Contemporary America," *Religion and American Culture: A Journal of Interpretation*, 21, no. 1 (2011); Krutzsch, *Dying to be Normal*.
8   Cobb, *God Hates Fags*, 6–7.
9   See Perry Miller, *Errand into the Wilderness* (Cambridge: Harvard University Press, 1956), and Sacvan Bercovitch, *The American Jeremiad* (Madison: University of Wisconsin Press, 1978).
10 Ibid., 9, 11.
11 Krutzsch, *Dying to Be Normal*, 49, 52–72.
12 Krutzsch, *Dying to be Normal*, 64.
13 For scholarship on prophetic rhetoric employing invective and agitation, see Andre Johnson, *No Future in This Country: The Pessimism of Bishop Henry McNeal Turner* (Jackson: University of Mississippi Press, 2020), 15–20.
14 Kenneth Burke *Proletariat Literature in the United States* (find publication info) 134
15 Kenneth Burke, *Philosophy of Literary Form* (Berkeley: University of California Press, 1969), 61.
16 René Girard theorizes "original sin" and the sacrificial violence of scapegoating stems from mimetic rivalry similar to Kenneth Burkes' negative or "Thou Shalt Nots" implicit in the concept of Order, Guilt, Purification, and Redemption. René Girard, *Violence and the Sacred* translated by Patrick Gregory (Baltimore: The Johns Hopkins University Press, 1972), 4, 8; 36–37. Danielle Allen, *Talking to Strangers: Anxieties of Citizenship Since Brown vs. Board of Education* (Chicago: University of Chicago Press, 2004), 28–29.
17 Danielle Allen, *Talking to Strangers*, 29.
18 Allen, *Talking to Strangers*, 107.
19 Quoted in Allen, *Talking to Strangers*, 107 footnote 8.
20 Kushner, "Matthew's Passion."
21 Kushner, "Matthew's Passion."
22 Kushner, "Matthew's Passion."
23 See Aristotle, *On Rhetoric: A Theory of Civic Discourse* 2nd ed. translated by George A. Kennedy (Oxford: Oxford University Press, 2007), 218–225. Also see Monica Westin, "Aristotle's Rhetorical *Energeia*: An Extended Note" *Advances in the History of Rhetoric*, 20, no. 3 (2017): 252–261; Cicero refers to this bringing-before-the eyes as "ocular demonstration;"

For Longinus it is a stylistic figure that aids in sublime writing; Ernesto Grassi characterized *energeia* as "catalytic imagination."
24 Kushner, "Matthew's Passion."
25 Fontanier, *Les Figures du discourse*, 371. Also see Jeanne Fahnestock, *Rhetorical Style: The Uses of Language in Persuasion* (Oxford: Oxford University Press, 2011), 291–300.
26 Cicero, *Rhetorica Ad Herennium*, 285.
27 Laurent Pernot, *The Subtle Subtext* (State College: The Pennsylvania State University Press, 2021), 129.
28 In defining apostrophe, Walter Ong remarked "the writer's audience is always a fiction." Walter Ong, *The Writer's Audience is Always a Fiction*, *PMLA* 90. 1 (1975): 9–21.
29 Kushner, "Matthew's Passion."
30 Kushner, "Matthew's Passion."
31 Kushner, "Matthew's Passion."

Chapter 3 Geopolitics, Violence, and Remembrance

1 C-SPAN, "Interfaith Meeting with Pope Francis at September 11 Memorial," C-SPAN video, 9:05, 29:34. September 25, 2015, https://www.c-span.org/video/?328181-1/interfaith-meeting-pope-francis-911-memorial; "Full Text: Pope Francis' speech at the 9/11 Memorial and Museum," *Catholic News Agency*, September 25, 2015, https://www.catholicnewsagency.com/news/32701/full-text-pope-francis-speech-at-the-911-memorial-and-museum. Public Domain.
2 J. Samuel Walker, *The Day That Shook America* (Lawrence, Kansas: University of Kansas Press, 2021), 15–17.
3 Walker, 17.
4 Alice M. Greenwald and Clifford Chanin, eds., *The Stories They Tell: Artifacts from the National September 11 Memorial Museum*, with foreword by Michael R. Bloomberg and introduction by Joe Daniels (Rizzoli International Publications, 2013), 7.
5 "September 11, 2001: The Day That Changed the World," National September 11 Memorial and Museum, published June 2021, https://www.911memorial.org/sites/default/files/inline-files/ALA-Poster-Final-20210629-SR.pdf.
6 Ernest R. May, *The 9/11 Commission Report with Related Documents*, 1st ed. (Boston: Bedford/St. Martin's, 2007). 39, 42.
7 May, *The 9/11 Commission Report*, 42.
8 May, *The 9/11 Commission Report*, 43.
9 May, *The 9/11 Commission Report*, 43, 44.
10 May, *The 9/11 Commission Report*, 44.
11 May, *The 9/11 Commission Report*, 47.
12 Stephen E. Atkins, ed., *The 9/11 Encyclopedia*, vol. 1, 2nd ed. (Santa Barbara, California: ABC-CLIO, 2011), 473.
13 Atkins, *The 9/11 Encyclopedia*, 34, 76.
14 Atkins, *The 9/11 Encyclopedia*, 78.
15 Atkins, *The 9/11 Encyclopedia*, 76–77.
16 Atkins, *The 9/11 Encyclopedia*, 78.

17 "Pope Francis to Visit Historic 9/11 Memorial and Museum" [Press Release], National September 11 Memorial and Museum, published June 30, 2015, https://911memorial.org/sites/default/files/inline-files/2015.6.30.pdf.
18 Laurie Goodstein, "In a Void Created by Religious Violence, Pope Francis Shares Prayers for Peace," *New York Times*, September 25, 2015, https://www.nytimes.com/2015/09/26/us/in-a-void-created-by-religious-violence-pope-francis-shares-prayers-for-peace.html.
19 Goodstein, "In a Void Created by Religious Violence."
20 Goodstein, "In a Void Created by Religious Violence."
21 Adrienne E. Hacker Daniels, "Rhetorology and Interfaith Dialogue," in *A Communication Perspective on Interfaith Dialogue*, ed. Daniel S. Brown, Jr. (Lanham, MD: Lexington Books, 2013), 65.
22 A. James Rudin, "The Interreligious Golden Age: Has It Ended?," in *Trialogue and Terror: Judaism, Christianity, and Islam after 9/11*, ed. Alan L. Berger (Eugene, OR: Cascade Books, 2012), 7.
23 Pope Paul VI, *Nostra Aetate*, released October 28, 1965, https://www.vatican.va/archive/hist_councils/ii_vatican_council/documents/vat-ii_decl_19651028_nostra-aetate_en.html.
24 Rudin, "The Interreligious Golden Age," 7–9.
25 Pope Paul VI, *Nostra Aetate*.
26 Amos Kiewe, *The Rhetoric of Antisemitism* (Lanham, MD: Lexington Books, 2021), 163–164.
27 Kiewe, *The Rhetoric of Antisemitism*, 161.
28 Pope Paul VI, *Nostra Aetate*.
29 Kathleen M. Edelmayer, "Function and Value of Interfaith Dialogue," Forward to *Interfaith Dialogue: Dialogue in Practice*, ed. Daniel S. Brown (New York: Fordham University Press, 2013), ix.
30 Daniel S. Brown, "Communication Theory Meets Interfaith Dialogue," in *Interfaith Dialogue: Dialogue in Practice*, ed. Daniel S. Brown (New York: Fordham University Press, 2013), 5.
31 Edelmayer, "Function and Value of Interfaith Dialogue," v-xv; Brown, "Communication Theory Meets Interfaith Dialogue," 3–22.
32 Kathleen Mary Black, "Interfaith/Interreligious? Worship/Prayer? Services/Occasions? Interfaith Prayer Gatherings," *Religions*, 13, no. 6 (2022): 2.
33 Jonathan Magonet, *Talking to the Other* (London: I.B. Taurus, 2003), 1–2.
34 Rabbi Herbert Bronstein, Helen Cahill, O.P., and Syafa'atun Elmirzana, "Prayer in the Abrahamic Faiths," *New Theology Review* (August 2003): 22–23.
35 Eugene J. Fisher, "9/11: Dialogue and Trialogue," in *Trialogue and Terror: Judaism, Christianity, and Islam after 9/11*, ed. Alan L. Berger (Eugene, OR: Cascade Books, 2012), 100.
36 Khaleel Mohammed, "Dialogical Interaction or Post-Honor Confrontation," in *Trialogue and Terror: Judaism, Christianity, and Islam after 9/11*, ed. Alan L. Berger (Eugene, OR: Cascade Books, 2012), 166.
37 Fisher, "9/11: Dialogue and Trialogue," 100.
38 Muhammad Shafiq, "Transformation Through Dialogue of a Muslim Scholar's Search for Identity," in *Trialogue and Terror: Judaism, Christianity, and Islam after 9/11*, ed. Alan L. Berger (Eugene, OR: Cascade Books, 2012), 225.
39 Sunggu A. Yang, "A Liturgical Model for Worship in the Multireligious Context: A Case Study Based on the Interfaith Service Held on September 25, 2015, at 9/11 Museum in New York City," *Religions*, 13, no. 6 (2022): 1.
40 Black, "Interfaith/Interreligious?," 1–2.
41 Bronstein, Cahill, and Elmirzana, "Prayer in the Abrahamic Faiths," 23.

42 Marcus Braybrooke, "The Issues," in *All in Good Faith*, ed. Jean Potter and Marcus Braybrooke (Oxford: The World Congress of Faiths, 1997), 31.
43 Black, "Interfaith/Interreligious?," 2.
44 "Pope Francis to Visit Historic 9/11 Memorial and Museum."
45 "Pope Francis to Visit Historic 9/11 Memorial and Museum."
46 "Pope Francis to Visit Historic 9/11 Memorial and Museum."
47 Marcus Braybrooke, "The Development of Interfaith Services," in *All in Good Faith*, ed. Jean Potter and Marcus Braybrooke (Oxford: The World Congress of Faiths, 1997), 22.
48 Marcus Braybrooke and Jean Potter, "Introduction," in *All in Good Faith*, ed. Jean Potter and Marcus Braybrooke (Oxford: The World Congress of Faiths, 1997), 1.
49 Braybrooke and Potter, "Introduction," 1.
50 Christopher Lewis, "The Argument for Interfaith Prayer and Worship," in *Interfaith Worship and Prayer*, ed. Christopher Lewis and Dan Cohn-Sherbok (London: Jessica Kingsley Publishers, 2019), 19.
51 Braybrooke, "The Development of Interfaith Services," 5.
52 Dan Cohn-Sherbok, "Introduction," in *Interfaith Worship and Prayer*, ed. Christopher Lewis and Dan Cohn-Sherbok (London: Jessica Kingsley Publishers, 2019), 13.
53 Cohn-Sherbok, "Introduction," 13.
54 Lewis, "The Argument for Interfaith Prayer and Worship," 17–18.
55 Lewis, "The Argument for Interfaith Prayer and Worship," 21.
56 Lewis, "The Argument for Interfaith Prayer and Worship," 22.
57 Braybrooke, "The Development of Interfaith Services," 22.
58 Braybrooke, "The Development of Interfaith Services," 22.
59 Braybrooke, "The Development of Interfaith Services," 22.
60 Marianne Moyaert, "Introduction: Exploring the Phenomenon of Interreligious Ritual Participation," in *Ritual Participation and Interreligious Dialogue*, ed. Marianne Moyaert and Joris Geldhof (London: Bloomsbury, 2015), 2.
61 Marianne Moyaert, "Introduction," 1–2.
62 Marianna Moyaert, "Broadening the Scope of Interreligious Studies: Interrituality," in *Interreligious Relations and the Negotiation of Ritual Boundaries*, ed. Marianne Moyaert (Np: Palgrave Macmillan, 2019), 6.
63 Moyaert, "Broadening the Scope," 6.
64 Moyaert, "Broadening the Scope," 6.
65 Marianne Moyaert, "Introduction," 2.
66 Black, "Interfaith/Interreligious?," 3.
67 Black, "Interfaith/Interreligious?," 4.
68 Black, "Interfaith/Interreligious?," 6.
69 C-SPAN, "Interfaith Meeting with Pope Francis at September 11 Memorial," C-SPAN video, 9:05, 29:34. September 25, 2015, https://www.c-span.org/video/?328181-1/interfaith-meeting-pope-francis-911-memorial.
70 Black, "Interfaith/Interreligious?," 6.
71 Black, "Interfaith/Interreligious?," 6.
72 Black, "Interfaith/Interreligious?," 6.
73 Black, "Interfaith/Interreligious?," 7.
74 Black, "Interfaith/Interreligious?," 7.
75 Black, "Interfaith/Interreligious?," 7; Marianne Moyaert, "Introduction," 6.

76   Marianne Moyaert, "Introduction," 6.
77   Marianne Moyaert, "Introduction," 7.
78   C-SPAN, "Interfaith Meeting with Pope Francis at September 11 Memorial."
79   C-SPAN, "Interfaith Meeting with Pope Francis at September 11 Memorial."
80   Tony Carnes, "Religions in the City: An Overview," in *New York Glory: Religions in the City*, ed. Tony Carnes and Anna Karpathakis (New York: New York University Press, 2001), 14.
81   Richard John Neuhaus, Preface to *New York Glory: Religions in the City*, ed. Tony Carnes and Anna Karpathakis (New York: New York University Press, 2001), xiii.
82   Alan L. Berger, "Introduction," in *Trialogue and Terror: Judaism, Christianity, and Islam after 9/11*, ed. Alan L. Berger (Eugene, OR: Cascade Books, 2012), 1.
83   C-SPAN, "Interfaith Meeting with Pope Francis at September 11 Memorial."
84   C-SPAN, "Interfaith Meeting with Pope Francis at September 11 Memorial."
85   "Spirituality, Identity, and What gets in the Way," Pardes Institute of Jewish Studies, accessed October 15, 2022, https://www.ramahdarom.org/wp-content/uploads/2020/05/Shavuot-5780-Spirituality-identity-and-what-gets-in-the-way-Pahad-Yitzchak-21-sourcesheet-font.pdf.
86   C-SPAN, "Interfaith Meeting with Pope Francis at September 11 Memorial."
87   *The Qur'an*, trans. and introduction by Tarif Khalidi (New York: Penguin Books, 2009), 287.
88   See Micah 4:3 in *Good News Bible: Catholic Study Edition* (New York: Sadlier, 1979).
89   C-SPAN, "Interfaith Meeting with Pope Francis at September 11 Memorial."
90   C-SPAN, "Interfaith Meeting with Pope Francis at September 11 Memorial."
91   *Good News Bible*, Matt. 5:3–14.
92   *Good News Bible*, Matt. 5:5–7.
93   *The Qur'an*, Sahih Muslim 592.
94   Ronald L. Eisenberg, *The JPS Guide to Jewish Traditions* (Philadelphia: The Jewish Publication Society, 2004), 87.
95   The United Synagogue of Conservative Judaism, *Siddur Sim Shalom for Shabbat and Festivals* (New York: The Rabbinical Assembly, 1998), 196.
96   The United Synagogue of Conservative Judaism, *Siddur Sim Shalom*, 48.
97   Lily Fisher Gomberg, "Ve'al Kol Yoshvei Tevel – Including our world in Tisha B'Av," *My Jewish Learning*, published August 7, 2019, https://www.myjewishlearning.com/2019/08/07/veal-kol-yoshvei-tevel-including-our-world-in-tisha-bav/.
98   Rita Ferrone, "Interfaith Service at 9/11 Memorial," *Pray Tell*, published September 26, 2015, https://www.praytellblog.com/index.php/2015/09/26/interfaith-service-at-911-memorial/.
99   Ferrone, "Interfaith Service at 9/11 Memorial."
100 Emma Green, "Pope Francis Assembles a Squad to Fight Religious Extremism," *Atlantic*, September 25, 2015, https://www.theatlantic.com/international/archive/2015/09/pope-francis-assembles-a-squad-to-fight-religious-extremism/407452/.
101 C-SPAN, "Interfaith Meeting with Pope Francis at September 11 Memorial."
102 Christopher Purdy, "The Pope and the Cantor at Ground Zero," *WOSU 89.7 NPR News*, September 28, 2015, https://news.wosu.org/classical-101/2015-09-28/the-pope-and-the-cantor-at-ground-zero.
103 Black, "Interfaith/Interreligious?," 5–7.
104 Lewis, "The Argument for Interfaith Prayer and Worship," 19–20.
105 Lewis, "The Argument for Interfaith Prayer and Worship," 23.
106 Lewis, "The Argument for Interfaith Prayer and Worship," 29.

107 Mar Griera, "Interreligious Events in the Public Space: Performing Togetherness in Times of Religious Pluralism," in *Interreligious Relations and the Negotiation of Ritual Boundaries*, ed. Marianne Moyaert (Np: Palgrave McMillan, 2019), 53.
108 Nicholas S. Paliewicz and Marouf Hasian, Jr. "Mourning Absences, Melancholic Commemoration, and the Contested Public Memories of the National September 11 Memorial and Museum," *Western Journal of Communication*, 80, no. 2 (2016), 142. For political controversy over the memorial see, Theresa Ann Donofrio, "Ground Zero and Place-Making Authority: The Conservative Metaphors in 9/11 Families' 'Take Back the Memorial' Rhetoric," *Western Journal of Communication*, 74, no. 2 (2010): 150–169.
109 Jacques Derrida, *Specters of Marx: The State of Debt, the Work of Mourning, and the New International*, trans. Peggy Kamuf (New York: Routledge, 1994), xviii.
110 Kenneth Burke, *Philosophy of Literary Form: Studies in Symbolic Action*, 3rd ed. (Berkeley: University of California Press, 1973), 65.
111 Nicholas S. Paliewicz, "Bent But Not Broken: Remembering Vulnerability and Resiliency at the National September 11 Memorial Museum," *Southern Communication Journal*, 82, no. 1 (2017): 3.
112 Quoted in Stephen Farrell, "9/11 Artifacts, and the Stories They Tell: The Keepers of 9/11" [video], *The New York Times*, May 14, 2014, https://www.nytimes.com/video/nyregion/100000002865373/the-keepers-of-911.html.
113 Simon Stow, "From Upper Canal to Lower Manhattan: Memorialization and the Politics of Loss," *Perspectives on Politics*, 10, no. 3 (2012): 689.
114 For a more in-depth discussion on prayer as rhetorical art of memory, see William Fitzgerald, *Spiritual Modalities: Prayer as Rhetoric and Performance* (State College: The Pennsylvania State University Press, 2012), 100–114.
115 Playing off Kenneth Burke's conception of *consolatio philosphia* in the *Philosophy of Literary Form: Studies in Symbolic Action*, 3rd ed. (Berkeley: University of California Press, 1973), 61, we explore the religious and prayerful symbolic action of Pope Francis's discourse of comfort and healing when applied to the 9/11 memorial and the collective memory of the tragic event.
116 Fitzgerald, *Spiritual Modalities*, 5.
117 Fitzgerald, *Spiritual Modalities*, 12
118 Fitzgerald, *Spiritual Modalities*, 98.
119 Paliewicz, "Bent But Not Broken," 3.
120 Paliewicz, "Bent But Not Broken," 101.
121 Paliewicz, "Bent But Not Broken," 102.
122 Allison M. Prasch, "Toward a Rhetorical Theory of Deixis," *Quarterly Journal of Speech*, 102, no. 2 (2016), 169.
123 Prasch, "Toward a Rhetorical Theory of Deixis," 169.
124 Prasch, "Toward a Rhetorical Theory of Deixis," 171. For excellent examples of rhetorical criticism that examine the religious, visual-spatial rhetoric of Pope Francis, see Chapter four, "'Welcome the Stranger': The Spatial Conversion of 'Birthplace,' Religious Freedom, Immigration, and the Lec'turn' of Inter-Contextual Synecdoche"; Christopher J. Oldenburg, *The Rhetoric of Pope Francis: Critical Mercy and Conversion for the Twenty-First Century* (Lanham: Lexington Books, 2018), 95–98; Christopher J. Oldenburg, "'Has Anyone Wept?' Pope Francis at Lampedusa: Migration, Indifference, and Pastoral Pastiche as Equipment for Forgiving," in *Understanding Pope Francis: Message, Media, and Audience*, ed. J. R. Blaney (Lanham, MD: Lexington Books, 2021), 97–117.
125 C-SPAN, "Interfaith Meeting with Pope Francis at September 11."

126 Joshua Gunn, *Modern Occult Rhetoric: Mass Media and the Drama of Secrecy in the Twentieth Century* (Tuscaloosa, AL: The University of Alabama Press, 2015), xxi.
127 C-SPAN, "Interfaith Meeting with Pope Francis at September 11."
128 For a description of the reflective pools, see https://www.911memorial.org/visit/memorial/about-memorial; Also see Paliewicz and Hasian, 148.
129 C-SPAN, "Interfaith Meeting with Pope Francis at September 11."
130 Jacques Derrida, *Of Grammatology* (Baltimore, Johns Hopkins University Press, 1998), 61.
131 "About the Memorial," 9/11 Memorial & Museum, https://www.911memorial.org/visit/memorial/about-memorial
132 "About the Memorial."
133 G. Roger Denson, "Michael Arad's 9/11 Memorial 'Reflecting Absence': More than a Metaphor or a Monument," *Huffington Post*, May 14, 2011. http://huffingtonpost.com/g-roger-denson/michael-arads-9ll-memoria_b_955454.html.
134 Denson, "Michael Arad's 9/11 Memorial 'Reflecting Absence.'"
135 Paliewicz and Hasian, Jr. "Mourning Absences," see footnote 3, 158. Also for a rhetorical analysis of Pope Francis's view of water's religious, environmental, and social justice status, see: Christopher J. Oldenburg, "Reviving Sister Water: Hydro-Anthropomorphism, Catholic Social Justice, and Pope Francis' Eco-rhetoric on the Care of Creation," in *Water, Rhetoric, and Social Justice: A Critical Confluence*, eds. Casey R. Schmitt, Theresa R. Castor, & Christopher S. Thomas (Lanham, MD: Lexington Books, 2020), 171–187.
136 Paliewicz and Hasian, Jr. "Mourning Absences," 150.
137 C-SPAN, "Interfaith Meeting with Pope Francis at September 11."
138 See chapter six of this book, Pope Francis, "Homily at Ciudad Juárez Fair Grounds," February 17, 2016; Pope Francis, *Fratelli Tutti: Encyclical Letter on Fraternity and Social Friendship* (Libreria Editrice Vaticana: Hijez Global Press, 2020), 34, 84; Cindy Wooden, "Theology of Tears: For Pope, Weeping Helps One See Jesus," *The Catholic News Service*, May 5, 2019, https://www.catholicsun.org/2016/05/05/theology-of-tears-for-pope-weeping-helps-one-see-jesus/. Christopher J. Oldenburg, "'Has Anyone Wept?' Pope Francis at Lampedusa: Migration, Indifference, and Pastoral Pastiche as Equipment for Forgiving," in *Understanding Pope Francis: Message, Media, and Audience*, ed. J. R. Blaney (Lanham, MD: Lexington Books, 2021), 109–112.
139 Cardinal Luis Antonio G. Tagle, "Tears," in *A Pope Francis Lexicon*, ed. Joshua J. McElwee and Cindy Wooden (Collegeville: Liturgical Press, 2018), 184.
140 Tagle, "Tears," 184.
141 C-SPAN, "Interfaith Meeting with Pope Francis at September 11."
142 C-SPAN, "Interfaith Meeting with Pope Francis at September 11."
143 Pope Francis, *Let Us Dream: The Path to a Better Future* (New York: Simon & Schuster, 2020), 53, 107. Also see Pope Francis, *Fratelli Tutti*, 87.
144 Richard A. Lanham, *A Handlist of Rhetorical Terms*, 2nd ed. (Berkeley: University of California Press, 2012), 148.
145 Kenneth Burke, *A Grammar of Motives* (Berkeley: University of California Press, 1969), 509.
146 David Tell, "Burke's Encounter with Ransom: Rhetoric and Epistemology in 'Four Master Tropes,'" *Rhetoric Society Quarterly*, 34, no. 4 (2004), 44.
147 C-SPAN, "Interfaith Meeting with Pope Francis at September 11."
148 C-SPAN, "Interfaith Meeting with Pope Francis at September 11."
149 C-SPAN, "Interfaith Meeting with Pope Francis at September 11."

150 Pope Francis, *Fratelli Tutti*, 115.
151 Pope Francis, *Fratelli Tutti*, 115.
152 For a more robust rhetorical analysis on the symbolism and narrative exposition of the Last Column, see Paliewicz, "Bent But Not Broken," 8–10.
153 C-SPAN, "Interfaith Meeting with Pope Francis at September 11."
154 Stephen Foley, "'We were able to put a hand on him, feel part of him. We're at peace now,'" *Independent*, September 12, 2011, https://www.independent.co.uk/news/world/americas/we-were-able-to-put-a-hand-on-him-feel-part-of-him-we-re-at-peace-now-2353169.html.
155 C-SPAN, "Interfaith Meeting with Pope Francis at September 11."
156 Paliewicz, "Bent But Not Broken," 5. For a similar analysis of encounters with the Vietnam Veterans memorial names, see Sonja K. Foss, "Ambiguity as Persuasion: The Vietnam Veterans Memorial," *Communication Quarterly*, 34, no. 3 (1986): 333–336.
157 "About the Memorial."
158 "About the Memorial."
159 C-SPAN, "Interfaith Meeting with Pope Francis at September 11."
160 C-SPAN, "Interfaith Meeting with Pope Francis at September 11 Memorial."
161 Black, "Interfaith/Interreligious?," 11.
162 Black, "Interfaith/Interreligious?," 11.

Chapter 4 Education and Violence

1 C-SPAN, "President Obama at Newtown, Connecticut Prayer Vigil," C-SPAN video, December 16, 2012, https://www.c-span.org/video/?309977-1/president-obama-newtown-connecticut-prayer-vigil. Public Domain.
2 Lazaro Gamio and Shawn Hubler, "Texas Masscre Is the Second-Deadliest School Shooting on Record," *New York Times*, May 24, 2022, https://www.nytimes.com/interactive/2022/05/24/us/texas-school-shooting-deaths.html; Elizabeth Williamson, *Sandy Hook: An American Tragedy and the Battle for Truth* (New York: Dutton, 2022), 3.
3 Williamson, *Sandy Hook*, 5.
4 James Barron, "Nation Reels After Gunman Massacres 20 Children at School in Connecticut," *New York Times*, December 14, 2012, https://www.nytimes.com/2012/12/15/nyregion/shooting-reported-at-connecticut-elementary-school.html.
5 C-SPAN, "President Obama at Newtown, Connecticut Prayer Vigil," C-SPAN video, December 16, 2012, https://www.c-span.org/video/?309977-1/president-obama-newtown-connecticut-prayer-vigil.
6 C-SPAN, "President Obama at Newtown, Connecticut Prayer Vigil."
7 C-SPAN, "President Obama at Newtown, Connecticut Prayer Vigil."
8 Sharon Otterman, "Pastor Apologizes to His Denomination for Role in Sandy Hook Interfaith Service," *New York Times*, February 7, 2013, https://www.nytimes.com/2013/02/08/nyregion/lutheran-pastor-explains-role-in-sandy-hook-interfaith-service.html.
9 Otterman, "Pastor Apologizes to His Denomination."
10 Otterman, "Pastor Apologizes to His Denomination."
11 Kera Bolonik, "Pastor apologizes for participating in Newtown memorial service," *salon*, February 8, 2013, https://www.salon.com/2013/02/08/read_the_apology_by_pastor_punished_for_participating_in_an_interfaith_service_after_newtown_massacre/.

12 Bolonik, "Pastor apologizes for participating."
13 Bolonik, "Pastor apologizes for participating."
14 Marc Santora, "After Rebuke, an Apology for Pastor in Newtown," *New York Times*, February 12, 2013, https://www.nytimes.com/2013/02/13/nyregion/rev-matthew-c-harrison-offers-apology-for-his-rebuke-of-newtown-pastor.html.
15 Caleb K. Bell, "Missouri Synod president apologizes for 'debacle,'" *Christian Century*, February 12, 2013, https://www.christiancentury.org/article/2013-02/missouri-synod-president-apologizes-newtown-interfaith-debacle.
16 Bell, "Missouri Synod president apologizes."
17 Kathleen Mary Black, "Interfaith/Interreligious? Worship/Prayer? Services/Occasions? Interfaith Prayer Gatherings," *Religions*, 13, no. 6 (2022): 6.
18 Black, "Interfaith/Interreligious?," 6.
19 Black, "Interfaith/Interreligious?," 6.
20 Black, "Interfaith/Interreligious?," 7.
21 Gary Wills, "Our Moloch," *The New York Review of Books*, December 15, 2012, https://www.nybooks.com/daily/2012/12/15/our-moloch/.
22 Lawrence W. Rosenfield, "The Practical Celebration of Epideictic," edited by E.E. White, *Rhetoric in Transition: Studies in the Nature and Uses of Rhetoric* (University Park: Pennsylvania State University Press), 135.
23 Our claim that Obama's speech as a rhetorical hybrid conflates both eulogy and a call for deliberative action and manifests through Obama's use of a parental theology of political responsibility. Such stylistic armature functions much like two related political-religious theories. First, Steven Mailloux argues for a political theology that "deals with the connection between political praxis and religious belief. It is any implicit or explicit theory relating worldly action within power relations to speculative thinking about a world beyond." Steven Mailloux, *Rhetorical Pragmatism: Essays in Rhetorical Hermeneutics* University Park: Pennsylvania State University Press, 2017, 198. For more on political theology, see Steven Mallioux, "Political Theologies of Sacred Rhetoric," in *Responding to the Sacred: An Inquiry into the Limits of Rhetoric* eds. Michael Bernard-Donals and Kyle Jensen, University Park: University of Pennsylvania State Press, 202, 77–98. Secondly, Pope Francis, in his most recent encyclical *Fratelli Tutti*, calls for "a better kind of politics" and argues we must strive towards "political love." Political love is rooted in a deep care for the commonweal and the common good. Political love transcends individual interests like using the second amendment to justify the manufacturing, sales, and ownership of high-capacity, high-impact assault weapons designed to kill many people and works instead to find solutions to the long-term crisis of gun violence. Political love does not end with a one-time eulogy but must represent a commitment to deliberative and civic action. See Pope Francis, *Fratelli Tutti: Enclycial Letter on Fraternity and Social Friendship* Vatican City: Libreria Editrice Vaticana, (2020): 180–192.
24 David Maraniss, People will long remember what Barack Obama said in Newtown…his Gettysburg address…[Tweet]. Retrieved from https://twitter.com/davidmaranisss/status/280510394437607426
25 David Frank, "Facing Moloch: Barack Obama's National Eulogies and Gun Violence" *Rhetoric & Public Affairs*, 17, no. 4 (2014): 658.
26 Karlyn Kohrs Campbell and Kathleen Hall Jamieson, *Form and Genre: Shaping Rhetorical Action* (Falls Church: Speech Communication Association, 1978).

27 "Interview with Oprah," YouTube, https://www.youtube.com/watch?v=2J6KZImZVKE. Obama expressed he was most disgusted and appalled by Congresses inaction on gun violence after Sandy Hook. Obama also referred to Sandy Hook as "the toughest day of his presidency." Barack Obama, "Remarks by the President on Reducing Gun Violence—Hartford CT" *The White House*, April 8, 2013. https://obamawhitehouse.archives.gove/the-press-office/2013/04/08/remarks-president-reducing-gun-violence-hartford-ct
28 Wills, "Our Moloch."
29 Craig Rood, "'Our Tears are Not Enough': The Warrant of the Dead in the Rhetoric of Gun Control," *Quarterly Journal of Speech*, 104, no. 1 (2018): 47–70. As an argumentative strategy, Rood explains the warrant of the dead is an explicit or implicit claim that the dead place a demand on the living. The warrant is expressed as the justificatory injunction, "since they died, we should do X."
30 Christopher M. Duerringer, "Dishonoring the Dead: Negotiating Decorum in the Shadow of Sandy Hook" *Western Journal of Communication*, 80, no. 1 (2016): 79–99.
31 David A. Frank, "Facing Moloch: Barack Obama's National Eulogies and Gun Violence," *Rhetoric & Public Affairs*, 17, no. 4 (2014): 655.
32 Frank, 658.
33 Frank, 658; Also see Renee C. Romano, "Narratives of Redemption: The Birmingham Church Bombing Trials and the Construction of Civil Rights Memory," in *The Civil Rights Movement in American Memory*, ed. Renee C. Romano and Leigh Raiford (Athens: University of Georgia Press, 2006), 97.
34 Scriptural evidence of the Almighty's fatherly status and his people as children of God abounds; see Malachi 2:10; Isaiah 8:18; Romans 8:14; 1 John 3:2; 2 Corinthians 6:18; Matthew 6:9.
35 Obama, Sandy Hook Interfaith Prayer Vigil.
36 Obama, Sandy Hook Interfaith Prayer Vigil. The fact that Obama would place rhetorical emphasis on the parent-child relationship is not surprising given the frequency with which Obama's discourse relies on familial metaphors. The family metaphor has appeared in the following Obama speeches: "A More Perfect Union," both his 2010 and 2011 State of the Union Addresses, "A Way Forward in Afghanistan", and "Together We Thrive: Tucson and America Memorial. Obama compares America to the family unit, using the same specific language in his "Together We Thrive: Tucson and America Memorial address and his 2011 State of the Union. In his Tucson address he observed that those who were killed are "part of our family, an American Family 300 million strong." His 2011 State of Union references the Tucson tragedy announcing "Tucson reminded us that no matter who we are or where we come from, each of us, each of us is part of something greater—something more consequential than party or political preference. We are part of the American family." The family metaphor has appeared in the following Obama speeches: "A More Perfect Union," both his 2010 and his 2011 State of the Union Addresses, and "Together We Thrive: Tucson and America' Memorial," January 12, 2012, https://www.americanrhetoric.com/speeches/barackobama/barackobamatucsonmemorial.htm.
37 Celeste Condit, "The Function of Epideictic: The Boston Massacre Orations as Exemplar," *Communication Quarterly*, 33, (1985): 291.
38 Obama, Sandy Hook Interfaith Prayer Vigil.
39 Obama, Sandy Hook Interfaith Prayer Vigil.
40 Frank, 667.
41 Obama, Sandy Hook Interfaith Prayer Vigil.

42 Kohrs Campbell and Hall Jamieson, *Form and Genre*.
43 Obama, Sandy Hook Interfaith Prayer Vigil.
44 Obama, Sandy Hook Interfaith Prayer Vigil.
45 Obama, Sandy Hook Interfaith Prayer Vigil.
46 Obama, Sandy Hook Interfaith Prayer Vigil.
47 Obama, Sandy Hook Interfaith Prayer Vigil.
48 Obama, Sandy Hook Interfaith Prayer Vigil.
49 See Richard A. Lanham, *A Handlist of Rhetorical Terms,* 2nd ed. (Berkeley: University of California Press, 1991), 9. Also see Mark Forsyth, *Elements of Eloquence: Secrets of the Perfect Turn of Phrase* (New York: Berkeley Books, 2013), 78.
50 Forsyth, *Elements of Eloquence*, 78.
51 Obama, Sandy Hook Interfaith Prayer Vigil.
52 Chaim Perelman and Lucie Olbrechts-Tyteca, *The New Rhetoric*: *Treatise on Argumentation* translated by John Wilkinson & Purcell Weaver (Notre Dame: University of Notre Dame Press, 1969), 49–50.
53 Obama, Sandy Hook Interfaith Prayer Vigil.
54 Obama, Sandy Hook Interfaith Prayer Vigil.
55 See Matthew 19:14 in American Bible Society, *Good News Bible* (New York: American Bible Society, 1976).
56 Emma Carson, "From (Someone Else's) Cold, Dead Hands: Disarming the PLCAA With the Sales and Marketing Predicate Exception Post Soto v. Bushmaster," *Journal of Law and Commerce*, 39, no. 2 (2021).
57 Nathan D. Harp, "Note: Imperfect Immunity: How State Attorneys General Could Sue Firearm Manufacturers Under The Predicate Exemption to the Protection of Lawful Commerce In Arms Act," *Cornell Journal of Law and Public Policy*, 30, no. 797 (2021): 799; Carson, "From (Someone Else's) Cold, Dead Hands," 181.
58 Harp, "Note: Imperfect Immunity," 804.
59 Carson, "From (Someone Else's) Cold, Dead Hands," 194.
60 Rick Rojas, Karen Zraick, and Troy Closson, "Sandy Hook Families Settle With Gunmaker for $73 Million Over Massacre," *New York Times*, February 15, 2022, https://www.nytimes.com/2022/02/15/nyregion/sandy-hook-families-settlement.html; Elizabeth Williamson, "How They Did It: Sandy Hook Families Gain Long-Awaited Legal Wins," *New York Times*, February 20, 2022, https://www.nytimes.com/2022/02/20/us/politics/sandy-hook-legal-victories.html.
61 Rojas, Zraick, and Closson, "Sandy Hook Families Settle."
62 Rojas, Zraick, and Closson, "Sandy Hook Families Settle"; Ana Radelat, "U.S. Supreme Court allows Sandy Hook suit against Remington to advance," *Connecticut Mirror*, November 12, 2019, https://ctmirror.org/2019/11/12/u-s-supreme-court-allows-sandy-hook-suit-against-remington-to-advance/.
63 Radelat, "U.S Supreme Court allows Sandy Hook suit."
64 Williamson, *Sandy Hook*, 28.
65 Elizabeth Williamson, "How They Did It: Sandy Hook Families Gain Long-Awaited Legal Wins," *New York Times*, February 20, 2022, https://www.nytimes.com/2022/02/20/politics/sandy-hook-legal-victories.html.
66 Williamson, "How They Did It."
67 Williamson, *Sandy Hook*, 310–311.
68 Williamson, "Judge Upholds $49 Million Verdict."

69 Williamson, *Sandy Hook*, 310–311.
70 Elizabeth Williamson, "Parents of Sandy Hook Victim at Alex Jones Trial Seek $150 Million in Damages," *New York Times*, July 26, 2022, https://www.nytimes.com/2022/07/26/us/politics/sandy-hook-alex-jones.html.
71 Elizabeth Williamson, "With New Ruling, Sandy Hook Families Win Over $1.4 Billion From Alex Jones," *New York Times*, November 10, 2022, https://www.nytimes.com/2022/11/10/us/politics/alex-jones-sandy-hook-damages.html; Jack c in punitive damages in Sandy "Hook defamation case," *Reuters*, November 10, 2022, https://www.reuters.com/legal/alex-jones-must-pay-473-million-punitive-damages-sandy-hook-defamation-case-2022-11-10/.
72 First Amendment Watch Staff and 1791 Delegates, "Teacher Guide."
73 Elizabeth Williamson, "Truth in a Post-Truth Era: Sandy Hook Families Sue Alex Jones, Conspiracy Theorist," *New York Times*, May 23, 2018, https://www.nytimes.com/2018/05/23/us/politics/alex-jones-trump-sandy-hook.html.
74 Tedford and Herbeck, *Freedom of Speech*, 80.
75 Tedford and Herbeck, *Freedom of Speech*, 79.
76 Williamson, "Sandy Hook Parents to Testify."
77 Williamson, "Parents of Sandy Hook Victim at Alex Jones Trial Seek $150 Million."
78 Williamson, "Judge Upholds $49 Million Verdict."
79 Williamson, "Judge Upholds $49 Million Verdict."
80 Williamson, "Judge Upholds $49 Million Verdict."
81 Robbie Parker, father of Emily Parker, 6, received 60 million dollars in defamation and slander damages, and 60 million dollars in emotional distress damages; David Wheeler, father of Ben Wheeler, 6, received 25 million in defamation and slander damages, and 30 million in emotional distress damages; Francine Wheeler, mother of Ben Wheeler, received 24 million in defamation and slander damages, and 30 million distress damages; Jacqueline Barden, mother of Daniel Barden, 7, 10 million in defamation and slander damages, and 18.8 million in emotional distress; Mark Barden, father of Daniel Barden received 25 million in defamation and slander, and 36.2 million in emotional distress damages; Nicole Hockley, mother of Dylan Hockley, 6, received 32 million in defamation in slander, and 31.6 million in emotional distress. Ian Hockley, father of Dylan Hockley, 38 million in defamation and slander, and 43.6 million in emotional distress. Jennifer Hensel, mother of Avielle Hensel, 6, received 21 million in defamation and slander, and 31 million in emotional distress. William Sherlach, husband of Mary Sherlach (Sandy Hook Elementary school psychologist), received 9 million in defamation and slander, and 27 million in emotional distress. Donna Soto, mother of Vicki Soto (first grade teacher) received 18 million in defamation and slander, and 30 million in emotional distress; Carlee Soto Parisi, sister of Vicki Soto, 30 million in defamation and slander, and 36 million in emotional distress. Carlos Mathew Soto, brother of Vicki Soto, received 18.6 million in defamation and slander, and 39 million in emotional distress. Jillian Soto-Marino, sister of Vicki Soto, received 30 million in defamation and slander, and 38.8 million in emotional distress. Erica Lafferty, daughter of Dawn Lafferty Hochsprung (principal), received 18 million in defamation and slander, and 58 million in emotional distress. William Aldenburg, the FBI agent who responded to the shooting and survived received 45 million in defamation and slander, and 45 million emotional distress. See Elizabeth Williamson, "How the jury divided $965 million in damages among the plaintiffs in the case," *New York Times*, October 12, 2022.
82 Williamson, "'We Told the Truth.'"

83 Williamson, "'We Told the Truth.'"
84 Williamson, "With New Ruling, Sandy Hook Families Win."
85 Williamson, "With New Ruling, Sandy Hook Families Win."
86 Tedford and Herbeck, *Freedom of Speech*, 130–132.
87 Tedford and Herbeck, *Freedom of Speech*, 463.
88 Tedford and Herbeck, *Freedom of Speech*, 83.
89 Williamson, "'We Told the Truth.'"
90 Williamson, "With New Ruling, Sandy Hook Families Win."
91 Elizabeth Williamson, "Jurors Award Sandy Hook Parents $4 Million in Damages," *New York Times*, August 4, 2022, https://www.nytimes.com/2022/08/04/us/politics/alex-jones-damages-sandy-hook.html.
92 Elizabeth Williamson, "With New Ruling, Sandy Hook Families Win."

Chapter 5: Part 1 Religion and Violence

1 Bytwerk, *Landmark Speeches*, 1.
2 Eastwood, *The Nuremberg Trial of Julius Streicher*, 2.
3 Bytwerk, *Julius Streicher*, 86–87.
4 Eastwood, *The Nuremberg Trial of Julius Streicher*, 2.
5 Reprinted from *Landmark Speeches of National Socialism*, edited and with translations by Randal L. Bytwerk by permission of Texas A&M University Press.
6 Randall L. Bytwerk, ed. and trans, *Landmark Speeches of National Socialism* (College Station: Texas A&M University Press, 2008), 1.
7 Bytwerk, *Landmark Speeches*, 2; Randall L. Bytwerk, *Bending Spines* (East Lansing: Michigan State University Press, 2004), 4.
8 Bytwerk, *Landmark Speeches*, 3.
9 Bytwerk, *Bending Spines*, 22.
10 Raul Hilberg, *The Destruction of the European Jews* (Eastford, CT: Martino Fine Books, 2019), 690.
11 Bytwerk, *Bending Spines*, 43.
12 Bytwerk, *Landmark Speeches*, 1.
13 Margaret Eastwood, *The Nuremberg Trial of Julius Streicher* (Lewiston: The Edwin Mellen Press, 2011), 1.
14 Eastwood, *The Nuremberg Trial of Julius Streicher*, 2.
15 Eastwood, *The Nuremberg Trial of Julius Streicher*, 2.
16 Eastwood, *The Nuremberg Trial of Julius Streicher*, 3.
17 Eastwood, *The Nuremberg Trial of Julius Streicher*, 19.
18 Gregory S. Gordon, foreword by Benjamin B. Ferencz, *Atrocity Speech Law: Foundation, Fragmentation, Fruition* (New York: Oxford University Press, 2017), 369.
19 Gordon, *Atrocity Speech Law*, 369.
20 Gordon, *Atrocity Speech Law*, 328.
21 Gordon, *Atrocity Speech Law*, 328.
22 Gordon, *Atrocity Speech Law*, 369.
23 Gordon, *Atrocity Speech Law*, 368.
24 Eastwood, *The Nuremberg Trial of Julius Streicher*, 29.

25 "Streicher Advises Foreigners on Jews," *New York Times*, September 16, 1936.
26 "Streicher Advises Foreigners on Jews."
27 Randall L. Bytwerk, "Julius Streicher and the Early History of 'Der Sturmer,' 1923–1933," *Journalism History*, 5, no. 3 (Autumn 1978): 74–79.
28 Eastwood, *The Nuremberg Trial of Julius Streicher*, 119; Randall L. Bytwerk, *Julius Streicher: Nazi Editor of the Notorious Anti-semitic Newspaper Der Sturmer* (New York: Cooper Square Press, 2001), 63.
29 Eastwood, *The Nuremberg Trial of Julius Streicher*, 119.
30 Eastwood, *The Nuremberg Trial of Julius Streicher*, 227.
31 Eastwood, *The Nuremberg Trial of Julius Streicher*, 237, 246–247; Nina Andrews, "Julius Streicher at Nuremberg: A Case of Justice Denied?" *The British Journal of Holocaust Education*, 3, no. 1 (Summer 1994): 39.
32 Eastwood, *The Nuremberg Trial of Julius Streicher*, 238.
33 Eastwood, *The Nuremberg Trial of Julius Streicher*, 238.
34 Eastwood, *The Nuremberg Trial of Julius Streicher*, 8.
35 Eastwood, *The Nuremberg Trial of Julius Streicher*, 9.
36 Joel E. Dimsdale, *Anatomy of Malice* (New Haven: Yale University Press, 2016), 103.
37 Dimsdale, *Anatomy of Malice*, 103.
38 Eastwood, *The Nuremberg Trial of Julius Streicher*, 243.
39 Eastwood, *The Nuremberg Trial of Julius Streicher*, 252.
40 Eastwood, *The Nuremberg Trial of Julius Streicher*, 253.
41 Eastwood, *The Nuremberg Trial of Julius Streicher*, 253.
42 Eastwood, *The Nuremberg Trial of Julius Streicher*, 2.
43 Eastwood, *The Nuremberg Trial of Julius Streicher*, 3.
44 Eastwood, *The Nuremberg Trial of Julius Streicher*, 246.
45 G. M. Gilbert, *Nuremberg Diary* (New York: Da Capo Press, 1995), 306.
46 Bytwerk, *Julius Streicher*, 1.
47 Dennis E. Showalter, *Little Man, What Now? Der Sturmer in the Weimar Republic* (Hamden, CT: Archon Books, 1982), 20, 29.
48 Showalter, *Little Man, What Now?*, 29.
49 Bytwerk, *Julius Streicher*, 199.
50 William P. Varga, *The Number One Nazi Jew-Baiter* (New York: Carlton Press, Inc., 1981), 95.
51 Varga, *The Number One Nazi Jew-Baiter*, 96.
52 Bytwerk, *Julius Streicher*, 9.
53 Bytwerk, *Julius Streicher*, 51.
54 Showalter, *Little Man, What Now?*, 31.
55 Andrews, "Julius Streicher at Nuremberg," 40.
56 Andrews, "Julius Streicher at Nuremberg," 40, 49.
57 Susanna Schrafstetter and Alan E. Steinweis, eds., *The Germans and the Holocaust* (New York Berghahn, 2016), 112.
58 Alan E. Steinweis, *Kristallnacht 1938* (Cambridge, MA: Belknap Press of Harvard University Press, 2009), 1; Martin Gilbert, *Kristallnacht: Prelude to Destruction* (New York: Harper, 2007), 31–35.
59 Steinweis, *Kristallnacht 1938*, 2.
60 Steinweis, *Kristallnacht 1938*, 3.
61 Hilberg, *The Destruction of the European Jews*, 29.

212 | NOTES

62 Steinweis, *Kristallnacht 1938*, 24.
63 Martin Gilbert, *The Holocaust: The Human Tragedy* (New York: RosettaBooks, 2014), 67.
64 Martin Gilbert, *Kristallnacht: Prelude to Destruction* (New York: Harper, /2007), 23; Gilbert, *The Holocaust*, 67.
65 Gilbert, *The Holocaust*, 66.
66 Gilbert, *Kristallnacht*, 23.
67 Varga, *The Number One Nazi Jew-Baiter*, 259.
68 Varga, *The Number One Nazi Jew-Baiter*, 251.
69 Gilbert, *The Holocaust*, 69.
70 Varga, *The Number One Nazi Jew-Baiter*, 259.
71 Varga, *The Number One Nazi Jew-Baiter*, 10.
72 Varga, *The Number One Nazi Jew-Baiter*, 71.
73 Varga, *The Number One Nazi Jew-Baiter*, 72.
74 Showalter, *Little Man, What Now?*, xiii.
75 Showalter, *Little Man, What Now?*, 59.
76 Varga, *The Number One Nazi Jew-Baiter*, 92.
77 Varga, *The Number One Nazi Jew-Baiter*, 92.
78 Varga, *The Number One Nazi Jew-Baiter*, 92.
79 Bytwerk, *Julius Streicher*, 56.
80 Bytwerk, *Julius Streicher*, 169.
81 Bytwerk, *Julius Streicher*, 168.
82 Norman Cohn, *Warrant for Genocide* (London: Serif, 1996), 221.
83 Cohn, *Warrant for Genocide*, 225.
84 Bytwerk, *Julius Streicher*, 59.
85 Shlomo Gliksman, *The Forgeries and Falsifications in the Antisemitic literature and my lawsuit Against Julius Streicher and Company* (New York: People's Institute for Dissemination of Biblical and Talmudic Jurisprudence, 1939), 83.
86 Gliksman, *The Forgeries*, 10–11.
87 Gliksman, *The Forgeries*, 20.
88 Bytwerk, *Julius Streicher*, 86–87.
89 Bytwerk, *Julius Streicher*, 88.
90 Bytwerk, *Julius Streicher*, 88.
91 Bytwerk, *Julius Streicher*, 88.
92 Bytwerk, *Julius Streicher*, 88.
93 Bytwerk, *Julius Streicher*, 75.
94 Bytwerk, *Julius Streicher*, 75.
95 Dimsdale, *Anatomy of Malice*, 113.
96 Dimsdale, *Anatomy of Malice*, 113.
97 Bytwerk, *Julius Streicher*, 46.
98 Bytwerk, *Julius Streicher*, 89.
99 Maurice M. Mizrahi, "Response to antisemitic distortions of the Talmud," June 2016, https://images.shulcloud.com/618/uploads/PDFs/Divrei_Torah/160615-Response%20to%20antisemitic%20distortions%20of%20the%20Talmud.pdf, 1.
100 Mizrahi, "Response," 2.
101 Mizrahi, "Response," 2.
102 Bytwerk, *Julius Streicher*, 90.

103　Bytwerk, *Julius Streicher*, 91.
104　Varga, *The Number One Nazi Jew-Baiter*, 163.
105　Varga, *The Number One Nazi Jew-Baiter*, 291.
106　Mary Mills, "Propaganda and Children During the Hitler Years," Yad Vashem, October 12, 1999, http://www.yadvashem.org/download/education/conf/Millsishedwithoutpic.pdf, 5–6.
107　Mills, "Propaganda and Children," 6.
108　"What Christ Said about the Jews," German Propaganda Archive, n.d., https://research.calvin.edu/german-propaganda-archive/story14.htm.
109　Bytwerk, *Landmark Speeches*, 91.
110　"Purim" in *Encyclopedia Judaica*, 2nd ed. (Detroit: MacMillan, 2007).
111　Dimsdale, *Anatomy of Malice*, 113.
112　Bytwerk, *Landmark Speeches*, 91.
113　Magda Teter, *Blood Libel* (Cambridge: Harvard University Press, 2020), 4.
114　"Blood Libel," Holocaust Encyclopedia, n.d., https://encyclopedia.ushmm.org/content/en/article/blood-libel; Cecil Roth, "The Feast of Purim and the Origins of the Blood Accusation," in *The Blood Libel Legend: A Casebook in Anti-Semitic Folklore*, Alan Dundes, ed. (Madison: The University of Wisconsin Press, 1991), 270.
115　Teter, *Blood Libel*, 2.
116　Teter, *Blood Libel*, 2, 4; Andrews, "Julius Streicher at Nuremberg," 39.
117　Teter, *Blood Libel*, 200; The issue included a "three-page 'annalistic' list of Jewish ritual murders from the times of Christ to 1932." See Teter, 200.
118　"Blood Libel," https://encyclopedia.ushmm.org/content/en/article/blood-libel.
119　"Blood Libel," https://encyclopedia.ushmm.org/content/en/article/blood-libel; Roth, "The Feast of Purim," 270.
120　Roth, "The Feast of Purim," 269.
121　Bytwerk, *Landmark Speeches*, 92.
122　Jeffrey Veidlinger, *In the Midst of Civilized Europe: The Pogroms of 1918–1921 and the Onset of the Holocaust* (New York: Metropolitan Books, 2021), 331; Carolyn J. Dean, *The Moral Witness: Trials and Testimony After Genocide* (Ithaca: Cornell University Press, 2019), 28.
123　Dean, *The Moral Witness*, 32.
124　Dean, *The Moral Witness*, 33.
125　Veidlinger, *In the Midst of Civilized Europe*, 339.
126　Veidlinger, *In the Midst of Civilized Europe*, 342.
127　Veidlinger, *In the Midst of Civilized Europe*, 340.
128　Bytwerk, *Landmark Speeches*, 92.
129　Bytwerk, *Landmark Speeches*, 92.
130　Bytwerk, *Julius Streicher*, 66.
131　Cohn, *Warrant for Genocide*, 261.
132　Bytwerk, *Julius Streicher*, 63.
133　Bytwerk, *Julius Streicher*, 193, 197.
134　Bytwerk, *Julius Streicher*, 43.
135　Gordon, *Atrocity Speech Law*, 2.
136　Gordon, *Atrocity Speech Law*, 30.
137　Gordon, *Atrocity Speech Law*, 4.
138　Gordon, *Atrocity Speech Law*, 6.
139　Gordon, *Atrocity Speech Law*, 22.

140 Gordon, *Atrocity Speech Law*, 4.
141 Gordon, *Atrocity Speech Law*, 21.
142 Telford Taylor, *The Anatomy of the Nuremberg Trials: A Personal Memoir* (London: Bloomsbury, 1993), 376.
143 Taylor, *The Anatomy of the Nuremberg Trials*, 590.
144 Eastwood, *The Nuremberg Trial of Julius Streicher*, 243.
145 Taylor, *The Anatomy of the Nuremberg Trials*, 590.
146 Beth Van Schaack, "*Crimen Sin Lege*: Judicial Lawmaking at the Intersection of Law and Morals," *The Georgetown Law Journal*, 97, no. 119 (2008): 119.
147 Christian Tomuschat, "The Legacy of Nuremberg," *Journal of International Criminal Justice* 4 (2006): 835.
148 Alan M. Olson, "Metaphysical Guilt," *Existenz*, 3, no. 1 (Spring 2008): 10.
149 Karl Jaspers, *The Question of German Guilt*, trans. E. B. Ashton with intro. by Joseph W. Koterski, S. J. (New York: Fordham University Press, 2000), 25–26.
150 Olson, "Metaphysical Guilt," 12; Jaspers, *The Question of German Guilt*, 25.
151 Olson, "Metaphysical Guilt," 12; Jaspers, *The Question of German Guilt*, 25.
152 Jaspers, *The Question of German Guilt*, 26.
153 Olson, "Metaphysical Guilt," 13.
154 Olson, "Metaphysical Guilt," 13.
155 Olson, "Metaphysical Guilt," 13.
156 Olson, "Metaphysical Guilt," 13.
157 Jaspers, *The Question of German Guilt*, 26.
158 Jaspers, *The Question of German Guilt*, 26.
159 Jaspers, *The Question of German Guilt*, 66.
160 Jaspers, *The Question of German Guilt*, 117.
161 Jaspers, *The Question of German Guilt*, 112.
162 Keegan Hankes, "Eye of the Stormer," The Southern Poverty Law Center, February 9, 2017, https://www.splcenter.org/fighting-hate/intelligence-report/2017/eye-stormer.
163 Hankes, "Eye of the Stormer."
164 Hankes, "Eye of the Stormer."
165 Hankes, "Eye of the Stormer."
166 Luke O'Brien, "Andrew Anglin: The Making of an American Nazi," *Atlantic*, December 15, 2017, https://www.theatlantic.com/magazine/archive/2017/12/the-making-of-an-american-nazi/544119/.
167 Talia Lavin, "The Neo-Nazis of the Daily Stormer Wander the Digital Wilderness," *New Yorker*, January 7, 2018, https://www.newyorker.com/tech/annals-of-technology/the-neo-nazis-of-the-daily-stormer-wander-the-digital-wilderness.
168 Jaspers, *The Question of German Guilt*, 93.
169 Trip Gabriel, "Trump Escalates Anti-Immigrant Rhetoric with 'Poisoning the Blood' comment," *New York Times*, October 5, 2023, https://www.nytimes.com/2023/10/05/us/politics/trump-immigration-rhetoric.html.
170 Michael Gold, "Trump Says He Wouldn't Be a Dictator, 'Except for Day 1,'" *New York Times*, December 5, 2023, https://www.nytimes.com/2023/12/05/us/politics/trump-fox-news-abuse-power.html.

Chapter 5: Part 2 Religion and Violence

1. Josef Schuster, "Speech by Dr. Josef Schuster, President of the Central Council of Jews in Germany, at the ceremony marking the 80th Anniversary of Reichspogromnacht," November 26, 2018, https://www.zentralratderjuden.de/aktuelle-meldung/artikel/news/speech-by-dr-josef-schuster-president-of-the-central-council-of-jews-in-germany/. By kind permission of Zentralrat der Juden in Deutschland.
2. For more on the 1938Project, see www.1938projekt.org.
3. Schuster, "Speech at the ceremony."
4. For more on the AfD, see Frank Decker, "The 'Alternative for Germany': Factors behind Its Emergence and Profile of a New Right-Wing Populist Party," *German Politics and Society*, 34, no. 2 (2016): 1–16. DOI:10.3167/gps.2016.340201. It is also worth noting that the AfD was the only German political party that was not invited to the Anniversary ceremony.
5. Karl Marx, *The Eighteenth Brumaire of Louis Bonaparte*, translated by D.D.L. (Monodial: Berlin, 2005), 1.
6. Miriam Bistrovic, "Germany Marks 80Years Since Kristallnacht with the 1938Projekt," *Leo Baeck Institute* November 9, 2018, https://www.lbi.org/news/germany-marks-80-years-kristallnacht-1938projekt/.
7. For more see Melissa Eddy, "Looking to History and Recent Events, German Leaders Defend Democracy and Pluralism," *New York Times*, November 9, 2018, https://www.nytimes.com/2018/11/09/world/europe/steinmeier-germany-democratic-patriotism.html?searchResultPosition=1.
8. See Eberhard Bethge, "Dietrich Bonhoeffer: One of the Silent Bystanders?" *European Judaism: A Journal for the New Europe*, 25, no. 1 (1992): 33–40. Also see David A. R. Clark, "Psalm 74:8 and November 1938: Rereading Dietrich Bonhoeffer's Kristallnacht Annotation in Its Interpretive Context," *Scottish Journal of Theology*, 71, no. 3 (2018): 253–66.doi:10.1017/S0036930618000315; Patrick D. Miller, "Dietrich Bonhoeffer and the Psalms," *Princeton Seminary Bulletin*, 15, no. 3 (1994): 280; Jeffery Worthen, "Praying the Psalms and the Challenges of Christian-Jewish Relations,'" *Studies in Christian-Jewish Relations*, 9, no. 1 (2014): 11.
9. Schuster, "Speech at the ceremony."
10. Schuster, "Speech at the ceremony."
11. Schuster, "Speech at the ceremony."
12. Michael Osborn, "Archetypal Metaphor in Rhetoric: The Light-Dark Family," *Quarterly Journal of Speech*, 53, no. 2 (1967): 123.
13. Schuster, "Speech at the ceremony."
14. Schuster, "Speech at the ceremony."
15. Schuster, "Speech at the ceremony."
16. Kenneth Burke, "The Rhetoric of Hitler's Battle," in *The Philosophy of Literary Form*, 3rd ed. (Berkeley: University of California Press, 1973), 191–220. Elsewhere Burke has argued that substance and motives are convertible terms and as Schuster has demonstrated they are also combustible terms. See *A Grammar of Motives* (Berkeley: University of California Press, 1969), 57.
17. Burke, "The Rhetoric of Hitler's Battle."
18. Schuster, "Speech at the ceremony."
19. Elie Wiesel, *The Forgotten*, trans. Stephen Becker (New York: Simon & Schuster, 1992), 193, 309.

216 | NOTES

20 Osborn, "Archetypal Metaphor in Rhetoric," 122.
21 Osborn demonstrates how Churchill rhetorically transformed the destructive conflagration of London by Nazi firebombs into a purifying fire of perseverance and resolve "kindled in British hearts," "a fire which will burn with a steady and consuming flame until the last vestiges of Nazi tyranny have been burnt out of Europe..." 123.
22 Kenneth Burke, *A Grammar of Motives* (Berkeley: University of California Press,1969), 506.
23 Paul Ricoeur, *The Rule of Metaphor: The Creation of Meaning in Language*, trans. Robert Czerny with Kathleen McLaughlin and John Costello, SJ (Toronto: University of Toronto Press, 1978), 6.

Chapter 6: Part 1 Borders/Immigration and Violence

1 Jeff Sessions, "Attorney General Sessions Addresses Recent Criticisms of Zero Tolerance by Church Leaders," *Justice News*, June 14, 2018, https://www.justice.gov/archives/opa/speech/attorney-general-sessions-addresses-recent-criticisms-zero-tolerance-church-leaders.
2 Jeff Sessions, "Attorney General Sessions Addresses Recent Criticisms of Zero Tolerance by Church Leaders."
3 Jeff Sessions, "Attorney General Sessions Delivers Remarks Discussing the Immigration Enforcement Actions of the Trump Administration," *Justice News*, May 7, 2018, https://www.justice.gov/opa/speech/attorney-general-sessions-delivers-remarks-discussing-immigration-enforcement-actions.
4 Julie Zauzmer and Keith McMillan, "Sessions Cites Bible passage Used to Defend Slavery in Defense of Separating Immigrant Families," *Washington Post*, June 14, 2018, https://www.washingtonpost.com/news/acts-of-faith/wp/2018/06/14/jeff-sessions-points-to-the-bible-in-defense-of-separating-immigrant-families/; Two other principals who conceived and operationalized the Zero Tolerance policy, according to Dickerson, are Kevin McAleenan, "Commissioner of Customs and Border Protection, which oversees the Border Patrol. In May 2018, McAleenan recommended that the Border Patrol start referring migrant parents for prosecution and separating them from their children." Tom Homan, "the intellectual 'father' of the idea to separate migrant families as a deterrent, who went on to serve as acting ICE director through the end of Zero Tolerance."
5 Jeff Sessions, "Attorney General Sessions Delivers Remarks Discussing the Immigration Enforcement Actions of the Trump Administration."
6 Caitlin Dickerson, "The secret history of the U.S. government's family-separation policy," *Atlantic*, August 7, 2022, https://www.theatlantic.com/magazine/archive/2022/09/trump-administration-family-separation-policy-immigration/670604/.
7 According to Caitlin Dickerson in "The secret history of the U.S. government's family-separation policy," as of November 30, 2017, 868 children were separated; as of January 24, 2018, 1,141; as of June 18, 2018, 4,335; as of August 1, 2018, 4,371; as of January 20, 2021, 5,569.
8 Megan Henry and Jordyn Hermani, "Attorney General Jeff Sessions: Zero-Tolerance Policy Isn't About Being 'Mean to Children,'" *Indy Star*, June 20, 2018, https://www.indystar.com/story/news/2018/06/14/jeff-sessions-immigration-fort-wayne-attorney-general/698894002/.
9 Julie Hirschfeld Davis and Michael D. Shear, "How Trump Came to Enforce a Practice of Separating Migrant Families," *New York Times*, June 16, 2018, https://www.nytimes.com/2018/06/16/us/politics/family-separation-trump.html.

10 Kathy L. Gilbert and Sam Hodges, "United Methodists Fight Separation of Immigrant Families," *United Methodist News Service*, June 13, 2018, https://www.umnews.org/en/news/united-methodists-fight-separation-of-immigrant-families.
11 Gilbert and Hodges, "United Methodists Fight Separation of Immigrant Families."
12 Gilbert and Hodges, "United Methodists Fight Separation of Immigrant Families."
13 Gilbert and Hodges, "United Methodists Fight Separation of Immigrant Families."
14 Julia Jacobs, "Sessions's Use of Bible Passage to Defend Immigration Policy Draws Fire," *New York Times,* June 15, 2018, https://www.pbs.org/newshour/politics/watch-live-attorney-general-jeff-sessions-talks-about-immigration.
15 "Watch: Sessions Cites Bible to Defend Separating Immigrant Families," *PBS News Hour,* June 14, 2018, https://www.pbs.org/newshour/politics/watch-live-attorney-general-jeff-sessions-talks-about-immigration.
16 Jeff Sessions, "Attorney General Sessions Addresses Recent Criticisms of Zero Tolerance by Church Leaders."
17 Jeff Sessions, "Attorney General Sessions Addresses Recent Criticisms of Zero Tolerance by Church Leaders."
18 Jeff Sessions, "Attorney General Sessions Addresses Recent Criticisms of Zero Tolerance by Church Leaders."
19 Jeff Sessions, "Attorney General Sessions Addresses Recent Criticisms of Zero Tolerance by Church Leaders."
20 Julie Menke, "Abuse of Power: Immigration Courts and the Attorney General's Referral Power," *Case Western Reserve Journal of International Law* 52 (2020), 599.
21 Menke, "Abuse of Power," 601.
22 Menke, "Abuse of Power," 601.
23 "A Complaint Regarding Jefferson Sessions," *United Methodist News Service*, July 18, 2018, chrome-extension://efaidnbmnnnibpcajpcglclefindmkaj/https://s3.amazonaws.com/Website_Properties/news-media/documents/A_Complaint_regarding_Jefferson_Sessions.pdf.
24 "A Complaint Regarding Jefferson Sessions."
25 "A Complaint Regarding Jefferson Sessions."
26 "A Complaint Regarding Jefferson Sessions."
27 Jeff Sessions, "Attorney General Sessions Addresses Recent Criticisms of Zero Tolerance by Church Leaders."
28 Jacobs, "Sessions's Use of Bible Passage to Defend Immigration Policy Draws Fire."
29 Zauzmer and McMillan, "Sessions Cites Bible passage Used to Defend Slavery."
30 Emily Stewart, "Jeff Sessions Cited a Bible passage used By American Slaveholders to Defend Trump's Family Separation Policy," *Vox*, June 15, 2018, https://www.vox.com/policy-and-politics/2018/6/15/17467772/jeff-sessions-bible-passage-slavery-romans-13; "Romans: Chapter 13," King James Bible Online, www.kingjamesbibleonline.org: "1: Let every soul be subject unto the higher powers. For there is no power but of God: the powers that be are ordained of God. 2: Whosoever therefore resisteth the power, resisteth the ordinance of God: and they that resist shall receive to themselves damnation. 3. For rulers are not a terror to good works, but to the evil. Wilt thou then not be afraid of the power? Do that which is good, and thou shalt have praise of the same: 4. For he is the minister of God to thee for good. But if thou do that which is evil, be afraid; for he beareth not the sword in vain: for he is the minister of God, a revenger to execute wrath upon him that doeth evil" (Romans 13:1–4).

31 "Romans: Chapter 13," *King James Bible Online*, www.kingjamesbibleonline.org.
32 "Romans: Chapter 12," *King James Bible Online*, www.kingjamesbibleonline.org.
33 Aristotle, *Poetics and Rhetoric*, trans. and ed. Eugene Garver (New York: Barnes and Noble Classics, 2005), 248.
34 Aristotle, *Poetics and Rhetoric*, 248.
35 Aristotle, *Poetics and Rhetoric*, 248.
36 Aristotle, *Poetics and Rhetoric*, 249.
37 Aristotle, *Poetics and Rhetoric*, 249, 251.
38 Aristotle, *Poetics and Rhetoric*, 251.
39 Aristotle, *Poetics and Rhetoric*, 251.
40 Aristotle, *Poetics and Rhetoric*, xiii.
41 Aristotle, *Poetics and Rhetoric*, 279.
42 Debbie Lord, "Clergy Group Brings Church Charges of Abuse Against Jeff Sessions Over Immigration Policy (Updated)," *Atlanta Journal-Constitution*, August 13, 2018, https://www.ajc.com/news/national/clergy-group-brings-church-charges-child-abuse-immorality-against-jeff-sessions-over-zero-tolerance-policy/F9ObosPmuSUj1wACeBMjpO/.
43 Gabriella Munoz, "United Methodist Church Leaders Dismiss Complaint Against Jeff Sessions," *Washington Times*, August 8, 2018, https://www.washingtontimes.com/news/2018/aug/8/jeff-sessions-complaint-dismissed-by-united-method/.
44 "A Complaint Regarding Jefferson Sessions," Immigration Courtside, June 2018, chrome-extension://efaidnbmnnnibpcajpcglclefindmkaj/https://s3.amazonaws.com/Website_Properties/news-media/documents/A_Complaint_regarding_Jefferson_Sessions.pdf; As Caitlin Dickerson says in "The secret history of the U.S. government's family-separation policy," "separating children was not just a side effect, but the intent." See Adam Serwer, *The Cruelty is the Point* (New York: One World, 2021) and given the evidence, that conclusion is ineluctable.
45 Lord, "Clergy Group Brings Church Charges of Abuse."
46 Elizabeth S. Belfiore, *Tragic Pleasures: Aristotle on Plot and Emotion* (Princeton, New Jersey: Princeton University Press, 1992), 145.
47 "*Shir Hashirim* – Song of Songs – Chapter 6," Chabad-Lubavitch Media Center, www.chabad.org.
48 Jacob Soboroff, *Separated: Inside an American Tragedy* (New York: HarperCollins, 2020); Sabrina Rodriguez, "'The Crisis is in Washington': Overwhelmed Border Officials Urge D.C. to Act," *Politico*, March 20, 2021; Jen Psaki and Alejandro Mayorkas, "Briefing by Press Secretary Jen Psaki and Secretary of Homeland Security Alejandro Mayorkas," *The White House*, March 1, 2021, https://www.whitehouse.gov/briefing-room/press-briefings/2021/03/01/press-briefing-by-press-secretary-jen-psaki-and-secretary-of-homeland-security-alejandro-mayorkas/; Jacob Soboroff, Julia Ainsley and Geoff Bennett, "Biden Administration Will Let Migrant Families Separated Under Trump Reunite Inside U.S.," *NBC*, March 1, 2021, https://www.nbcnews.com/politics/immigration/biden-admin-expected-let-migrant-families-separated-under-trump-reunite-n1259141; Nancy Cook and Jordan Fabian, "Biden Immigration Chief Blasts Trump for 'Gutted System,'" *Bloomberg*, March 1, 2021, https://news.bloomberglaw.com/immigration/biden-immigration-chief-blasts-trump-for-gutted-u-s-system; Alejandro N. Mayorkas, "Statement by Homeland Security Secretary Alejandro N. Mayorkas Regarding the Situation at the Southwest Border," *Department of Homeland Security*,

March 16, 2021, https://www.dhs.gov/news/2021/03/16/statement-homeland-security-secretary-alejandro-n-mayorkas-regarding-situation; Linda Qiu, "Fact-Checking Claims on the Migrant Surge at the U.S.-Mexico Border," *New York Times*, March 20, 2021, https://www.nytimes.com/2021/03/20/us/politics/fact-check-immigration-border.html; Michael D. Shear and Zolan Kanno-Youngs, "Biden Issues Orders to Dismantle Trump's 'America First' Immigration Agenda," *New York Times*, February 3, 2021, https://www.nytimes.com/2021/02/02/us/politics/biden-immigration-executive-orders-trump.html; Katie Benner and Charlie Savage, "Immigration and Family Separation, Live Updates."; Caitlin Dickerson, "Parents of 545 Children Separated at the Border Cannot Be Found," *New York Times*, October 21, 2020, https://www.nytimes.com/2020/10/21/us/migrant-children-separated.html; Julia Ainsley and Jacob Soboroff, "Lawyers Have Found the Parents of 105 Separated Migrant Children in Past Months," *NBC*, February 24, 2021, https://www.nbcnews.com/politics/immigration/lawyers-have-found-parents-105-separated-migrant-children-past-month-n1258791; Aishvarya Kavi, "Biden's 17 Executive orders and other Directives in Detail," *New York Times*, January 21, 2021, https://www.nytimes.com/2021/01/20/us/biden-executive-orders.html.
49 Jen Psaki and Alejandro Mayorkas, "Briefing by Press Secretary Jen Psaki and Secretary of Homeland Security Alejandro Mayorkas," *The White House*, March 1, 2021, https://www.whitehouse.gov/briefing-room/press-briefings/2021/03/01/press-briefing-by-press-secretary-jen-psaki-and-secretary-of-homeland-security-alejandro-mayorkas/.
50 Jen Psaki and Alejandro Mayorkas, "Briefing by Press Secretary Jen Psaki and Secretary of Homeland Security Alejandro Mayorkas."
51 Jen Psaki and Alejandro Mayorkas, "Briefing by Press Secretary Jen Psaki and Secretary of Homeland Security Alejandro Mayorkas."
52 Jen Psaki and Alejandro Mayorkas, "Briefing by Press Secretary Jen Psaki and Secretary of Homeland Security Alejandro Mayorkas."
53 Jen Psaki and Alejandro Mayorkas, "Briefing by Press Secretary Jen Psaki and Secretary of Homeland Security Alejandro Mayorkas."
54 According to Caitlin Dickerson in "The secret history of the U.S's family-separation policy," of the present, 700 families have not been reunited with their children
55 Carl Hulse, "On the Border, Republicans Set a Trap, Then Fell Into It," *New York Times*, February 6, 2024, https://www.nytimes.com/2024/02/06/us/politics/border-republicans-ukraine-bill.html.
56 Karoun Demirjian, "House Republicans Impeach Mayorkas for Border Policies," *New York Times*, February 13, 2024, https://www.nytimes.com/2024/02/13/us/politics/mayorkas-impeachment-house.html.
57 Demirjian, "House Republicans Impeach Mayorkas."
58 Hulse, "On the Border."

Chapter 6: Part 2 Borders/Immigration and Violence

1 Pope Francis, "Homily at Ciudad Juárez Fair Grounds," February 17, 2016, http://www.vatican.va/content/francesco/en/homilies/2016/documents/papa-francesco_20160217_omelia-messico-ciudad-juarez.html. © Dicastero per la Communicazione-Libreria Editrice Vaticana.
2 Rick Gladstone, "Displaced Population Hit Record in 16, U.N. Says," *New York Times*, June 19, 2007, A5.

3   Pope Francis first uttered the phrase "globalization of indifference" in his homily at Lampedusa on July 8, 2013. In that homily, Francis characterized indifference as becoming numb to the suffering of others, it is no longer our concern nor our business. Francis went on to contend that the globalization of indifference has robbed us of the ability to experience compassion and rendered us incapable of weeping. Pope Francis, "Visit to Lampedusa Holy Mass in the 'Arena' Sports Camp," July 08, 2013,http://www.vatican.va/content/francesco/en/homilies/2013/documents/papa-francesco_20130708_omelia-lampedusa.html; By far Francis's most extensive explication of several types of indifference and the Christian responses of solidarity, fraternity, mercy, and dialogue to them occurs in his "Message for the Celebration of the XLIX World Day of Peace: Overcome Indifference and Win Peace." Francis acknowledged that while indifference, the problem of people closing their hearts and eyes to the needs of others, avoiding encounter with the suffering of the other, is not a new problem, he observed that it has amplified and intensified beyond a personal matter and today encompasses a much larger scope. See Pope Francis, "Message for the Celebration of the XLIX World Day of Peace: Overcome Indifference and Win Peace," January 1, 2016,http://www.vatican.va/content/francesco/en/messages/peace/documents/papa-francesco_20151208_messaggio-xlix-giornata-mondiale-pace-2016.html; Also see Pope Francis, *Evangelii Gaudium (The Joy of the Gospel)* (Washington, D.C.: United States Conference of Catholic Bishops, 2013), 54; Pope Francis, "Message for the World Day of Migrants and Refugees 2016: Migrants and Refugees Challenge Us. The Response of the Gospel of Mercy," January 17, 2016. In this message, Francis linked indifference and silence to "complicity whenever we standby as people are dying of suffocation, starvation, violence and shipwreck. Whether large or small scale, these are always tragedies, even when a single human life is lost." http://www.vatican.va/content/francesco/en/messages/migration/documents/papa-francesco_20150912_world-migrants-day-2016.html; For an articulation of indifference towards the environment and the poor, see Pope Francis, *Laudato Si': On the Care of Our Common Home* (Vatican City: Vatican Press, 2016), 14, 25, 52, 91, 92, 232; For economic and consumer indifference, see Pope Francis, "Misericordiae Vultus: Bull of Indiction of the Extraordinary Jubilee of Mercy," April 11, 2015,http://www.vatican.va/content/francesco/en/bulls/documents/papa-francesco_bolla_20150411_misericordiae-vultus.html; For more recent discussions of indifference, see Pope Francis, *Fratelli Tutti (All Brothers)* (Libreia Editrice Vaticana: Hijez Global Press, 2020), 30, 57, 68, 73, 199; and for indifference during a pandemic, see Pope Francis, *Let Us Dream: The Path to A Better Future* (New York: Simon & Schuster, 2020), 13, 18–20, 47, 98–99,106, 120, 125.

4   Francis Pontifical Council for the Pastoral care of Migrants and Itinerant People, May 24, 2013.

5   See https://www.infomigrants.net/en/post/20055/migrant-deaths-19-000-in-mediterranean-in-past-6-years, 19,000 migrants have been reported missing or dead since October 2013.

6   Pope Francis, "Visit to Lampedusa."

7   Jim Yardley, "Pope Francis Takes 12 Refugees Back to the Vatican After Trip to Greece," *New York Times*, April 16, 2016. https://www.nytimes.com/2016/04/17/world/europe/pope-francis-visits-lesbos-heart-of-europes-refugee-crisis.html.

8   See Jim Yardley and Azam Ahmed, "Pope Francis Wades into U.S. Immigration Morass With Border Trip," *New York Times*, February 17, 2016,http://www.vatican.va/content/francesco/en/homilies/2016/documents/papa-francesco_20160217_omelia-messico-ciudad-juarez.html and Joshua Partlow and Gabriela Martinez, "Pope Francis ends his Mexico tour praying for migrants at the U.S. border," *The Washington Post*, February 17, 2016,https://www.washingtonpost.com/world/the_americas/pope-francis-will-finish-his-mexico-tour-looking-straight-at-the-us-border/2016/02/16/3bff6154-8eb1-4aed-b7f7-49cea05698d0_story.html.

9 Yardley and Ahmed, "Pope Francis Wades into U.S. Immigration"; Partlow and Martinez, "Pope Francis ends his Mexico tour."
10 Phil Pullella, "Full text of Pope Francis' in-flight interview from Mexico to Rome," *Catholic News Agency,* February 18, 2016, https://www.catholicnewsagency.com/news/full-text-of-pope-francis-in-flight-interview-from-mexico-to-rome-85821.
11 Sari Horwitz and Maria Sacchetti, "Sessions vows to prosecute all illegal border crosser and separate children from their parents," *The Washington Post,* May 7, 2018, https://www.washingtonpost.com/world/national-security/sessions-says-justice-dept-will-prosecute-every-person-who-crosses-border-unlawfully/2018/05/07/e1312b7e-5216-11e8-9c91-7dab596e8252_story.html.
12 Pope Francis, *Let Us Dream: The Path to a Better Future* (New York: Simon & Schuster 2020), 72–73.
13 Pope Francis, "Homily at Ciudad Juárez Fair Grounds."
14 Pope Francis, "Homily at Ciudad Juarez Fair Grounds."
15 Pope Francis, *Let Us Dream: The Path to a Better Future* (New York: Simon & Schuster 2020), 76.
16 See Elizabeth S. Belfiore, *Tragic Pleasures: Aristotle on Plot and Emotion* (Princeton: Princeton University Press, 1992), 218.
17 Eszter Timár, "The body of shame in affect theory and deconstruction," *Parallax,* 25, no. 2 (2019): 200.
18 Timár, "The body of shame in affect theory and deconstruction," 201.
19 I am exceedingly grateful to Sergio Peña for sharing his knowledge of affect theory and his inventive insights on Francis's rhetorical construction and deployment of shame with me. This analysis is prodigiously enhanced by Peña's illuminating interpretations and applications.
20 Pope Francis, "Homily at Ciudad Juarez Fair Grounds."
21 Pope Francis, "Homily at Ciudad Juarez Fair Grounds."
22 Pope Francis, "Homily at Ciudad Juarez Fair Grounds."
23 St. Augustine, *The Four Books of St. Augustine on Christian Doctrine* (Sun Valley: Indo-European Publishing, 2014), Chapter 24 section 53, 160–161.
24 John Lesley, *An Epithrene: or Voice of Weeping Bewailing the Want of Weeping. A Meditation* (Augustine Mathewes, 1631), 43.
25 Pope Francis, *Fratelli Tutti: Encyclical Letter on Fraternity and Social Friendship* (Libreria Editrice Vaticana: Hijez Global Press, 2020), 84.
26 Pope Francis, *Fratelli Tuti*, 84.
27 Cardinal Luis Antonio G. Tagle, "Tears," in *A Pope Francis Lexicon* edited by Joshua McElwee and Cindy Wooden (Collegeville: Liturgical Press, 2018), 184.
28 Tagle, "Tears," 184.
29 Elizabeth Belfiore, *Tragic Pleasures*, 263.
30 *Catechism of the Catholic church*, 2nd ed. (Libreria Editrice Vaticana, 1997), 1431.
31 *Catechism of the Catholic Church*, 1434.
32 Quoted in Cindy Wooden, "Theology of Tears: For Pope, Weeping Helps One See Jesus," *The Catholic News Service,* May 5, 2019, https://www.catholicsun.org/2016/05/05/theology-of-tears-for-pope-weeping-helps-one-see-jesus/.

Afterword

1. Nilay Saiya, "Why Christian nationalism is a global problem," *ABC*, July 11, 2022, https://www.abc.net.au/religion/christian-nationalism-is-a-global-problem/13968062.
2. Saiya, "Why Christian nationalism is a global problem."
3. "2023 anti-trans bills tracked," *Trans Legislation Tracker*, accessed May 26, 2023, https://translegislation.com/; Unfortunately, this afterward joins a growing scholarly record accounting for the development and escalation of trans necropolitical legislation and violence.
4. "2023 anti-trans bills tracked."
5. Conor Friederdorf, "That's Not What Grooming Means," *The Atlantic*, April 6, 2022, https://www.theatlantic.com/newsletters/archive/2022/04/thats-not-what-grooming-means/629501/; James Bickerton, "Florida Republicans Set to Pass Multiple Bills Targeting Transgender People," *Newsweek*, April 19, 2023, https://www.newsweek.com/florida-republicans-set-pass-multiple-bills-targeting-transgender-people-1795381.
6. H.B. 1521, Leg. Sess. 125(R) (Fl. 2023), https://legiscan.com/FL/text/H1521/2023.
7. S.B. 1438, Leg. Sess. 125(R) (Fl. 2023), https://flsenate.gov/Session/Bill/2023/1438.
8. S.B. 254, Leg. Sess. 125(R) (Fl. 2023), https://legiscan.com/FL/bill/S0254/2023.
9. Maria Serrano, "'Fear and tears': Nurse practitioners restricted from providing gender transition care," *Spectrum News 13*, May 23, 2023, https://www.mynews13.com/fl/orlando/news/2023/05/24/nurse-practitioners-cannot-prescribe-meds-for-transgender-patients-going-through-gender-transition.
10. Jack Selzer, "Habeas Corpus: An Introduction," in *Rhetorical Bodies*, edited by Jack Selzer and Sharon Crowley (Madison, WI: The University of Wisconsin Press, 1999), 10.
11. Jack Selzer, "Habeas Corpus: An Introduction," 10.
12. Michael Lechuga, "An anti-colonial future: Reassembling the way we do rhetoric," *Communication and Critical/Cultural Studies*, 17, no. 4 (2020): 380.
13. Lechuga, "An anti-colonial future," 381.
14. Saiya, "Why Christian nationalism is a global problem."
15. Emily Mae Czachor, "'Florida is where woke goes to die,'" Gov. Ron DeSantis Says after reelection victory, *CBS News*, November 9, 2022, https://www.cbsnews.com/news/ron-desantis-florida-where-woke-goes-to-die-midterm-election-win/.
16. CBS News Miami, "Gov. DeSantis Signs Bill On School Books, Term Limits," *CBS News*, March 25th, 2022, https://www.cbsnews.com/miami/news/gov-desantis-signs-bill-on-school-books-term-limits/; Matt Lavietes, "As Florida's 'Don't Say Gay' law takes effect, schools roll out LGBTQ restrictions," *NBC News*, June 30, 2022, https://www.nbcnews.com/nbc-out/out-news/floridas-dont-say-gay-law-takes-effect-schools-roll-lgbtq-restrictions-rcna36143; Anthony Izaguirre, "Florida blocks high school African American studies class," *AP*, January 19, 2023, https://apnews.com/article/ron-desantis-florida-race-and-ethnicity-education-353417231de0a790c8e290479a5e52b8; Anthony Izaguirre, "DeSantis to expand 'Don't Say Gay' law to all grades," *AP*, March 22, 2023, https://apnews.com/article/dont-say-gay-desantis-florida-gender-d3a9c91f4b5383a5bf6df6f7d8ff65b6; C Mandler, "Florida bill targets 'diversity, equity or inclusion,' on college campuses," *CBS News*, March 26, 2023, https://www.cbsnews.com/news/florida-hb-999-diversity-equity-inclusion-college-campus-bill-advances/.
17. S.B. 1718, Leg. Sess. 125(R) (Fl. 2023), https://www.flsenate.gov/Session/Bill/2023/1718.
18. Joseph, Drexler-Dreis, *Decolonial Love: Salvation in Colonial Modernity* (Fordham University Press, 2018), 11.

Speaking of Religion

Daniel S. Brown, *Series Editor*

Speaking of Religion grows from a scholarly attentiveness to the role that religion plays in the public sphere. The decline of religious thought in public affairs is a common yet false narrative in the United States. Americans remain a devout people who are motivated to action by their faith commitments. Several contemporary, interdisciplinary scholars including Jürgen Habermas, Charles Taylor and Tariq Ramadan point us toward the privilege that religion and faith enjoys in public life. Collectively their work asserts that the world has entered a post-secular era: Secularism is dead and faith is alive. Speaking of Religion features short books, no more than 60,000 words or approximately 150 pages in length.

For additional information about this series or for the submission of manuscripts, please contact:

> Erika Hendrix, Acquisitions Editor
> e.hendrix@peterlang.com

To order books, please contact our Customer Service Department:

> peterlang@presswarehouse.com (within the U.S.)
> order@peterlang.com (outside the U.S.)

Or browse online by series at www.peterlang.com

www.ingramcontent.com/pod-product-compliance
Lightning Source LLC
Chambersburg PA
CBHW052018290426
44112CB00014B/2284